THE NEW MANAGEMENT

Democracy and Enterprise
Are Transforming Organizations

WILLIAM E. HALAL

Berrett-Koehler Publishers
San Francisco

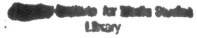

Berrett-Koehler Publishers, Inc.
155 Montgomery Street
San Francisco, CA 94104- 4109
Tel.: (415) 288-0260   Fax: (415) 362-2512

ORDERING INFORMATION

Individual sales. Berrett-Koehler publications are available through most bookstores. They can also be ordered direct from Berrett-Koehler at the address above.

Quantity sales. Special discounts are available on quantity purchases by corporations, associations, and others. For details, contact the "Special Sales Department" at the Berrett-Koehler address above.

Orders for college textbook/course adoption use. Please contact Berrett-Koehler Publishers at the address above.

Orders by U.S. trade bookstores and wholesalers. Please contact Publishers Group West, 4065 Hollis Street, Box 8843, Emeryville, CA 94662. Tel.: (510) 658-3453; 1-800-788-3123. Fax: (510) 658-1834.

Printed in the United States of America.

Printed on acid-free and recycled paper that is composed of 85% recovered fiber, including 15% postconsumer waste.

Library of Congress Cataloging-in-Publication Data

Halal, William E.
    The new management : democracy and enterprise are transforming organizations / William E. Halal.
        p.   cm.
    Includes bibliographical references and index.
    ISBN 1-881052-53-2 (alk. paper)
    1. Management. 2. Corporate culture.   I. Title.
HD31.H2283   1996
658—dc20   96-7027
                                                                            CIP

First Edition

2000 99 98 97 96   10 9 8 7 6 5 4 3 2 1

DEDICATION

TO THOSE UNSUNG HEROES who keep societies working everywhere—the managers of modern organizations. While television shows like *ER, LA Law,* and *NYPD Blue* glorify doctors, lawyers, police, and other more popular professions, millions of men and women bear the responsibility of managing today's interlocking maze of business corporations, government agencies, schools, hospitals, TV stations, newspapers, armies, and other institutions that make up the social order. I hope this book can help guide these stewards of our daily lives as their demanding jobs spiral to new heights of complexity.

CONTENTS

FOREWORD

IT IS INCREASINGLY CLEAR that current approaches to managing are not going
to work in the 21st century. The growing pressures of global competition, the
speed of technological change, and the demands of sophisticated customers
for high-quality, efficiently produced customized goods and services are
motivating a search for what William Halal calls "the New Management."

Professor Halal's book explores this modern dilemma and prescribes
two premises to guide managers toward the design of organizations capable of responding to an increasingly complex and challenging business and
social environment. Halal's first premise is that the hierarchical "command" economy that guided traditional organizations from the top down
will give way to a disaggregated, "internal market" economy in which myriad autonomous profit centers produce a self-organizing form of control
that operates from the bottom up. His second building block is that these
internal markets will operate within a broader management system that is
guided by the informed involvement of numerous stakeholders—a governance system that he defines as "corporate community," a simple form of
economic democracy.

The premise that 21st century organizations will demand broad economic empowerment of their members is well supported, and Halal's pre-
scription of internal markets as the mechanism for this empowerment is
well argued and illustrated by useful company examples. Decentralizing the

decision process to meet diverse and accelerating demands has logical appeal, and Information Age profit centers would appear to have what they need to make good decisions: information, competence, and hard criteria.

The second central premise is far more complex and thus more challenging to both Halal and his readers. The need for broadening the concept of democracy to provide recognition and voice for all major corporate stakeholders is clearly presented. The "how" of this process is not as clear. Halal, like most of us, runs up against the fact that our society, as the late Aaron Wildavsky lamented, does not have a strong philosophical foundation to explain collaborative behavior. That is, while we have libertarian philosophies rationalizing the positive effects of individual initiatives and collectivist philosophies positing the social gains of shared efforts and rewards, we do not have a clear-cut logical system laying out the costs and benefits of behavior motivated simultaneously by personal desires and an awareness of external obligations.

Thus, Halal is forced to make his own arguments, to provide his own definitions and supply his own rationale and conclusions. In general, the case is clearly enough made for my needs, but then I have made similar forays in my own writings. Certainly not all will agree and readers may demand more precision, more evidence, more debate. Indeed, if the book generates that debate, it will have largely succeeded. The governance mechanisms necessary for 21st-century organizations will always be more complex than those of most current forms and will turn on hard realities with soft definitions—trust, human capital, empowerment, etc. In the creation of these mechanisms, debate and inventions will be our most useful companions.

Part Two of the book provides both Halal and his readers another challenge. In this section, he seeks to build conceptual linkages across the legal and social contracts connecting the firm to its customers, its employees, and its ecological community. Underlying this entire section is an argument that includes but goes beyond enlightened self-interest. The sweep of this argument is so broad it defies easy treatment but I believe, as does Halal, that these issues are related and must be managed from an integrated perspective. In an Information Age organization, full responsiveness to customers can only be provided by largely self-managing organization members and the social costs of the enterprise must be addressed by both its members and its clients.

In Part Three, Halal argues that informed, empowered organizational members, operating in systems that allow agile, efficient responses to market forces, are the essential elements of an effective, decentralized global economy. The notion that leadership is best exercised by empowering others, whether at the organizational, national, or international level has always been challenging, even though it is a founding assumption of our society. This section does not put the argument to rest, as no treatment is likely to, but it does remind us that levels of economic institutions and activities are rapidly compressing and that every economic decision is increasingly a global action.

I have know Professor Halal since his days as a doctoral student in the Haas School of Business at the University of California at Berkeley. As his earlier writings have shown, he has never been afraid to accept the challenge of tough and complex issues. In all, this provocative book provides a strong statement of the demands faced by today's and tomorrow's managers and offers them a conceptual path through the new economic and organizational jungle. New paths are seldom smooth nor completely clear. I commend Professor Halal for both his contributions and his courage. I believe the reader will do the same.

RAYMOND E. MILES

RAYMOND E. MILES is the Trefethen Professor of Organizational Behavior at the Haas School of Business, University of California at Berkeley. Professor Miles was also dean of the school from 1983 to 1990. His most recent book is Fit, Failure, and the Hall of Fame *(New York: Free Press, 1994).*

ACKNOWLEDGMENTS

IT'S ALWAYS IMPOSSIBLE TO acknowledge the many people who assist the birth of a book, but a few stand out. I am grateful to my publisher, Steve Piersanti, and the following staff members at Berrett-Koehler for their help in guiding this manuscript from its gestation to its audience: Pat Anderson, Beverly Butterfield, Robin Donovan, Kate Fuller, Susan Malikowski, Elizabeth Swenson, and Debbie Uyeshiro. I owe a particular debt to the many managers and scholars whose work is described throughout these pages; this book builds on their contributions that I have incorporated into a conceptual framework. The finished manuscript would have been far less readable had it not been for Charles Dorris, my developmental editor, and the many people who reviewed earlier drafts; Barbara Shipka carefully critiqued the entire book and helped me to see my own biases, while Ronald Schmidt, Steve Wallman, Paul Malone, and Ann Lehman provided general suggestions and reviewed various chapters. My students deserve recognition for assisting with the surveys reported here and for seriously considering my early thoughts on the New Management when they were half-baked ideas. Special thanks are extended to my colleagues at George Washington University for providing an intellectual home that supports this work. I want to acknowledge the help of my graduate assistant, Michael Kull, who is there when I need him. My deepest affection is reserved for my wife and children whose support is always indispensable.

INTRODUCTION

Another Step Toward a New Economic System

ECONOMIC UPHEAVAL HAS BECOME a way of life during the past few decades, but I am struck by the abrupt shifts in direction that leave us puzzled as to where this profound transition is heading.

Can you recall the heady vision of the 1960s in which a "postindustrial society" would bore people with too much leisure? Do you remember how the 1970s witnessed an emotional outpouring as "organizational development" exposed inner conflicts? And then the bright hope for "corporate social responsibility" that turned into an empty piety when business had to struggle to survive? What about the use of "strategic planning" in the eighties that was abandoned when it became clear that the result was usually more bureaucracy? Then we had the "Reagan Revolution" that left a legacy of nagging budget deficits. In the nineties this search for answers has produced such a flood of hot new practices that corporate changes are being called the "flavor of the month."

These were all genuine, useful attempts to come to grips with a different era, and many of these innovations will continue to serve an important purpose. But reaching that much-proclaimed "new economic paradigm" would be far easier if we possessed a set of basic principles on which to build a new economic foundation. Without some generally agreed upon principles, the search for a new economic system often becomes an endless exercise in bewildering change.

A NEW FOUNDATION BUILT ON OLD IDEALS

I want to suggest that a well-established foundation is readily available if we would simply look in the right place. America's heritage of democracy and free enterprise could serve us exceedingly well in the uncharted frontier of the Information Age. The main obstacle is that we tend to relegate these enduring ideals to their occasional use in political elections and in competition between firms. But if managers could learn to extend the liberating power of democracy and enterprise *inside* business corporations, government agencies, and other social institutions that govern the daily flow of ordinary life, their widespread application would have profound implications.

This is not some hopelessly utopian quest because I intend to illustrate that trends are moving us rapidly in this direction.

To survive a world of constant change, massive diversity, and intense competition, monolithic corporations are dissolving into fluid collections of entrepreneurial units. This need to cope with a difficult era should bring the power of enterprise to fruition as organizations melt even further into a churning sea of "internal markets," connected by information networks into a near-perfect global economy—I call it "the flowering of enterprise."

The move to democracy is equally apparent in the way managers now work closely with tough competitors, empowered employees, and discriminating clients. After a long history of authoritarian control, collaborative working relations have become one of the most powerful forces in economics because of the hard realization that cooperation is now efficient. Some progressive companies such as GM Saturn are uniting their stakeholders into vital "corporate communities"—think of this as "the extension of democracy."

If American managers could take a fresh look at these rich but often misunderstood trends from the perspective of our traditions, the emerging pattern could guide our way ahead with confidence. As this book will demonstrate, the power of democracy and enterprise promises to transform institutions for a new economic era.

Why would we be surprised? This is the philosophical foundation that gave birth to the United States and that has been bringing down dictatorship after dictatorship in recent years. Free markets and democratic governance are the twin pillars supporting modern civilization, the social axes that orient our very thoughts, our guiding vision of an effective social order. The difference today is that these principles are no longer relegated to lofty domains but are moving into the heart of management.

If these trends hold, the foundation of a "New Management" built on democracy and enterprise will support far more powerful institutions that are entrepreneurial yet human-oriented, intensely competitive but also highly collaborative. As the chapters in this book show, business and government are then likely to become serving enterprises that raise our quality of life, intelligent workplaces that advance knowledge, organizations that are ecologically benign, quick to adapt, good for the soul, and a civilizing local force in a global economy.

ORIGINS OF *THE NEW MANAGEMENT*

This conclusion is the result of my studies on the transition to a new economic era. A critical point in this work occurred in 1986 with the publication of *The New Capitalism*.[1] To understand such an embryonic transformation, I surveyed innovative practices, distilled hundreds of examples into trends, and clustered trends into key concepts. In struggling to make sense of this mass of data, a dominant pattern constantly presented itself through the changes taking place: the emerging economic system can be best understood as an extension of democracy and enterprise into organizations.

The present book integrates this theme and more recent work into a practical yet thought-provoking guide to the many innovations that are now transforming all institutions. Whereas *The New Capitalism* was an intellectual effort to explore a new economic frontier, *The New Management* is designed to offer managers a practical, comprehensive, yet stimulating survey of where their craft is heading. It should serve as a supplementary text for the Organization and Management course in the typical M.B.A., a resource for training programs in the private and public sectors, and the professional reading of managers and scholars.

The conceptual framework developed for *The New Capitalism* remains largely unchanged in this book. I've updated my research and reorganized the original concepts a bit, but the basic ideas remain valid because this approach has proved robust enough to withstand a decade of brutal change. As before, I've also reviewed the scholarly and popular literature, interviewed prominent executives and scholars, drawn on my consulting work, and generally used anything else available to advance our thinking.

This book breaks new ground by presenting data on new management practices from an international survey of 426 managers, the *Corporations in Transition* (CIT) study.[2] (See Appendix C.) Results confirm that the New Management is not simply a theory but a growing body of progressive practice that managers consider essential to thrive in the Knowledge Age. Indeed, many think these changes are needed to survive.

My guiding intention, then, is to continually revise these methods, data, and concepts in order to periodically update our understanding of the new system of business and economics. In other words, the idea is to "track the transition as it unfolds."

To serve the needs of busy managers, I've tried to present these complex ideas in a lively, readable style that is to the point and free of technical or intellectual baggage. I've also been personal occasionally, rather than writing in the detached voice that is traditionally used to convey authority and objectivity. The reality is that the work of even the most rational scientist is derived ultimately from his or her underlying human qualities, so I think it is more honest to admit this openly. At appropriate times, then, I offer experiences from my life and work, I may speak directly to the reader on crucial points, acknowledge my own biases, and admit ignorance of some issue.

Each chapter opens with an interesting example to highlight the central theme. Three major sections then examine the underlying problem and provide a conceptual solution, move on to guiding principles and illustrative applications, and conclude with implications for managers. A focus on issues facing business, government, and other institutions is used throughout to address the troublesome problems that concern the average manager today.

While I realize "management" may be out of favor now because of the keen need for "leadership," my view of management is broadly conceived to include the most enlightened leadership. Managers today need to lead, but leadership alone cannot address the technical, organizational, and economic complexities of modern institutions.

THE PURPOSE OF THIS BOOK

I hope this book will serve as a source that managers everywhere will find useful as today's transition to a knowledge-based, global economy gathers force. Despite the doubt and controversy that are stirred up when institutions change so fundamentally, events of the nineties have made it clear that the new economic system many of us have studied and practiced so long is coming vividly to life now. Its central ideas are working effectively in scattered places, and the main challenge is to bring them into the mainstream.

That is the goal of this book. It represents another small step toward realizing the potential of a new economic era. I can think of no more exciting purpose than to envision a better way of life that is made possible by the revolutionary forces of our time, and to help make that better way a reality. I invite you to join me in this effort by considering the ideas in this book, and then by using whatever response they elicit to achieve your own goals.

WILLIAM E. HALAL
Washington, D.C.
September 1995

Notes

1. William E. Halal, *The New Capitalism* (New York: Wiley, 1986).
2. William E. Halal, *Corporations in Transition* (an unpublished study in progress). The author expresses his gratitude for the assistance of the following graduate students: Ed Adelman, Fabiola Antezana, Bill Baldwin, Adam Coacher, David Dugan, Brian Duncan, Jung-An Huang, Jongril Hyun, Jose Ibarra, Jennifer Johnson, Lisa King, Adrienne Laster, Kyu-Hwan Lee, Jim Lucas, Ramsey Meiser, Tom Notaro, David O'Connell, Robert Pugh, Antonia Rao, San Retna, Regan Rosenfeld, Steve Rubley, Carlos Ruis, Thelma Staples-Jones, Brooke Toni, Kerry Tremayne, Sonia Vaid, Asir Vedamuthu, Gary Weinfeld, David Wieser, Maggie Yang, and Roger Yu.

1

Management in Transition

*Bridging That Divide Between
the Old and the New*

Civilization today is poised at the brink of a great divide between an old way of life that is dying and a new way of life that is still being born. Behind lies an Industrial Age that lavished wealth on a world that was poor—but which also left a polluted planet, quarrelsome societies, and empty lives. Ahead lies the much heralded promise of the Information Age—but its growing contours continue to surprise and shock us. Who would have thought that a global economy would appear almost overnight? That the Soviet Union would just disintegrate? That the United States would slip into decline?[1]

There are many ways to examine such complex issues, but basically these are problems of managing social institutions. As a knowledge economy spreads around the world, the largest professional group today is the rising managerial class that guides a growing infrastructure of complex organizations.[2] Most of the worries that dominate the news emanate from the interaction of corporations, governments, schools and universities, hospitals, news media, armies, and other institutions that support modern life. Peter Drucker described it this way: "Because a knowledge society is one of organizations, its central organ is management. Management alone makes effective all of today's knowledge."[3]

And as events accelerate to produce ever more complex technologies, intense competition, and turbulent, constant change, the aging foundation

1

of this entire institutional system is failing everywhere. Witness antigovernment sentiment in the United States, the crisis in health care, and demands to reform education. IBM, once regarded as the best-managed corporation in the world, recorded the biggest business loss in history recently, which was soon exceeded by General Motors (GM). Confidence in institutions has fallen from 52 percent in 1966 to 22 percent in 1994, and no recovery is in sight.[4]

Out of all this confusion, a workable new social order must be constructed to manage a radically different world. This book describes the organizing principles that are emerging to master this challenge—*The New Management*—and it offers guides on how managers can lead their old institutions into this new era.

WHAT REALLY IS THE NEW MANAGEMENT?

Most people have an intuitive grasp of management because we are raised in a world of organizations, so at an early age we absorb the basic concepts of working life. That's why management education is often dismissed as "common sense."

But it is exactly this commonly understood sense, or "paradigm," that is the problem. Prevailing management concepts were conceived for an industrial past, so they are not useful for a vastly different economy based on knowledge. The founding fathers of management would be baffled to hear modern managers talk of "networks," "telecommuting," and "virtual organizations."

The Evolution of Management

The classic theories of Henri Fayol, Max Weber, and Frederick Taylor defined the traditional view of "mechanistic" organizations to manage the simple conditions of the Industrial Age. What could be more reasonable in an "age of machines" than to construct institutions as "social machines"? Today, however, a more complex world described by the "supertrends" in Box 1.1 has made this model obsolete.[5]

The force driving this transformation is the inexorable increase in computer power by a factor of ten every few years. Forty percent of American homes now have personal computers (PCs), and the number is growing 30 percent per year. The average household uses computers twice as

BOX 1.1. GLOBAL SUPERTRENDS.

An Information Society. Sometime between 2000 and 2010, today's PCs will seem as primitive as a slide rule in comparison to a new breed of far more convenient, intelligent systems that should increase computing power roughly a million times. Small portable computers will become indispensable assistants helping us manage "smart" homes, offices, and autos, while larger parallel processors containing thousands of chips will provide the muscle power to cruise the information superhighways of a planetary society. People will thereby gain access to a wealth of knowledge at the touch of a finger: conversations with anyone across the globe on full motion video, data on any topic, libraries of books and periodicals, current news around the world, and a cornucopia of entertainment.

Technical Mastery. The Information Revolution exerts an enormous multiplier effect as it advances our ability to acquire knowledge, the heart of scientific progress. The result is historic breakthroughs in all fields. As one example, biogenetics will soon gain such control over life processes that any conceivable type of organism may be created, just as physical science now confers the power to create hydrogen bombs and explore space.

A Unified Globe. The electrifying force of information technology is wiring the globe into a single, unified whole. Just as people thought the idea of a United States of Europe and a North American Free Trade Agreement were unthinkable a few years ago, today's economic blocs are likely to merge in a decade or so, producing open trade among most nations, huge new developing markets, some form of coherent global governance, and the free movement of capital, information, and people across borders.

The Ecological Transformation. The rise of a middle class in Asia, South America, and possibly Africa is almost certain to increase the level of industrialization dramatically, possibly tenfold, producing a commensurate strain on an already decaying ecological system. The industrialization of China alone should at least double the load on the environment. Thus, present technological, economic, and social systems must inevitably be transformed into some as yet unknown new system that is ecologically benign.

Social Diversity. The information revolution seems to invariably release keen needs for personal achievement, cultural identity, and spiritual meaning, driving almost uncontrollable diversity. That is why the world is wracked with social conflagrations in the Middle East, the former Communist bloc, and even the United States; and the problem may become more intense.

Source: William E. Halal, "Global Strategic Management in a New World Order," *Business Horizons* (December 1993).

much as it uses TV, and computers are also connecting people together through the Internet and information services like America Online, CompuServe, The Microsoft Network, and Prodigy. In 1994, the first three-dimensional virtual meeting was held across the Pacific between teams of Japanese and Americans whose images "met" in a virtual conference room. One participant described the experience this way: "We've been dreaming of cyberspace for a long time. Here it is, the way people really interact." Bill Gates claims all these capabilities will be in common use by the year 2000.[6]

By the end of this decade, then, average people should be able to work, vote, learn, shop, play, and conduct almost all other aspects of their lives electronically, using multimedia PCs that combine the intelligence of a supercomputer, the communications of a portable telephone, and the vivid images of high-definition TV. These trends foretell a transformation of the entire social order, and the battle to define a new social order will be waged in the way we design and manage institutions.

Managers have begun to restructure their organizations in recent years as Total Quality Management (TQM), alliances, reengineering, self-directed teams, empowerment, community, and other innovations suddenly burst on the scene. A recent issue of *Fortune* even announced "The End of the Job,"[7] and Kunhee Lee, chairman of Samsung Corporation, the largest Korean conglomerate, told his managers, "Change everything except your wife and kids."[8] Figure 1.1 outlines this rich body of emerging thought, showing how the introduction of major new concepts has progressively moved the practice of management toward an "organic" focus. The entries are not exhaustive, but they offer a general guide to the rapid evolution of management today.

The neat concepts of classical management were challenged in the 1950s when Abraham Maslow, Elton Mayo, and Douglas McGregor showed that the field was expanding to include human and social factors. Later, in the sixties and seventies, bolder insights burst the boundaries of the old management altogether. Chester Barnard, an executive at American Telephone and Telegraph (AT&T), described management in terms of social systems. Paul Lawrence and Jay Lorsch discovered that effective organizations consist of diverse parts united into a coherent whole. Warren Bennis foresaw the need to replace authoritarian control with democracy. And Henry Mintzberg found that managers are engaged in an action-oriented flow of people and information rather than sterile problem solving.[9]

FIGURE 1.1. THE ADVANCE OF MANAGEMENT THOUGHT.

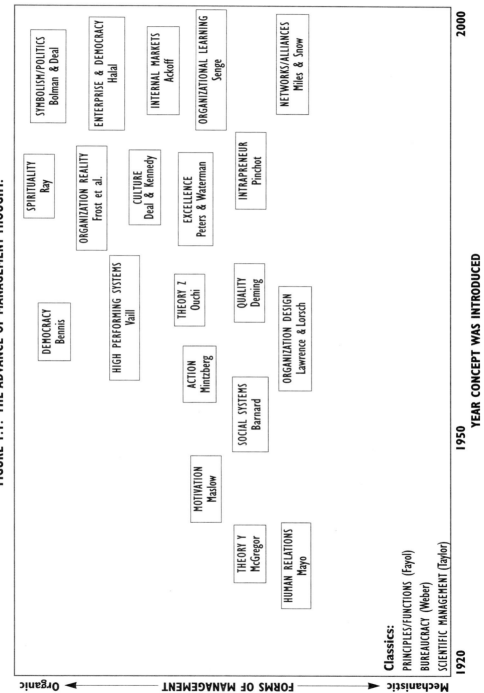

SYMBOLISM/POLITICS
Bolman & Deal

ENTERPRISE & DEMOCRACY
Halal

INTERNAL MARKETS
Ackoff

ORGANIZATIONAL LEARNING
Senge

NETWORKS/ALLIANCES
Miles & Snow

SPIRITUALITY
Ray

ORGANIZATION REALITY
Frost et al.

CULTURE
Deal & Kennedy

EXCELLENCE
Peters & Waterman

INTRAPRENEUR
Pinchot

DEMOCRACY
Bennis

HIGH PERFORMING SYSTEMS
Vaill

ACTION
Mintzberg

THEORY Z
Ouchi

QUALITY
Deming

SOCIAL SYSTEMS
Barnard

ORGANIZATION DESIGN
Lawrence & Lorsch

MOTIVATION
Maslow

THEORY Y
McGregor

HUMAN RELATIONS
Mayo

Classics:

PRINCIPLES/FUNCTIONS (Fayol)

BUREAUCRACY (Weber)

SCIENTIFIC MANAGEMENT (Taylor)

1920

1950

2000

YEAR CONCEPT WAS INTRODUCED

FORMS OF MANAGEMENT

Mechanistic ◄————————————————► Organic

Although these were radical ideas at the time, they can now be understood more clearly as the first wave in a flood of organic concepts that swept through the 1980s and 1990s. W. Edwards Demming and J. M. Juran pioneered the quality revolution. William Ouchi, Tom Peters and Robert Waterman, and Peter Vaill helped us see that excellent managers instilled purpose and meaning. Ray Miles and Charles Snow showed that modern organizations consisted of networks. Gifford Pinchot and Russell Ackoff brought free enterprise inside the firm. Peter Senge outlined the principles of organizational learning. Terrence Deal, Allen Kennedy, Peter Frost and his colleagues, Lee Bolman, and Michael Ray revealed how institutions form their own cultures and spiritual beliefs. And my book *The New Capitalism* showed that all this change flows from traditional Western ideals of enterprise and democracy.[10]

The Old Versus the New Management

While it is clear that a new stream of management has appeared, there is great confusion over what this New Management will consist of when it matures. A quick scan of the business media shows a bewildering blur of new management ideas extolling everything from "greed is good" to "business ethics," and an authoritative survey recently concluded that there is little agreement on today's management paradigm.[11]

This confusion is particularly severe because it often rages across a great divide separating the past from the future. The economic history of our time will likely be told as a tugging and pulling between the old versus the new: power versus participation, hierarchical control versus market freedom, profit versus society, growth versus the environment, and so on.

On the "new" side of this divide, many proponents of progressive change are caught up in a revolutionary zeal that proclaims the virtues of "empowered people," working in "fluid structures," to serve "human needs" and "protect the environment," all energized by "spirituality." These are exciting ideas, but they often appear naive to managers who are struggling to survive a hard world. Managers who responded to the CIT survey offered the following reactions: "Just because an idea is old does not mean it is bad," and "There will never be a substitute for the discipline and accountability of the old system." One executive put it this way, "The implication that we've come to a crossroads in business management is full of hot air. . . . We need to remember, follow, and reinforce the good old ideas . . . no one has discovered any new secrets of management."[12]

On this "old" half of the divide, it's true that many executives are stuck in outdated views. Listen to some typical comments from managers in the CIT survey: "It is incredible to witness just how terrified senior managers are of change. They paid their dues in the old system, and now they feel a right to privileges within that system," and "Some people must exert total control over every aspect of their business." These are valid criticisms; however, adherents to the Old Management raise crucial objections that test new ideas, and their influence maintains a healthy continuity with the past. Serious change is going to require more than lofty sentiments.

For instance, it is refreshing to see attempts to empower employees sweep across the land, but these innovations often fail because of unrealistic expectations. Weirton Steel excited the nation when it became the largest employee stock ownership plan (ESOP) in America, yet now the company has fallen on hard times and so it has been forced to take drastic measures, including the same type of layoffs often associated with "heartless corporations." Weirton's owner-workers are justifiably angry: "How can we be laid off if we own the company?" asked a puzzled shareholder.[13]

The road to a New Management is littered with the ruins of such noble failures, so it would be wise to acknowledge their cause honestly if we want to avoid them. In the Weirton Steel case, avid proponents failed to recognize the enduring truth that "authority must be commensurate with responsibility." While workers were enthusiastic about their newfound powers, they were unprepared to suffer losses because they did not realize that ownership incurs the *risk* of control as well as the right of control. The same fatal flaw is damaging employee governance in Europe.

These forms of worker participation have been a beacon for enlightened management, but they accorded employees dominant control over their enterprises without ensuring that this power was used responsibly, allowing workers to reward themselves without commensurate gains in performance. The most brilliant management innovations cannot repeal the iron laws of economic reality that require us to live within our means. A New Management can offer people the power to control their lives, but it must also hold them accountable for performance as well—just as the Old Management did.

The reverse is also true: demands to improve productivity mean little unless they are accompanied by the power to control one's work life. The use of downsizing and other attempts to reduce costs are often disappointing because they are usually imposed from the top down in a rather arbitrary way, causing fear, stress, and resentment at being treated unfairly. At a time when CEOs routinely claim "our employees are our greatest asset," this is precisely the wrong approach. Top-down change disempowers people and prevents local solutions that are usually superior—hallmarks of the New Management.

These confusing conflicts between outmoded practices and untested promises are the principal obstacle to economic progress. We can't go back to a past that no longer works, and yet we seem to be having difficulty finding solid ground to move ahead. How can organizations be productive when managers seem confused over what they expect from their employees? Will American companies lose the product markets of the future to global competitors as they did before in electronics and automobiles? Most importantly, the full impact of this upheaval will hit when the next wave of information systems arrives about the year 2000. Will we be ready to handle this enormous untamed power of the Information Revolution? The question can no longer be avoided: What really is the New Management?

The New Foundation of Management: Democracy and Enterprise

I believe a new foundation of management is emerging that can bridge this divide between the old and the new. Not only can this conflict be resolved, the *New Management absorbs the Old Management into a broader, more powerful framework that makes sense of all the concepts, problems, and innovations that confuse managers today. The key to understanding this crucial resolution is to see that the two complementary principles of democracy and enterprise are now transforming organizations into a balanced whole.*

Managers have always worked in a market economy, of course, and we all live in a democratic society, so what is really new? What's new is that these practices have been notably absent in organizations. There has been precious little entrepreneurial freedom *inside* corporations or governments because they were traditionally managed as centrally planned hierarchies, and the mere thought of democracy was anathema in business. Even the Catholic Church acknowledges that it is not democratic.

But within the past few years, these two principles have been bringing a fresh new vitality into corporate life. As we will see, today's movement toward smaller business units, entrepreneurial freedom, accountability for economic results, and other enterprise principles is likely to culminate in complete "internal markets." Likewise, a similar trend toward empowerment, participation, collaborative working relations, human values, and other democratic ideals should lead toward "corporate communities."

Please note that there is a difference between the concepts of "enterprise" and "internal markets," and between "democracy" and "corporate community."

The power of free enterprise is introducing some aspects of market behavior in organizations, but it is hard to envision hostile takeovers of corporate divisions. So organizations are unlikely to become completely free markets. But as Chapter 2 will show, if managers encourage the starting of internal ventures, provide the wide operating freedom that enterprises need to thrive, and reward entrepreneurs for their success, these conditions constitute what I call an "internal market."

Likewise, the ideals of democracy are moving into organizations, but this is not likely to be a legal system of representative government. Webster's dictionary defines "democracy" as originating from the Latin *demos*, meaning "the people." In this broader sense, democracy is a system of governance based on the rights of people. As we will see in Chapter 3, the application of democracy in organizations usually takes the practical form of collaborative working relations that form a corporate community.

Thus, internal markets and corporate community are defined here as "organizational equivalents of enterprise and democracy." These two concepts together offer such breadth of understanding that they provide managers a unified, practical body of principles. No single framework is able to explain all aspects of management, but I estimate that most, and possibly as much as 70 to 90 percent, of today's management innovation flows from these two key principles.

If this view is valid, the union of democratic and entrepreneurial principles should resolve the clash between the Old and the New Management noted above. In fact, it does exactly that: "empowered people" must assume both rights *and* responsibilities, "fluid structures" require freedom *and* accountability, "human needs" include the welfare of social constituencies and profit for investors, *and* spirituality—ah, spirituality!

Spirituality has become a powerful new entry in management recently, as we will see later. Lawrence Perlman, CEO of Ceridian Corporation said, "Ultimately, the combination of head and heart will be a competitive advantage."[14] But I think much of this interest is misleading. Some of my most disappointing experiences have occurred in organizations that profess spiritual values. Because we tend to equate spirituality with "goodness," people often avoid discussing the hard necessities of economic life—conflict, poor performance, and so on—thereby allowing such problems to fester until they explode. After all, the history of religion abounds with war. Tom Peters ignited a controversy when he said, "I find the idea of spirituality in the workplace appalling."[15]

It seems to me that spirituality is destined to become part of the New Management, but it will be more broadly conceived. As we will see later, the spirit is both the source of our highest ideals and a practical discipline that leaders use to resolve intense differences among demanding clients, empowered workers, and tough business partners. Our approach to the spirit cannot be limited to traditional dogma nor New Age mysticism. As Walt Whitman told us, life is a sacred whole that encompasses all. Institutions are no less an integral part of life, ablaze with endless meaning that encompasses the messy, disturbing realities as well. The spirit that animates life permeates *all* life, not just those aspects we prefer.

A FORECAST OF THE NEW MANAGEMENT PARADIGM

The concepts comprising the New Management paradigm, or system, are outlined in Table 1.1, in contrast with the corresponding features of the Old Management. Of course, we can't "prove" where this revolutionary transition will lead. By approaching the task in a systematic way using the research method described in the Introduction, however, I think we can provide a reasonably sound forecast that sketches out the new system.

The following chapter summaries explain the concepts in Table 1.1 and thereby provide an overview of the book. As shown, the book is divided into three parts. Part One lays a conceptual foundation by describing how the two central themes of internal markets and corporate commu-

TABLE 1.1. THE TRANSITION TO A NEW MANAGEMENT.

Chapter	Feature	Industrial Age: The Old Management	Information Age: The New Management
2	Organization structure	Hierarchy	Internal Market
3	Goals and governance	Profit	Corporate Community
4	Management system	Mechanistic	Organic
5	Client relations	Selling	Serving Enterprise
6	Work roles	Employee	Knowledge Entrepreneur
7	Ecological interface	Unbounded Growth	Intelligent Growth
8	Strategy formation	Planning	Continuous Change
9	Guidance and control	Authority	Inner Leadership
10	World system	The Old Capitalism vs. The Old Socialism	Democratic Enterprise

nity form a new management system. Part Two focuses on building three structures that constitute the heart of this system: the organization's relationships with its clients, its workers, and the environment. Part Three explores how modern managers can lead this type of organization effectively in an era of constant change, empowered people, and global markets.

Each of these three parts is introduced by a table that more fully outlines the logic of this transition from Old Management concepts to their corresponding New Management concepts. As these tables—1.2, 1.3, and 1.4—show, the most prominent feature of this transition is synthesis, the creative integration of old practices and new trends in the Hegelian sense: the old status quo (the "thesis" of the Old Management) is combined with opposing evolutionary forces (the "antithesis" of change) to produce a new status quo (the "synthesis" of the New Management).

It is important to observe that what many consider the New Management actually consists of the opposing forces or trends alone (the antithesis). This limited nature of so many hot but ephemeral management fads explains why the overhyped promises noted earlier often earn the disdain of main-stream managers. One executive complained to me of "New Age business babble," and another thought "the New Management in many cases is business school claptrap."

To avoid this problem, the concepts listed in Table 1.1 are firmly rooted in economic reality. I've carefully integrated successful management innovations to produce a blend of theory and practice based on the work of creative executives: leaders such as Richard (Skip) LeFauve, chairman of GM-Saturn, who expanded the old focus on profit to include the interests of workers, clients, and other stakeholders; Anita Roddick, founder of the Body Shop, who set a new standard for high-quality products that provide genuine value and protect the environment; and Bert Roberts, CEO of MCI, who created a dynamic organization that continues to outperform AT&T.

Principles are shown to flow out of hundreds of such examples, illustrated with anecdotes, cases, quotes, data, figures, and exercises to provide a vivid, realistic understanding of how creative leaders design and manage organizations today. While the book focuses on American business, it also covers government and other institutions within the context of today's global economy.

TABLE 1.2. PART ONE: REDEFINING THE FOUNDATION OF MANAGEMENT.

Chapter	The Old Management (thesis)	Forces of Change (antithesis)	The New Management (synthesis)
2	Organization structure: *Hierarchy*	Complexity, diversity, economic change, global competition, information networks	*Internal Market:* Small enterprises cooperating within a large organization
3	Goals and governance: *Profit*	Human & social values, stakeholder power, cooperation becomes efficient	*Corporate Community:* Coalition of all stakeholder rights & responsibilities
4	Management system: *Mechanistic*	Information revolution	*Organic Organization:* Creative tension between internal markets and corporate community

Chapter 2. From Hierarchy to Enterprise: Internal Markets Are the New Form of Organization Structure

Large corporations are disbanding their former hierarchies, but surely there must be a new model that is more precise than "flat structures," "flexible organizations," "networks," and other popular terms.

Just as former socialist nations are moving to markets, so too are leading-edge corporations such as MCI, Hewlett-Packard (HP), and Asea Brown Bovari (ABB)—"internal markets." Internal markets bring the power of free markets *inside* organizations by defining all units as small internal enterprises working together within a supportive corporate infrastructure.

This cooperative cluster of internal enterprises offers the creativity of small business ventures and the economic power of large corporations. Markets have their drawbacks, but they are spreading throughout the new social order because they provide the dynamic foundation needed to manage complexity and change.

Chapter 3. From Profit to Democracy: Corporate Community Is the New Form of Organization Governance

The conflict between profit and social welfare has been a long, bitter struggle waged continuously over the same tired ground. Social responsibility enjoyed popularity in the 1970s, but became an empty piety when the Reagan era restored a focus on profit. Either view alone is unrealistic since the broader reality is that business is a socioeconomic institution.

A wholistic perspective is emerging as it becomes clear that any organization is a political system composed of five main constituencies: investors, employees, customers, business partners, and the public. Since success hinges on the support of all these groups, progressive firms such as GM-Saturn, IKEA, and the Body Shop strive to create a political coalition that serves all interests better, including making profits for investors.

This can be seen as "a better way to make money," but the New Management presents a more powerful perspective. The role of business is expanding to form a "corporate community" composed of all stakeholders, with profit being a critical but limited goal.

Chapter 4. The New Management Synthesis: Uniting Internal Markets and Corporate Community

The themes of internal markets and corporate community are integrated here into a conceptual foundation for the New Management. It may appear that these concepts oppose one another. Markets are associated with conservative values of enterprise, competition, and profit, while community is thought of in terms of liberal values of democracy, cooperation, and social welfare.

But these orientations are essential parts of any social system. Western society has always struggled to reconcile markets and community, which is why free enterprise and democracy are the two pillars supporting modern civilization. In institutions, this union is symbolized by the metaphor of an "organization tree": a living organism rooted into its economic terrain by internal enterprises and guided by the social values of its community.

Excellent managers create more powerful organizations based on a creative tension between these two halves of the New Management. Internal markets are needed to master a diverse complex world, yet this diversity must be pulled together into corporate communities that are economically productive and socially harmonious.

TABLE 1.3. PART TWO: BUILDING AN ENTREPRENEURIAL COMMUNITY.

Chapter	The Old Management (thesis)	Forces of Change (antithesis)	The New Management (synthesis)
5	Client relations: *Selling*	Demand for value, quality of life, global competition	*Serving Enterprise:* Working relationship with clients to improve quality of life
6	Work roles: *Employee*	Economic change, need for productivity, achievement values	*Knowledge Entrepreneur:* Pay for performance combined with freedom of operations
7	Ecological inter-face: *Unbounded Growth*	Ecological crisis, global industrialization, appreciation of nature	*Intelligent Growth:* Innovative economic progress that is ecologically sound

Chapter 5. The Serving Enterprise: Relinquishing Our Grip on Self-Interest

One of the harshest features of previous business practice was the sell-at-any-cost marketing that turned television into a cultural wasteland, urged shoddy products on a gullible public, and failed to serve a growing need for improving the quality of life.

This chapter shows that global competition, demanding clients, and growing social problems are moving marketing away from simply selling goods toward a client-driven focus on improving the quality of life. Creative business is becoming a "serving enterprise" that uses sophisticated information systems to understand social needs, customize products and services, evaluate client satisfaction, and make advertising more useful.

The result is a working partnership between organizations and their customers that benefits both parties. If managers can relinquish their immediate self-interest, the difficult problems that abound today can be converted into limitless opportunities.

Chapter 6. Knowledge Entrepreneurs: A Working Contract of Rights and Responsibilities

Employee empowerment is becoming common now, but global competition has forced employers to cut costs and boost productivity. Even the Japanese are laying off workers. Suddenly, working relations no longer seem as promising as they once did.

Such conflicting trends signal a historic shift in work. The old lifetime employment system of the Industrial Age is yielding to a more sharply focused contractual system that links rewards to output. A new breed of "knowledge entrepreneurs" is emerging in which teams act as quasi business partners with the corporation, sharing both the rights and responsibilities of management.

Some organizations will continue to provide traditional work relationships, but the same forces that are driving the world to market economies are forcing employees to assume entrepreneurial roles. People will thereby have to become more self-reliant, but they will also gain the benefits entrepreneurs have always enjoyed.

Chapter 7. Intelligent Growth: Balancing Ecological Health and Economic Progress

After decades of conflict over economic growth versus the environment, the concept of "sustainability" has been widely accepted. But how can sustainability be attained when the industrialization of less developed nations will inevitably increase the load on the environment by a factor of five to ten?

We are not likely to resolve this issue by insisting on either a pristine environment or unchecked growth. A form of "intelligent growth" is appearing as business accepts the necessity for a healthy environment and turns its problem-solving skills to this end. Progressive firms now consider a clean manufacturing cycle—from product design to disposal—a sound competitive advantage.

If environmentalists, government officials, and businesspeople can resolve the difficult problems involved, the industrial world could be transformed into a new economic system that is able to improve the lives of ten billion people while safeguarding the environment. Indeed, there is little choice.

TABLE 1.4. PART THREE: LEADING IN THE NEW ECONOMIC ORDER.

Chapter	The Old Management (thesis)	Forces of Change (antithesis)	The New Management (synthesis)
8	Strategy formation: *Planning*	Turbulent environment, organic organization	*Continuous Change:* Organizations integrated with forces of change in their surroundings
9	Guidance and control: *Authority*	Power shift, rise of informal organization, participation, risk and uncertainty	*Inner Leadership:* Resolution of differences between leaders and followers
10	World system: *The Old Capitalism vs. The Old Socialism*	Free enterprise, democracy, globalization	*Democratic Enterprise:* Global networks of entrepreneurial community

Chapter 8. Continuous Change: Rooting the Organization into Its Environment

Strategic planning faded in the 1980s when companies found that it usually produces bureaucracy rather than actual change. The problem is that any type of planning coordinated from the top will incur the disadvantages common to all centralized controls.

The New Management comprises a more powerful form of strategic change that harnesses the energy of outside forces. Internal markets and corporate community integrate organizations into their environment, allowing the ebb and flow of external events to produce "continuous change" throughout the institution.

Individual organizations may favor different aspects of the New Management. But in an age when the only constant is change, the organic, fluid, messy nature of living systems must provide the creative behavior needed to survive a turbulent world.

Chapter 9. Inner Leadership: How to Handle the Coming Power Shift

Participative leadership has become essential now, but it is leading to a profound shift in power as the informal organization rises to challenge authority with conflicting demands. How can leaders marshal the talents of their followers while avoiding this disintegration into a cacophony of diverse interests?

Good leaders resolve these challenges by drawing on the power of their personal intuition, insights, and spiritual awareness—"inner leadership" that acts from the inside out. The leader welcomes disagreements in a constructive spirit, listens carefully to critical opposition, acknowledges his or her own weaknesses, holds followers responsible for meeting their goals, and relies on inner wisdom to guide the organization through stress and uncertainty.

When leaders and followers are joined in such an intense existential dialogue, more useful guidance can be wrought that is steadfast and unerring. The truth usually emerges for all to see, and leaders may then embrace it on behalf of their followers.

Chapter 10. Managing a Unified World: Global Order out of Local Institutions

This concluding chapter examines the macroeconomic implications of the New Management. The United States is suffering from a lack of direction, Russia is facing doubts about Western-style capitalism, and social support is disappearing as welfare states are abandoned. All these dilemmas pose the same basic problem: how can a decentralized world of free markets provide the guidance needed by the West, the security demanded by the East, and the social support people require everywhere?

The New Management suggests a middle ground between government planning and unguided markets: a local blend of enterprise and community at the grassroots level. We will see that the rapid spread of huge new consumer markets around the world is encouraging robust competition, albeit guided by alliances among business partners, employees, governments, and other stakeholders. For the West, the result may be a "New Capitalism" that encourages cooperation among autonomous economic actors. The same concept offers the East a "New Socialism" that draws on their cohesive cultures to manage free markets in a more orderly and productive manner.

This illustrates that *the same principles of the New Management apply to all economic levels.* Whether it is a team of knowledge workers managing its own affairs, a complex organization guided by executives, or a national economy led by government, all require a similar blend of enterprise and democracy.

APPLYING NEW CONCEPTS TO A CHANGING WORLD

Let's briefly review the logic of this introductory chapter to put the transition to a New Management in perspective:

1. Like the Industrial Revolution, the Information Revolution is transforming business, government, and other institutions.

2. A wave of innovation is under way that promises to replace the Old Management with a New Management.

3. However, conflicts between "old" and "new," "left" and "right," and so on create confusion over the New Management paradigm.

4. The confusion is resolved by seeing that democracy and enterprise are transforming organizations into internal markets guided by corporate communities.

This transition to a New Management is supported by the CIT Study. As Table 1.5 shows, many of these concepts were widely practiced in 1995, although some are lagging because they provoke resistance. The data also show that 83 percent of the respondents think the New Management is needed, 74 percent estimate it should enter the mainstream in five to ten years, and 78 percent say companies that do not change will fail or suffer a marginal existence. Listen to how typical managers view the prospects: "Things are changing rapidly but we still have a long way to go," "Some are using the New Management now," "I think it's already entered the main-stream to varying degrees," "More companies will make the transition in 1996–1998," and "If we don't see changes soon, business will lose effectiveness." (Details of this study are reported in later chapters.)

TABLE 1.5. APPLICATION OF NEW MANAGEMENT CONCEPTS.
(SAMPLE = 426 CORPORATE MANAGERS.)

Concept	Not Practiced (0–3)	Partially Practiced (4–6)	Fully Practiced (7–10)	Mean (0–10)
Internal Markets	48%	17%	35%	4.3
Corporate Community	19	13	68	6.9
Serving Enterprise	24	17	59	6.4
Knowledge Entrepreneur	45	22	33	4.4
Intelligent Growth	37	24	39	4.9
Continuous Change	13	23	64	6.9
Inner Leadership	11	23	66	7.1

Source: William E. Halal, Corporations in Transition (an unpublished study in progress). Note that data in the first three columns ("Not Practiced," etc.) are aggregated by collapsing portions of the questionnaire scale as shown ("0–3," etc.). See the questionnaire in Appendix C.

It's obvious that implementing the New Management will prove daunting because the opposition to institutional change is always intense. I recall the struggle of getting managers to seriously consider the need for change during the seventies and eighties. Even the prospect of a Knowledge Revolution seemed outlandish to many competent people. It would have been difficult to act then, but bold leadership could possibly have avoided the fall of GM, IBM, and other great companies, the loss of American markets to foreign competition, and today's slide into social decline. Could a similar cynicism divert us today?

It's always possible, but unusually powerful forces are at work because a knowledge-based world introduces new economic imperatives. As we will show later, democracy and enterprise have now become economically *efficient*. This shift in the laws of economics is one of the pivotal events of our time. It may seem a bit theoretical, but there is no stopping an idea whose time has arrived. We have just witnessed the power of the Information Revolution in the fall of Communism, the decline of big government, restructuring of corporations, and other historic changes that are caused basically by the spreading of information technology.[16]

While the concepts in this book may be appealing, then, they are always argued on the basis of economic value because that is the test of good management. As information flows around the world instantaneously, it also moves capital, knowledge, and labor to their point of greatest productivity.[17] Peter Drucker predicts the new economy "will inevitably be far more competitive than anything yet known." Even "New Age" companies are yielding their altruism to the necessity of increasing productivity, cutting prices, and improving marketing. Arnold Hiatt, former CEO of Stride Rite Shoes, says, "The first act of social responsibility is to make money."[18]

Meeting this test of economic reality does not mean that we must slavishly accept business practices we may not approve of. Organizations, like families and societies, are so infinitely rich that they defy any one approach to understanding; each is characterized by a special blend of people, skills, and other conditions. The New Management offers valid principles, but they must be interpreted to suit the unique needs of each individual acting in each situation.[19] Here's how managers in the CIT survey expressed it: "The New Management must vary for different organizations and human resources," and "It depends entirely on the company, industry, the competition in the field, and the type of leadership."

If the New Management requires us to embrace everything in a spirit of wholism, how can we possibly find our way through such a limitless range of possibilities? What criteria can guide us? I think the answer is that managers should practice their profession in the same manner all skilled practitioners have traditionally done: by systematically discovering what best works for *them*.

From this view, management is much like science. Scientists propose a theory to explain how the world behaves, they test the theory against empirical evidence, revise it accordingly, and continue this cycle to perfect a theory's explanatory power. In like manner, good managers approach their profession with a mental model or philosophy that explains how their *organization* behaves. They test the concept against the outcome using trial and error, and revise it to improve their management abilities. Ask any seasoned manager and you will get a carefully built, detailed personal philosophy that has been honed to perfection over years of hard experience.

I conclude that faith in the concepts of a New Management is essential to create a different future, but it must be based on healthy skepticism. In a changing, complex world where bewildering new ideas are emerging constantly, leaders must test their vision to avoid half-truths or fantasy. There is simply no other way to forge the hard new understanding needed to distinguish between outmoded practices of the past and grandiose claims for the future.

As we've seen, the New Management favors neither power nor freedom, profit nor society, material growth nor the environment. It is all these and more, presenting managers with an enormous responsibility for learning to act in the face of complexity, change, and sheer mystery. So it seems to me that managers will need everything we can our lay hands on in the years ahead, including those ideas inherited from our ancestors and those yet to come.

Notes

1. I realize that the contention that the United States is in decline may be controversial, but later chapters will show that, although the American economy is successful in many ways, the nation as a whole is showing serious signs of

decline. For instance, average wages rose steadily throughout the industrial past, yet they have been flat, at best, for the past two decades.

2. The U.S. Bureau of Labor Statistics reports that 15.4 million people were managers in 1994, making managers by far the largest professional group. Also, the study of management now enrolls the greatest number of students at colleges.

3. Peter Drucker, *The New Realities* (New York: Harper & Row/Perennial, 1989), p. 223. Peter Drucker, "The Age of Social Transformation," *Atlantic Monthly* (November 1994), p. 72.

4. Louis Harris, "What in the World Is Going on in This Nation?" *Vital Speeches of the Day* (August 15, 1994), pp. 663–666. William E. Halal, "The Deeper Cause of National Decline: American Institutions Need American Ideals," *By George* (November 6, 1992).

5. The new science of complexity is described by Mitchell Waldrop in *Complexity: The Emerging Science at the Edge of Order and Chaos* (New York: Simon & Schuster, 1992), and by David Freedman in "Is Management Still a Science?" *Harvard Business Review* (November-December, 1992)

6. "Home Computer Sales Explode as PCs Turn into All-Purpose Information Appliances," *BusinessWeek* (November 28, 1994). Bill Richards, "Test of Virtual Reality Spans the Pacific," *Wall Street Journal* (November 16, 1994). Elizabeth Corcoran, "Bill Gates Heads Home," *Washington Post* (November 13, 1994).

7. William Bridges, "The End of the Job," *Fortune* (September 19, 1994).

8. This statement was quoted to me by Korean managers.

9. Abraham Maslow, "A Theory of Human Motivation," *Psychological Review* (1943), Vol. 50, pp. 370–396. Elton Mayo, *The Social Problems of an Industrial Civilization* (Cambridge, Mass.: Harvard University Press, 1945). Douglas McGregor, *The Human Side of Enterprise* (New York: McGraw-Hill, 1960). Chester I. Barnard, *The Functions of the Executive* (Cambridge, Mass.: Harvard University Press, 1968). Warren Bennis, *Beyond Bureaucracy* (New York: McGraw-Hill, 1966). Paul Lawrence and Jay Lorsch, "Differentiation and Integration in Complex Organizations," *Harvard Business Review* (June 1964). Henry Mintzberg, "The Manager's Job," *Harvard Business Review* (July-August 1975).

10. W. Edwards Deming, *Out of the Crisis* (Cambridge, Mass.: MIT Press, 1986). J. M. Juran, *Juran on Leadership for Quality* (London: Collier Macmillan, 1989). William Ouchi, *Theory Z* (Reading, Mass.: Addison-Wesley, 1981). Tom Peters and Robert Waterman, *In Search of Excellence* (New York: Harper & Row, 1982).

Peter Vaill, *Managing as a Performing Art* (San Francisco: Jossey-Bass, 1991). Gifford Pinchot, *Intrapreneuring* (New York: Harper & Row, 1985). Russell Ackoff, *Creating the Corporate Future* (New York: Wiley, 1981). Raymond Miles and Charles Snow, *Fit, Failure, and the Hall of Fame* (New York: Free Press, 1994). Peter Senge, *The Fifth Discipline* (New York: Doubleday, 1990). Terrence Deal and Allen Kennedy, *Corporate Cultures* (Reading, Mass.: Addison-Wesley, 1982). Peter Frost et al., *Organizational Reality* (Santa Monica, Calif.: Goodyear, 1978). Lee Bolman and Terrence Deal, *Reframing Organizations* (San Francisco: Jossey-Bass, 1991). Michael Ray, "The Emerging New Paradigm in Business," in John Renesch (ed.), *New Traditions in Business* (San Francisco: Berrett-Koehler, 1992). William E. Halal, *The New Capitalism* (New York: Wiley, 1986).

11. For instance, see a fine review of this confusion by Martha Nichols, "Does New Age Business Have a Message for Managers?" *Harvard Business Review* (March-April 1994), and the responses reported in "Letters to the Editor," *Harvard Business Review* (May-June 1994), pp. 144–148. Jeffrey Pfeffer, "Barriers to the Advance of Organizational Science," *The Academy of Management Review* (October 1993), pp. 599–621.

12. The executive is quoted from "Changing Times in the Automotive Industry," *Academy of Management Executive* (February 1988).

13. "Weirton Steel Workers Are Furious That Their ESOP Can't Save Jobs," *BusinessWeek* (September 9, 1991). Robert L. Rose and Erle Norton, "ESOP Fables," *Wall Street Journal* (December 5, 1993).

14. "Companies Hit the Road Less Travelled," *BusinessWeek* (June 5, 1995).

15. See *The New Leaders* (September-October 1994).

16. Walter B. Wriston, *The Twilight of Sovereignty: How the Information Revolution Is Transforming Our World* (New York: Scribner, 1992).

17. See "Borderless Finance: Fuel for Growth," in the special issue of *BusinessWeek* titled *21st Century Capitalism,* (1994), which illustrates how global money markets increasingly govern the management of corporations and even governments.

18. Udayan Gupta, "Cause-Driven Companies' New Cause: Profits," *Wall Street Journal* (November 8, 1994). Leslie Kaufman-Rosen, "Being Cruel to Be Kind," *BusinessWeek* (October 17, 1994).

19. This point is well made by George Harrar, "The Tools of Success," *Enterprise* (October 1994), and Andrew Serwer, "Lessons from America's Fastest Growing Companies," *Fortune* (August 8, 1994).

Part One

●

Redefining the Foundation of Management

Like the foundation of a building, the foundation of management must support the entire structure by anchoring it securely to its environment. These three chapters of Part One redefine the conceptual foundation of modern management to anchor today's institutions in the Information Age.

Chapter 2 refutes the age-old universal assumption that organizations must be controlled by "superiors" from the top down. This hierarchical foundation was good for the simple conditions of the Industrial Age, but a new foundation based on enterprise is emerging to contain the turbulence of an Information Age. Modern organizations master complexity by having entreprenuerial units manage themselves from the bottom up—"internal markets."

Chapter 3 challenges the other major pillar that buttressed an industrial society—the profit-centered firm. The Information Revolution is introducing a new form of economic behavior in which cooperation has become productive. This shift in economic reality knits social and financial interests into a more powerful system that serves both needs better—a "corporate community."

Chapter 4 integrates these two central concepts into a unified, organic whole—think of it as an "organization tree." The roots of this "tree" are internal markets of small enterprises drawing nourishment at the grass roots of economic life. And its leaves are the diverse views of investors, workers, clients, business partners, and the public, who orient this corporate community to serve the needs of society. Thus the foundation of the New Management is a synthesis of democracy and enterprise.

2

From Hierarchy to Enterprise

*Internal Markets Are the New Form
of Organization Structure*

It has become a cliché to note that business schools are notorious for their poor management. Mine was no exception. An especially irksome problem was getting the copy center to work properly. Professors thrive on paper, yet we couldn't seem to get copies made in less than a week. We knew that our local Kinko's could get them done in a day, but we would have to pay. Since the copy center was free, we kept using it despite bad service. In fact, that's one reason why the service was bad: we overused this free good, clogging the system. Repeated attempts to get the copy center to improve its operations and the faculty to curb their excessive usage had little effect.

The problem was that we were relying on a hierarchical assignment of tasks that were too complex for this approach. We needed good service. We needed faculty accountability. We needed a copy center manager who was motivated to help us. We needed a choice of providers. In short, we needed a market.

After much argument, we asked the copy center manager (let's call him Art) if he would like to turn the operation into "his own business." He could still use the school's copiers and facilities to serve the faculty's needs,

Note: Earlier versions of this chapter appeared in my publications *Internal Markets: Bringing the Power of Free Enterprise Inside Your Organization* (New York: Wiley, 1993), *The New Portable MBA* (Wiley, 1994), and *The Academy of Management Executive* (November 1994).

but his income would be based on a percentage of the profits. The faculty would get his budget and could use it to either patronize Art or other copy centers. Art had an entrepreneurial streak, so he welcomed the opportunity.

Well, everything changed within days. A few people went to Kinko's, which got Art thinking about how to improve operations. And having to pay now, the faculty carefully considered whether they really needed fifty copies of their latest tome. Our copy center's service soon matched Kinko's, Art became a celebrated hero, and the problem was solved—by an internal market.

This little story illustrates that the most fundamental problem in management today is the bureaucracy that results almost invariably from large hierarchies. The hierarchical model of organization built civilization, from the pyramids of ancient Egypt, to the medieval church, to modern industry. It continued to dominate the Industrial Age because it was good at managing routine tasks performed by uneducated workers.

But the Information Age is releasing such revolutionary forces that the world is becoming an incomprehensible maze, thereby rendering today's hierarchies obsolete.[1] When Max Weber first defined the "theory of bureaucracy" based on principles of hierarchy at the start of the Industrial Age, the concept promised a Utopia of efficiency and order. Today the most damning thing one can say about an organization is to call it a "bureaucracy." Some hierarchy will always be needed because the universe is naturally organized in a hierarchical fashion. But the former management system in which decisions flowed from the top down is now history.

This chapter shows how today's wave of restructuring within "electronic organizations" is leading to an organic network of self-managed internal enterprises that operates more like an intelligent market system. We first examine the limitations of present approaches to restructuring and the evolution of market organizations. Then, principles for creating internal markets are described using examples of progressive companies. We conclude by exploring the implications of this profound shift from hierarchy to enterprise that makes up one-half of the new management foundation.

RISE OF THE ENTREPRENEURIAL ORGANIZATION

Today's exploding complexity challenges our most basic assumptions about management. Hierarchy is too cumbersome under these conditions, so modern economies require organic systems composed of numerous small, self-guiding enterprises that can adapt to their local environment more easily by operating from the bottom up.[2] Gerhard Schulmeyer, CEO of Siemens, put it best: "It's not important anymore to be big . . . but to be fast and innovative."[3]

Limits of Downsizing, Reengineering, and Networks

Companies have been moving in this direction with a vengeance as competition drives lower costs and faster innovation, as powerful new information systems automate jobs and streamline operations, and business processes are reengineered into cross-functional teams. These changes allowed CEOs to eliminate roughly one-third of their employees and layers of management during the past few years, producing flat, decentralized organizations. The pressure to downsize is so strong that it has become a way of life, even when profits are up. The chairman of Procter & Gamble said, "Our competitors are getting leaner and quicker, so we have to run faster," while a Xerox manager added: "I know it sounds heartless when the company's making money, but it's the new reality."[4]

This same imperative is being felt abroad. In Japan, the traditional system of lifetime employment is passing as Japanese corporations reduce management levels, lay off workers, and introduce merit pay. Here's how a Japanese manager saw the change: "The era of waving the company flag to motivate people is over."[5]

Considering the enormous impact of these difficult changes, we should not be surprised that restructuring has become very controversial. A 1995 survey of 1,800 CEOs showed that 94 percent of companies had implemented various forms of restructuring, but the economic gains have proven meager. Roughly two-thirds of these programs have failed to improve productivity or reduce costs. In addition, ten million Americans lost their jobs during the past decade, forcing U.S. wages down to the point where European and Japanese companies now open plants in the United States to take advantage of *America*'s cheap labor. In organizations across the land, employees have become traumatized by the fear of layoffs and are overstressed from doing the work of others. CEOs themselves know this is a problem. "If you keep [downsizing], you destroy morale and paralyze the organization," said the CEO of Scott Paper. Jim Stanford, CEO of Petro-Canada, put it best: "You can't shrink to greatness."[6]

How did intelligent, well-meaning people get into such a mess? These are genuine attempts to create high-performing organizations to survive a complex global economy. But present restructuring is ineffective because it is largely an extension of the hierarchical system. Most restructuring is arbitrary because it originates from senior managers who are often out of touch with operations, slashing the staffs of good and poor units alike, and it is forced on unwilling people who have little interest in its success. The predictable result is that the disadvantages of hierarchy remain, while managers feel confused and guilty for laying off their co-workers—at the very time they are also urged to empower people and to collaborate. Here's how one manager experienced it: "This year, I had to downsize my area by 25 percent. It's emotionally draining. I find myself not wanting to go to work because I'll have to push my people to do more. But they're not going to complain because they don't want to be the next 25 percent."[7]

The most feasible successor to the hierarchy currently is the concept of "organizational networks." In this model, temporary teams use groupware to form strategic alliances, producing a fluid network that can mobilize to meet changing market needs quickly.[8] But the concept does not go far enough.

The network model is a good description of how organizations should look, but it does not tell us how they should *work* in economic terms. How do we know whether teams create value or destroy it? How much freedom is allowed? How is accountability ensured? How are resources allocated? Who has the authority to make decisions? If the answers to these questions come from top management, we once again incur the disadvantages of hierarchy. After all, GM was awash in powerful alliances even as it floundered in bureaucracy. If teams are just allowed to be "flexible," what prevents anarchy? The Internet is a great network, but it is hardly a well-managed system.

Other metaphors that purport to replace the hierarchy suffer from the same limitation. There is the "federal" system of loosely connected units, the "pizza" or "circular" organization, the "horizontal" workplace, the "boundaryless" corporation, the "intelligent" or "learning" organization, fleet-footed "gazelles," the "agile" company, the "starburst," "spider's web," "fishnet," and so on. In the absence of sound answers to the questions about values, accountability, and authority raised earlier, however, these remain fluid variations of hierarchy rather than true bottom-up systems. The issue remains: how can any organization be managed without impairing local autonomy?

Fundamentally, this problem will resist solution as long as we instinctively continue to think of management within a hierarchical framework. Major corporations comprise economic systems that are as large and complex as national economies, yet they are commonly viewed as "firms" to be managed by executives who move resources about like a portfolio of investments, form global strategies, restructure the organization, and set financial targets. How does this differ from the central planning that failed in the Communist bloc? Why would such control be bad for a national economy but good for a *corporate* economy? Can *any* fixed structure remain useful for long in a world of constant change?

The Internal Market Perspective

For years a dramatically different concept has been quietly emerging that realizes the ideal of bottom-up systems.

Figure 2.1 illustrates the evolution of organizational structure from the hierarchy, to the matrix, and now to networks of decentralized, entreprenuerial units. Today, progressive organizations have become clusters of small business units that behave as separate firms in their own right. Some global corporations, such as Asea Brown Bovari (ABB), have thousands of such profit centers with their own products, clients, and competitors. At times they may buy and sell to other units within the parent corporation, compete with one another, and even work with outside competitors. The same trend can be seen in efforts to reinvent government; for instance, the concept of parental "choice" is gaining acceptance in education to force schools to compete for students.[9]

These structures cannot be explained with hierarchical concepts, and so an entrepreneurial economic framework has been proposed by Jay Forrester, Russell Ackoff, Gifford and Elizabeth Pinchot, and myself that views organizations as markets—"internal markets."[10] Just as the post-Communist bloc is adopting markets, so too are large corporations. Tom Peters urged: "Force the market into every nook and cranny of the firm."

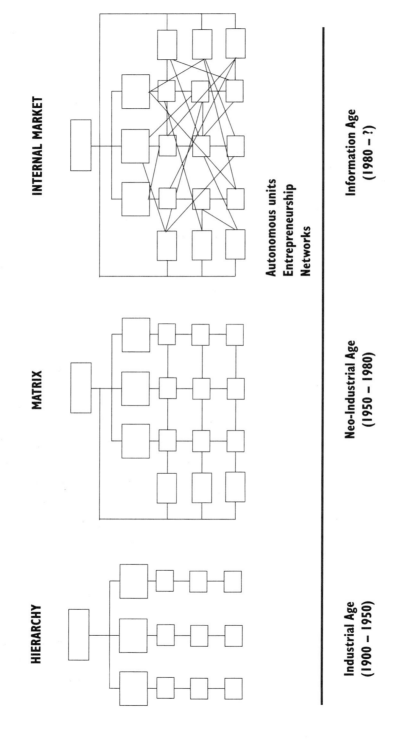

FIGURE 2.1. THE EVOLUTION OF ORGANIZATIONAL STRUCTURE.

HIERARCHY

MATRIX

INTERNAL MARKET

Autonomous units
Entrepreneurship
Networks

Industrial Age
(1900 – 1950)

Neo-Industrial Age
(1950 – 1980)

Information Age
(1980 – ?)

As shown in Box 2.1, internal markets are *meta*structures, or processes, that transcend ordinary structures. Unlike fixed hierarchies or centrally coordinated networks, they are *complete internal market economies* designed to produce continual, rapid structural change, just as external markets do. Although only a few companies have implemented this idea as yet, Table 2.1 shows fairly wide acceptance of some key features, and the examples in Box 2.2 demonstrate various approaches that have been used.

People are initially skeptical about internal markets because the idea breaks so sharply from the hierarchy. At first the notion seems fraught with conflict, and it is certainly true that internal markets incur the same risks, turmoil, and other drawbacks of any market system. But these doubts occur precisely because the concept represents a dramatically different form of logic. Once we grasp the central idea that an internal market replicates an external market, the behavior of such a system becomes almost self-evident.

As hierarchical controls are replaced by market forces, the release of entrepreneurial energy produces roughly the same self-organizing, creative

---

BOX 2.1. PRINCIPLES OF INTERNAL MARKETS.

1. Transform the Hierarchy into Internal Enterprise Units. "Internal enterprises" form the building blocks of an internal market system. All line and staff units are transformed into enterprises by not only becoming accountable for performance but also gaining control over their operations, as an external enterprise does. Alliances between internal enterprises link corporations together into a global economy.

2. Create an Economic Infrastructure to Guide Decisions. Executives design and regulate the infrastructure of this "organizational economy," just as governments manage national economics—by establishing common systems for accounting, communications, incentives, governing policies, an entrepreneurial culture, and the like. Management may also encourage the formation of various business arrangements that exist in an economic system: venture capital firms, consultants, distributors, and so on.

3. Provide Leadership to Foster Collaborative Synergy. An internal economy is more than a laissez-faire market, it is a community of entrepreneurs that fosters collaborative synergy in the forms of joint ventures, sharing of technology, mutual problem-solving, and so on, among both internal and external partners. Corporate executives provide the leadership to guide this internal market by encouraging the development of various strategies.

interplay that makes external markets so advantageous. Experience shows that solutions to difficult problems emerge far more quickly and almost spontaneously, permitting a rush of economic growth that can rarely be planned by even the most brilliant managers of hierarchical systems.

Markets can be chaotic, but they are spreading around the globe because they excel over the other alternative—central planning—whether in communist governments or capitalist corporations. *In both nations and organizations, planned economies are too cumbersome to cope with a complex new era, while free enterprise—either internal or external—offers an economic philosophy able to produce adaptive change rapidly and efficiently.*

TABLE 2.1. ADOPTION OF INTERNAL MARKET PRACTICES.
(SAMPLE = 426 CORPORATE MANAGERS.)

Practice	Not Practiced (0–3)	Partially Practiced (4–6)	Fully Practiced (7–10)	Mean (0–10)
Line units are treated as semiautonomous enterprises that have control over their own operations and keep most of their revenue.	38%	20%	42%	4.9
Staff and support units (HRD, Legal, IS, etc.) are treated as profit centers that obtain revenue by selling their services to other units.	73	8	19	2.5
Line units are generally allowed to buy products and services from any organization, inside or outside the company.	37	18	45	5.2
Staff and support units are generally allowed to sell their services to any organization, inside or outside the company.	62	12	26	3.3
Apart from proprietary secrets, employees have access to central information systems that contain all available company information.	30	24	46	5.6
Means	48%	17%	35%	4.3

Source: William E. Halal, *Corporations in Transition* (an unpublished study in progress). Note that data in the first three columns ("Not Practiced," etc.) are aggregated by collapsing portions of the questionnaire scale as shown ("0–3," etc.). See the questionnaire in Appendix C.

BOX 2.2. EXEMPLARS OF INTERNAL MARKETS.

MCI has become the second largest communications company in the U.S. by designing an entrepreneurial organization in which new ventures are started by anyone, resources are allocated to reward performance, and units compete with one another.

Johnson & Johnson's 168 separately chartered companies form their own strategies, relationships with suppliers and clients, and other business affairs. CEO Ralph Larsen says the system "provides a sense of ownership that you simply cannot get any other way."

Motorola uses autonomous units that compete with one another to produce the most successful products in America. One manager said: "The fact that I may conflict with another manager's turf is tough beans. Things will sort themselves out in the market."

Cypress Semiconductor defines each business unit as a separate corporation, and support units from manufacturing subsidiaries to testing centers sell their services to line units. The CEO, T. J. Rodgers, says "We've gotten rid of socialism in the organization."

Merck & Company has been rated the top Fortune 500 company because researchers pool their efforts in projects they choose, merging talents and resources into a new team. The CEO said: "Everybody here gravitates around a hot project. It's like a live organism."

Clark Equipment survived Chapter 11 by requiring all business units—including a staff of 500 people—to become self-supporting enterprises. Within months staff decreased by 400 positions, costs were reduced across the company, and sales moved upward.

Alcoa revitalized a bureaucracy by converting all units into suppliers or clients that were free to conduct business with outside competitors. This dose of economic reality doubled productivity, and support groups brought in outside business.

Xerox is transforming itself from a functional hierarchy into an internal market composed of nine independent business units, each including dozens of self-managed teams. Teams and business units are held accountable for performance and rewarded with bonuses.

Koch Industries has grown from a small firm to one of the largest private corporations in the world as a result of its system of "market-based management." The CEO, Charles Koch, defines all corporate functions in terms of market equivalents.

Matsushita allows its research labs, product groups, and sales units to choose the internal "business partners" they prefer to work with. The result is intense internal competition to develop successful products.

Semco has thrived in the turbulent economy of Brazil by forming dozens of internal enterprises, which it calls "satellites." The CEO, Ricardo Semler, says, "Semco has abandoned traditional business practices [to] the discipline of our own community marketplace."

Source: William E. Halal et al., *Internal Markets* (New York: Wiley, 1993).

PRINCIPLES OF INTERNAL MARKETS

The three central principles shown in Box 2.1 are described below more fully, illustrated by the experiences of companies my colleagues and I have studied and worked with.

Transform the Hierarchy into Internal Enterprise Units

Rather than think of units as "divisions," "departments," and other hierarchical concepts, the logic of internal markets transforms line, staff, and all other units into their entrepreneurial equivalents—an "internal enterprise," or what the Pinchots call an "intraprise." This change may require creative reengineering of existing structures, but it is usually feasible if an external or internal client can be identified, and that is almost always possible, as we will show. An AT&T manager told me: "We link internal suppliers with internal and external customers."

Units are converted into intraprises by accepting controls on *performance* in return for freedom of *operations*. Hewlett-Packard is famous for its entrepreneurial system, which holds units accountable for results but gives them wide operating latitude. As one HP executive described it, "The financial controls are very tight, what is loose is how [people] meet those goals." This sharply focused understanding enhances both control and freedom to provide two major strengths:

1. All units are accountable for results.

2. Creative entrepreneurship is encouraged.

There is wide agreement that performance should be evaluated using customer satisfaction, product quality, and other measures to ensure a realistic balance that avoids overemphasizing short-term profit. Managers are then held accountable through incentive pay, stock plans, budget allocations, or outright dismissal. The ideal arrangement is to treat each unit as a small, separate company, free to manage its own operations and resources. It is important to allow all units the freedom to conduct business transactions both inside and outside the firm. Without that freedom, managers are subject to the bureaucracy of central controls, about the same way the Soviets overcontrolled their economy.

Although the decentralization of line units is well known, Box 2.3 shows how the concept is being applied to staff units, manufacturing facilities, information system (IS) departments, research and development (R&D), marketing and distribution, employee work teams, starting new ventures, government, and even the CEO's office. This reminds us of the key principle for creating internal markets: all market functions should ideally be replicated within organizations. Raymond Smith, CEO of Bell Atlantic, described the logic:

> We are determined to revolutionize staff support, to convert a bureaucratic roadblock into an entrepreneurial force. Staffs tend to grow and produce services that may be neither wanted nor required. I decided to place the control of discretionary staff in the hands of those who were paying for them . . . line units. . . . The most important thing is that spending for support activities is now controlled by clients.[11]

Figure 2.2 illustrates the internal market that results from "privatizing" an organization with product, functional, and geographic structures. The heart of the system consists of new ventures spun off by product divisions to become independent business units that develop products or services. Functional support units are profit centers that sell their assistance to other units or external businesses. Geographic areas are also profit centers, distributing the full line of products and services to clients in their region. The network of business relationships formed by the intersection of these product, functional, and regional units constitutes the internal market economy.

From this view, the organization is no longer a pyramid of power but a web of changing business relationships held together by clusters of internal enterprise—as in any market. This system may appear radically different, but it simply represents an extension of the trend that began decades ago when large corporations decentralized into autonomous product divisions.

Create an Economic Infrastructure to Guide Decisions

With operational matters relegated to internal enterprises, executives focus on designing an infrastructure of performance measures, financial incentives, communication systems, an entrepreneurial culture, and other corporatewide frameworks. This infrastucture then allows market forces to guide

BOX 2.3. CONVERTING HIERARCHICAL FUNCTIONS INTO ENTERPRISES.

Support Units. IBM converted its HR unit into a business, "Workforce Solutions," which sells its services to IBM units and other companies. The U.S. Government is breaking up the monopoly of the General Services Administration and the Government Printing Office by allowing agencies to patronize other suppliers.

Manufacturing. Many companies treat their manufacturing units as "internal job shops" that produce goods for internal and external clients. A manager said: "Manufacturing is becoming a service function, making products for different companies."

Information Systems. Companies such as Brown-Foreman and Sunoco allow users to choose between the company's information systems (IS) office and outside competitors. The U.S. Government is forming "information utilities" that charge internal clients for computer time, electronic mail, and other IS services.

Research and Development. Bell Labs, Phillips Electronics, and Esso Canada are converting their R&D departments into profit centers that sell research services. Instead of relying on the debatable allocation of resources from the top, the value of research is determined by the willingness of profit-center managers to pay.

Marketing, Logistics, and Service. These units can be reorganized into "internal distributorships" that handle the full line of a company's products for a given region. Johnson & Johnson established common customer units that provide all sales and distribution services to retailers.

Work Teams. Market principles can be carried to the grass roots by organizing workers into self-managed profit centers. A paper-making company helped loggers form teams that were paid for the amount of timber they produced, thereby eliminating job classes, performance evaluations, and foremen. Loggers became keenly motivated because they could "run their own business," and they earned more, while management gained higher productivity and lower overhead.

New Ventures. Scores of companies have set up venture capital systems that welcome business proposals from any employee to start a new venture, which is then nursed to life as if in a "business incubator." Many states now allow teachers, parents, and administrators to form "charter schools."

The CEO's Office. Clark Equipment redefined the CEO's office as a profit center in which revenue was derived from assets invested in business units (similar to a venture capital firm), and from a portion of sales (like a "tax" by the "corporate government"). Like any profit center, the CEO must then keep the costs charged to managers down and the value they receive up to add value to these "clients."

Government. City, state, and federal bureaucracies are becoming enterprises. Mayor Steve Goldsmith of Indianapolis tells me that years of TQM and reengineering had little impact on reining in costs. Upon out-sourcing functions and allowing city departments to compete with their external counterparts, costs typically dropped by half or more.

FIGURE 2.2. EXAMPLE OF AN INTERNAL MARKET ORGANIZATION.

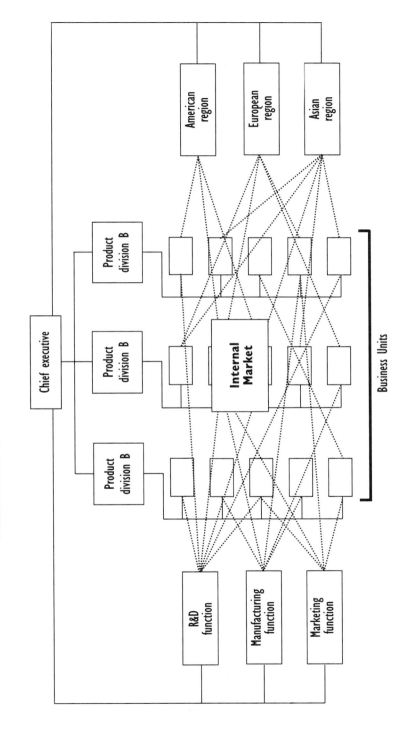

decisions instead of relying on administrative fiat. The behavior of this market system is then regulated, monitored for weaknesses and failures, and corrective changes are made to improve its performance.

When Alcoa moved to an internal market economy, its managers soon realized that decisions previously had been based on faulty estimates of costs and revenues. Like many corporations, the finances of operating units were pooled into larger divisions, absorbed by corporate overhead, and otherwise not identified accurately for individual units. Upon converting all units into autonomous enterprises with their own profit and loss statements, the newfound awareness of actual costs and revenues immediately altered decisions in more realistic directions. AT&T realized the same benefits when its large groups were divided into forty or so profit centers to highlight their individual performance. "The effect was staggering," said James Meehan, the CFO.

A striking example of the power of incentives to change behavior can be seen when converting staff units into profit centers. In the typical organization, IS services are provided free to line units, with the predictable result that people waste resources carelessly. Stories abound of line units demanding multiple copies of huge computer printouts that are never read, of overseas offices equipped with international phones lines used by clerks to call home every day. But when presented with monthly bills by the IS department, there is a marked change in attitude, causing line managers to select less costly systems that often provide better service as well.[12] Conversely, giving line units the freedom to choose among competing IS sources causes these internal suppliers to shape up equally fast.

There is also a need to instill the subtle norms of a social system. MCI has learned that an internal market must be augmented by an entrepreneurial culture that stresses taking initiative, embracing change, and supporting employees. The MCI culture constitutes a commonly understood, informal management system that guides human behavior effectively. Since this system exists in the minds of people rather than in cumbersome written policies, it is far more flexible because it is a shared idea. MCI employees and the company are one and the same, allowing quick agreement on a new product, organizational change, and other complex undertakings.

The impact of these various aspects of infrastructure illustrates the crucial need to design organizations as complex, interacting systems. As Jay

Forrester and Peter Senge point out, managers today must become organizational *designers,* in addition to *operators,* by creating a new class of adaptive, high-performing, intelligent organizations.[13]

Provide Leadership to Foster Collaborative Synergy

This model of entrepreneurial management raises tough questions about the role of executives and the very nature of corporations. If an organization is no longer a fixed, centrally controlled structure, but a fluid tangle of autonomous units going their own way, what gives it an identity that makes it more than the sum of its parts? What is best for the individual units and for the organization as a whole? How does this array of business units differ from an ordinary market economy? Why should they remain together at all? In short, what truly *is* a modern corporation, and how should it be managed?

CEOs may give up much of their formal authority in a market system, but they lead by ensuring accountability, resolving conflict, encouraging cooperation, forming alliances, providing inspiration, and other forms of strategic guidance that shape this system into a more productive community. One of Hewlett-Packard's great strengths is that its executives guide by persuasive leadership rather than fiat. The CEO, Lewis Platt, said, "In HP, you really can't order people to do anything. My job is to encourage people to work together, to experiment."[14]

MCI provides a good example in which corporate executives work hard to turn contentious issues into advantageous solutions. Top management understands that the autonomy of operating managers must remain inviolate, so executives avoid imposing decisions. Yet the company's entrepreneurial stance often provokes heated controversy over risky ventures. A new product concept, like MCI's Friends & Family, may be proposed by sales, engineering, or any other group, and is then the subject of a debate over the merits of the idea. Rather than squelch this conflict, MCI executives embrace it as a stimulant for tough, creative argument. By providing an acceptable form of constructive exchange among diverse viewpoints, a solid course of action usually emerges that all can support with confidence.

Johnson & Johnson (J&J) encourages coalitions of business units that serve everyone better. J&J's 166 separate companies retain their fierce autonomy because it "provides a sense of ownership that you simply cannot get any other way," says the CEO, Ralph Larsen. But the company's big clients, Wal-Mart, Kmart, and other retailers, want to avoid being bombarded by sales calls from dozens of J&J units. The CEO's solution was to urge his operating managers to pool such efforts into "customer support centers" that operate as internal distributorships to coordinate sales, logistics, and service for each major retailer.

These examples illustrate the resolution of two opposing sets of difficult demands. Modern executives must permit operating managers entrepreneurial freedom to gain their commitment, creativity, and flexibility. Yet they must also avoid disruptive conflict, needless duplication, and unnecessary risk. A market can provide this combination of freedom and control, but not by remaining a laissez-faire system. Leadership is essential to reconcile these opposing demands into a synergistic corporate community that adds net value to its internal enterprises.

Indeed, without the creation of net value there is little to justify uniting business units into a larger parent organization. The breakup of AT&T into three separate companies during 1995 illustrates a lack of this synergy. Hierarchical organizations may contain units that *destroy* value, but this is not apparent because the internal economic behavior of the system is masked by its bureaucratic structure. An internal market strips away the bureaucracy by regarding each unit as an enterprise, setting the stage for more realistic management.

Thus, an internal market is not simply a laissez-faire economy, but a *guided* economy, a vehicle for reaching common goals that is more effective than either a laissez-faire market or an authoritarian hierarchy. As these principles show, corporate executives guide an internal market by designing an economic infrastructure, setting policies to regulate the system, resolving critical issues, sharing valuable knowledge, and encouraging cooperative strategies. These benefits create the synergy that adds value which outside enterprises cannot match working alone.

THE FLOWERING OF ENTERPRISE

Surveying the evolution of organizational structure, the move from hierarchy to enterprise constitutes one of the most profound changes in management. The old pyramid has now become a decentralized network of semiautonomous units loosely coordinated by vestiges of the old chain of command. I estimate that the development of complete internal market systems is likely to form the next major phase in this process, entering the mainstream over the next decade or so as the Information Age matures.

If this estimate holds, the idea of hierarchy may soon seem as archaic as the divine right of kings. Most organizations will then be self-organizing clusters of roaming intrapreneurs who work together over communication networks, creating a seamless global economy in which power, initiative, and control flow from the bottom up—the flowering of enterprise.

Note that a market structure does not *ensure* effective management, but it is an essential starting point. Talented people, inspiring leadership, clever strategy, and other factors are also necessary, of course. But these are secondary causes. The Russians are highly educated, talented people with a wealth of resources, yet their economy was trapped in an archaic system for decades.

A similar problem faces managers in capitalist societies today. Capable, well-intentioned people working in corporations, governments, and other institutions are trapped in outmoded hierarchical structures. This impending shift to a market form of organization presents roughly the same challenges and opportunities posed by the restructuring of socialist economies. What are the implications of this profoundly different philosophy?

The Advantages and Disadvantages

Naturally, internal markets incur the same disorder, risk, and general turmoil of external markets, but they also permit some compelling advantages. As shown in Table 2.2, the organization's environment determines which approach is best, which then fixes the type of accountability, motivational system, and culture needed, as well as the corresponding advantages and disadvantages.

Economists argue that hierarchies are superior because markets produce transaction costs in searching for alternatives, managing financial transactions, and so on. But the Information Revolution is reducing transaction costs, and any cost increases can be offset by decreased overhead and gains in innovation. Western Airlines eliminated five hundred management jobs, and the resulting decrease in bureaucracy saved huge costs and

TABLE 2.2. CONTROL VERSUS FREEDOM.

	Hierarchical Control	Market Freedom
Environment:	Stable, simple	Turbulent, complex
Accountability:	Supervision	Performance
Motivation:	Security	Reward, challenge
Culture:	Efficiency	Enterprise
Disadvantages:	Bureaucracy	Disorder, risk
Advantages:	Order, equity	Client focus, innovation, adaptive change

improved performance. Studies by Thomas Malone at MIT show that decreasing information technology costs "should lead to a shift from [management] decisions . . . to the use of markets."[15]

Many think that markets increase conflict as units pursue different goals and compete for resources. My experience shows that market systems can *resolve* the abundant conflict that persists now. Peter Drucker observed that conflict within corporations is *more* intense than conflict between corporations, largely because decisions are often imposed arbitrarily and the choices are minimal, if any; so relations are usually fraught with tension and misunderstanding. In a market, however, decisions are clearly defined, voluntary, and selected from a range of options, providing a rational basis for sound working relationships that can replace office politics with openly reached agreements.

Even the troublesome aspects of internal markets can actually represent useful organizational adjustments. Is a manager in a free market organization unable to staff his unit? In the outside world this means that working conditions are poor. Are some units suffering losses? A market would let them fail because they do not produce value. Do differences in income exist? Wage inequalities can motivate good performance, and they urge poor workers to shape up. Thus, what appears to be disorder in a market is often vital information about economic reality that should be heeded.

Although markets are superior under most conditions today, it is important to emphasize that there are no perfect organizational designs, and there are infinite ways to organize a market system. As Table 2.2 suggests, the creative destruction of markets may unleash reservoirs of energy, but this energy can turn into anarchy if not guided into useful paths. Conversely, hierarchical control may avoid this disorder, but it also inhibits creative freedom.

We should hold no illusion that some universal structure can be applied in an all-encompassing way. Internal markets are no panacea. They are not useful in military operations, space launches, and other situations requiring close coordination of thousands of people and intricate plans, nor in routine operations facing a relatively simple, stable environment.

The "Organization Exercise" in Appendix A can help managers experience these differences. When conducting two sets of tasks of varying complexity, groups almost invariably develop a hierarchical structure for the simple task and a network structure for the complex task. You can thereby vividly appreciate the reasons for these two different structures and how they would work and feel.

Thus, organizations will have to trade off the costs and gains of each approach. The prudent executive will combine varying degrees of hierarchical control and market freedom to find the mix that best suits his or her organization.

Living with Market Systems

The drawbacks of enterprise seem especially severe now as mergers, bankruptcies, layoffs, and other changes are increasing unemployment, ending corporate loyalty, and generally making work life more traumatic. If internal markets introduce more of the same, how will we tolerate working in market organizations?

These turbulent changes are unavoidable because the world is in the throes of massive economic restructuring that exerts two major demands: accountability for performance in order to survive, and creative entrepreneurship to adapt to chaotic change—the two major strengths of internal markets. This explains the new role now emerging for individuals in a fast-moving, temporary society. Whereas it made sense for people to function as *employees* in a hierarchical economy, an internal market system requires people to assume the role of *entrepreneurs*.

Thus, the former paternalistic employment relationship in which people were paid for holding a *position* is yielding to a "self-employed" role in which people are offered an *opportunity*. The old "work ethic" is becoming an "enterprise ethic" that values the freedom and self-reliance, as well as the rewards and risks, that form the complementary rights and responsibilities of entrepreneurship (as we will see in Chapter 6). In fact, these are the roles preferred by the majority of businesspeople today.[16]

If organizations can make this adjustment, we may find that an internal market is less harsh. By decentralizing responsibility to small, self-managed units, the demands of a turbulent economy could be better resolved through voluntary layoffs, growing the business, tolerating lower rewards, or other local solutions. Self-management thereby permits constant, small adjustments to the ebb and flow of market forces, avoiding the large periodic crashes that now result from having executives bear this unreasonable burden alone.

For instance, a market organization can help make downsizing, reengineering, and other forms of restructuring more successful. Just as any external business can manage its affairs better without government interference, these approaches are likely to work best if they originate voluntarily from autonomous units that are accountable for serving their clients. Managers who treat units as internal enterprises will almost invariably improve operations beyond their expectations. Ralph Larsen, CEO of J&J, says: "Managers come up with better solutions and set tougher standards for themselves than I would impose."[17] In place of forced downsizing, then, this bottom-up approach produces self-initiated rightsizing throughout the organization—"self-sizing."

Likewise, studies show that two-thirds of TQM programs fail because they are imposed from the top down.[18] The principles of TQM are valuable, but they are not likely to be effective without first creating a keen sense of responsibility for some team to serve its clients—again, an internal enterprise. There is simply no substitute for the dedication, ingenuity, and, yes, even the mad zealotry of entrepreneurs committed to *their* business.

Finally, markets can help manage organizational networks. In a hierarchical structure, top managers control alliances to ensure that they are economically sound, but this is time-consuming and undermines operating managers. In a market organization, however, unit managers handle alliances because that is the way everyday relationships are managed. For instance, Corning, one of the leading companies in forming alliances, currently has fifty or so joint ventures among its semiautonomous product divisions, foreign subsidiaries, and business partners around the world.[19]

Corporate executives may provide advice and support, but they could not possibly control the explosion of networking that lies ahead. A proliferation of R&D consortia, supplier-manufacturer-distributor linkages, networking among "virtual" corporations, joint ventures among competitors, and business-government partnerships are rapidly connecting all corporations, governments, and universities together in a dense social infrastructure, as depicted on the cover of this book.[20] Internal markets will facilitate the operation of this global network.

The most useful role for top management is to form a collaborative corporate community that helps ameliorate the turmoil of a turbulent world, as we will see in the next chapter. It would also be useful to develop a working environment hospitable to creative people, emulating the hundreds of business incubators that have sprung up to nurture new ventures. One of IBM's most successful actions was the Independent Business Unit concept that created the PC in a year and a half. GM's new electric car project is spearheaded by an autonomous team of two hundred people.

Our views may change as organizations evolve, but internal market systems seem the logical conclusion of current restructuring efforts. By designing organizations as self-managed clusters of internal enterprises, downsizing, reengineering, TQM, networks, and other restructuring practices are likely to become more effective.

Corporate Perestroika

The major conclusions about organizational structure presented in this chapter can be summarized as follows:

1. As economies become more complex, they must be managed by "organic" systems operating from the bottom up.

2. Present restructuring concepts are limited because they are largely modifications of the top-down hierarchy.

3. A different perspective based on principles of enterprise is evolving to create complete "internal market economies" that are designed and managed roughly like "external market economies."

4. Internal markets are not appropriate in all cases, but they
   are best for most organizations today because they offer
   the dynamic qualities needed to navigate a complex world.

Transforming organizations into market systems is formidable because it involves a profound social upheaval; it could be thought of as "Corporate Perestroika," somewhat like the struggle facing the post-socialistic bloc. Experiences of companies that have made this transition offer some guidelines, as shown in Box 2.4. The CEO described how ABB created the system described in Box 2.5: "We took our best people and gave them six weeks to design the restructuring. We called it the Manhattan Project."[21]

BOX 2.4. GUIDES TO REORGANIZING INTO MARKET SYSTEMS.

The following guidelines were derived by examining the experiences of companies that have successfully transitioned to internal market systems:

- Learn about the concept of internal markets to gain a solid grasp of the possibilities and the problems involved.
- Start small in some limited part of the organization with willing, enterprising volunteers who will see the effort through.
- Provide thorough training in the business skills needed to succeed in a market environment.
- Plan the change collectively and sketch out a realistic vision of how it will work.
- Prepare people by shaping an entrepreneurial culture.
- Most importantly, give the reorganization top priority.

Many other corporations are moving in this same direction. In the late 1980s when computer companies had become bloated, Hewlett-Packard restructured to avoid the bureaucracy that swamped IBM (see Box 2.6). "We had too damn many committees. If we didn't fix things, we'd be in the same shape as IBM is today," said David Packard. HP dismantled unneeded controls to renew its belief that each division should be a self-managed enterprise. Former CEO John Young endorsed the development of radical new products—such as HP's first desktop printer that competed with the company's existing products—which would have been heresy at IBM.

Today the LaserJet line accounts for 40 percent of HP's sales. HP was valued at one-tenth of IBM in 1990; through this skillful blend of enterprise and support, HP is now worth roughly as much as IBM.

Although corporations are using market mechanisms, managers do not yet generally understand the broader concept of an internal market economy. Table 2.1 shows that most corporations do not allow profit centers adequate freedom, they impose limits on outsourcing, and their support units are rarely profit centers. The result is that, throughout large companies, business units strain against corporate bureaucracies that burden operations with excessive overhead and monopoly power.[22] Managers in the CIT survey reported: "We can't use outside sources if a product or service is available inside," and "I know of no company where staff units are nothing but profit drains; they are the most sacred of cows." So there is a long way to go before we realize the potential of internal markets.

In the final analysis, a market form of organization seems almost inevitable because it offers the only way of adapting to an age of constant, rapid change. Instead of relying on the heroic but risky judgment of executives to move the organization in some wholesale direction, the units of an internal market feel their way along like the cells of a superorganism possessing a life of its own, producing a constant stream of adaptive change. To use a phrase from chaos theory, the central advantage of an internal market system is that it "creates spontaneous order out of chaos."

The knowledge society lying dead ahead will present more complex intricacies than we can imagine, and much less control. This unpredictable nature of the modern world can be managed only by a local form of intelligence that guides average people to meet complexity where it begins—at the grass roots. Information technology will provide the communication for this system, and markets will provide the economic foundation.

Many will think this challenge is too enormous, but that is exactly what we once thought about the prospect of changing the Soviet Union. The move to market organizations seems likely to roll on because internal markets offer the same powerful advantages that inspired the overthrow of Communism: opportunities for personal achievement, liberation from authority, accountability for performance, entrepreneurial initiative, creative innovation, high quality and service, ease of handling complexity, fast reaction time, and flexibility for change. Imagine Corporate America's

BOX 2.5. ABB'S INTERNAL MARKET FOR A GLOBAL CORPORATION.

Percy Barnavik, the CEO of Asea Brown Bovari (ABB) corporation, has been described as "moving more aggressively than any CEO to build the new model of competitive enterprise." He described his firm's structure as follows:

A Confederation of Entrepreneurs: "We are a federation of national companies . . . a collection of local businesses with intense global coordination."

Multidimensional Structure: "Along one dimension ABB is structured into fifty business areas operating worldwide. Alongside this structure are 1,200 local companies that do the work of business areas in different countries."

Decentralization: "Our operations are divided into 4,500 profit centers with an average of fifty employees. We are fervent believers in decentralization. People can aspire to meaningful career ladders in units small enough to be committed to."

Support Units as Profit Centers: "You can go into any centralized corporation and cut its headquarters staff by 90 percent. You spin off 30 percent into free-standing service centers that perform real work and charge for it. You decentralize 30 percent into line organizations. Then 30 percent disappears through reductions."

Internal Enterprises: "Our managers need well-defined responsibilities, clear accountability, and maximum degrees of freedom. I don't expect them to do things that hurt their business but are good for ABB. That's not natural. We always create separate legal entities to allow real balance sheets with real cash flow and dividends. Managers inherit results year to year through changes in equity."

A Strategic Information System That Unites the Firm: "We have a glue of transparent reporting through a management information system called Abacus."

Employee Entrepreneurs: "I don't sit like a godfather, allocating jobs. What I guarantee is that every member of the federation has a fair shot at the opportunities."

Facilitating Leadership: "Real communication takes time, and top managers must be willing to meet with . . . the company CEOs in an open, honest dialogue."

Source: William Taylor, "The Logic of Global Business," Harvard Business Review (March-April 1991).

creative managers, engineers, and workers being turned free to launch myriad ventures, all guided by top management teams that provide a supportive infrastructure and inspiring leadership. Yes, many of these ventures would fail, but many more would thrive to create a new breed of dynamic, self-organizing institutions.

Managers could realize all these benefits by harnessing the abundant

---

BOX 2.6. HEWLETT-PACKARD'S INTERNAL MARKET SYSTEM.

Hewlett-Packard has become the second largest American computer maker by creating an entrepreneurial organization that allows it to constantly lead in technological innovation. HP's profits grow at an annual rate of 30 percent. Although management may not think of their organization as an internal market, it contains most elements of the market model.

Decentralized Structure. The company's 96,000 employees are organized into small, global, cross-functional units that never exceed 1,500 people, creating a decentralized, constantly changing structure that produces thousands of products.

Internal Enterprises. Each unit is an enterprise that "owns its business." Units plan their own strategy, work with their suppliers and customers, reinvest their profits in the unit, and have their own financial statements. "Our profit-and-loss statement is like any other small company's," said one unit manager.

Internal Competition. Units are accorded almost complete freedom to manage their affairs as they feel is best, including competing against other HP units and doing business with HP competitors. For instance, the HP laser printer competes with the ink-jet printer, and another unit chose to buy millions of chips from a competitor because the price was lower than HP's. Said one manager, "We don't feel an allegiance to any other part of HP. We feel an allegiance to our customer."

Internal Cooperation. Units also cooperate when it is useful by offering the benefits of their experience, sharing technology, organizing joint ventures, and so on. "I've never seen anyone say no if you ask for help," said a woman manager.

Facilitating Leadership. Corporate executives avoid making operating decisions that intrude on unit autonomy, but focus instead on facilitating cooperative relationships, offering advice, holding units accountable, and providing leadership. "The best I can do is bring people together and hope they mate," said Lewis Platt, the CEO.

Source: Alan Deutschman, "How HP Continues to Grow and Grow," *Fortune* (May 2, 1994).

---

entrepreneurial talent now languishing beneath the layers of today's bureaucracies. The first step is to recognize that organizations must be designed and managed as market economies in their own right.

Notes

1. A summary of the changes under way is provided by William E. Halal, "Global Strategic Management in a New World Order," *Business Horizons* (December 1993).

2. See Margaret Wheatley, *Leadership and the New Science* (San Francisco: Berrett-Koehler, 1992).

3. "Putting the Byte Back into Siemens Nixdorf," *BusinessWeek* (November 14, 1994).

4. Frank Swoboda, "The Case for Corporate Downsizing Goes Global," *Washington Post* (April 9, 1995). Matt Murray, "Amid Record Profits, Companies Continue to Lay Off Employees," *Wall Street Journal* (May 4, 1995).

5. "Japan, Wracked by Recession, Takes Stock of Its Methods," *Wall Street Journal* (September 29, 1993).

6. Ronald Henkoff, "Getting Beyond Downsizing," *Fortune* (January 10, 1994). Rahul Jacob, "TQM: More than a Dying Fad?" *Fortune* (October 18, 1993). Joann S. Liblin, "Don't Stop Cutting Staff," *Wall Street Journal* (September 27, 1994).

7. Reported in "Rethinking Work," *BusinessWeek* (October 17, 1994).

8. The network perspective is best represented by Raymond Miles and Charles Snow, *Fit, Failure, and the Hall of Fame* (New York: Free Press, 1994), and Jessica Lipnack and Jeffrey Stamps, *The Age of the Network* (Essex Junction, Vt.: Oliver Wight/Omneo, 1994).

9. David Osborne and Ted Gaebler, *Reinventing Government* (Reading, Mass.: Addison-Wesley, 1992).

10. Jay Forrester, "A New Corporate Design," *Industrial Management Review* (Fall 1965), pp. 5–17; Russell Ackoff, *Creating the Corporate Future* (New York: Wiley, 1981); Gifford and Elizabeth Pinchot, *The End of Bureaucracy and the Rise of the Intelligent Organization* (San Francisco: Berrett-Koehler, 1994); William E. Halal et al., *Internal Markets: Bringing the Power of Free Enterprise INSIDE Your Organization* (New York: Wiley, 1993).

11. Rosabeth Moss Kanter, "Championing Change: An Interview with Bell Atlantic's CEO Raymond Smith," *Harvard Business Review* (January-February 1991).

12. See William E. Halal, *Fee-For-Service in IS Departments* (A report of the International Data Corporation, 1992).

13. See Halal et al., *Internal Markets,* Chapters 3 and 5.

14. Alan Deutschman, "HP Continues to Grow," *Fortune* (May 2, 1994).

15. See Oliver Williamson, *Markets and Hierarchies* (New York: Free Press, 1975). The Western example is from David Clutterbuck, "The Whittling Away of Middle Management," *International Management* (November 1982), pp. 10–16.

Thomas Malone et al., "The Logic of Electronic Markets," *Harvard Business Review* (May-June 1989).

16. Paul Leinberger and Bruce Tucker, *The New Individualists* (New York: Harper-Collins, 1992). John Kotter, *The New Rules: How to Succeed in Today's Corporate World* (New York: Free Press, 1995).

17. Brian O'Reilly, "J&J Is on a Roll," *Fortune* (December 26, 1994).

18. R. Krishnan et al., "In Search of Quality Improvement," *Academy of Management Executive*, 7, (4) (1993).

19. Jordan Lewis, *Partnerships for Profit* (New York: Free Press, 1990).

20. "Learning from Japan: How a Few U.S. Giants Are Trying to Create Home-grown Keiretsu," *BusinessWeek* (January 27, 1992). Rosabeth Moss Kanter, "Pooling, Allying, and Linking Across Companies," *The Academy of Management Executive* (August 1989).

21. William Taylor, "The Logic of Global Business," *Harvard Business Review* (March-April 1991).

22. For a good analysis of this problem, see Craig Cantoni, *Corporate Dandelions* (New York: Amacom, 1993).

3

From Profit to Democracy

*Corporate Community Is the New Form
of Organization Governance*

A division manager of a large corporation I know (Steve) was struggling with a chronic dilemma. He was under pressure from senior management to increase his unit's profits, but all attempts failed. Raising prices and cutting corners to lower costs merely irritated his clients as they began to feel gouged. Making greater demands of employees backfired because they felt overworked. And negotiating tough terms with suppliers and creditors also provoked resistance. After discussing the problem at length with Steve, I suggested that he might be focusing too exclusively on profitability—any goal can become elusive if one tries too hard.

The idea seemed to catch his interest, setting off a serious reexamination of his goals and working relations. A few months later Steve's division was absolutely humming with energy. He had redefined his unit as a "cooperative enterprise" jointly managed by himself, his employees, suppliers, and even his clients. This was the result of much serious soul-searching and frank discussion, leading to the realization that the best way to gain the support of people was to engage their interests.

Now Steve's employees were designing and managing their own operations, and they were eager to take on these responsibilities because they

---

Note: Portions of this chapter are adapted from Chapter 6 of my earlier work, *The New Capitalism* (New York: Wiley, 1986).

received a generous share of the division's profits. The division's clients became faithful patrons after visiting Steve's staff to describe their special needs and to work out problems. A similar relationship was developed with suppliers.

The outcome: Steve's division reached its higher profit goals, but it did so by focusing on the needs of its constituents. Steve also felt delighted at the new spirit of his organization. Rather than the demanding boss he had been, he could enjoy working with these people in a constructive way.

Human nature is not turning altruistic, but progressive managers like Steve are creating a new form of corporate governance that unifies the goals of all parties. This chapter describes the democratic half of the New Management that focuses on integrating an enterprise into a harmonious whole—a corporate community.[1] Secretary of Labor Robert Reich observes that a telling sign of good management is that employees speak of the company in terms of "us" and "we" rather than "them" and "they."

The following pages outline the limitations of the old profit-centered model of business and the social responsibility model. Then we examine the evolution of corporate goverance toward collaboration among all stakeholders of the firm. This move from profit to democracy implies creating a coalition of investors, employees, customers, business partners, and the public, thereby forming a corporate community that serves all interests better.

I conclude that economics is likely to be elevated to include a broader concern for social and human values. This should not harm the financial goals of business because they are compatible with social goals. In fact, the pursuit of both goals may be a "better way to make money." From the view of the New Management, however, the concept of corporate community could prove so effective that the profit-centered system once thought to be intrinsic to the marketplace may soon become an artifact of the industrial past.

THE EVOLUTION OF ECONOMIC COOPERATION

The issue of corporate goverance has always been contentious because of basic assumptions about economic behavior. Throughout industrialization, business was usually considered a zero-sum game in which one party gained at the loss to another. This conflict is most apparent in the continuing controversy over whether companies should focus on making money or serving society. But with the onset of a knowledge economy, all that has changed. As today's rush to alliances demonstrates, cooperation has now become efficient.[2]

Limits of the Profit Motive

The profit motive is so deeply ingrained in present economies that most of us cannot imagine how business could be conducted otherwise. Ask an average American if business should focus on profit, and you will probably get a blank stare at such a dumb question. Indeed, you are likely to hear an adoration of wealth because most Americans hold out the hope of striking it rich themselves. Making money is part of the American dream.

In general, Americans have faith in the capitalist theory that profit is the driving force of economic progress. The profit motive should motivate business to satisfy customer needs, employ workers effectively, use scarce resources efficiently, and otherwise serve society. The problem, of course, is that the messy realities of economic life do not fit this theory very well.

A major cause of this problem is that in the zealous pursuit of money, managers are often encouraged to disregard social consequences. As we can commonly observe, many companies make lavish profits—even as they lay off workers, evade taxes, pollute the environment, and cause other social disorders. A study by Amitai Etzioni found that 62 percent of the Fortune 500 companies had been involved in illegal practices over the last ten years.[3] Other studies estimate the cost of price fixing, pollution, bribes, work injuries, product defects, and other white-collar crime to total several hundred billions dollars per year, a major portion of the U.S. gross domestic product (GDP).[4]

Let's be clear about what is going on here. The cause is not primarily attributable to "greed," as we often hear, because most business managers are moral, dedicated professionals trying to do a difficult job as best they can. Rather, the problem is systemic. As shown in Figure 3.1, the profit-centered model is based on an ideological system that focuses on serving the interests of those owning capital—shareholders. In this view, the interests of employees, customers, the public, and other stakeholders are not really goals of the firm, but simply a means to making money.

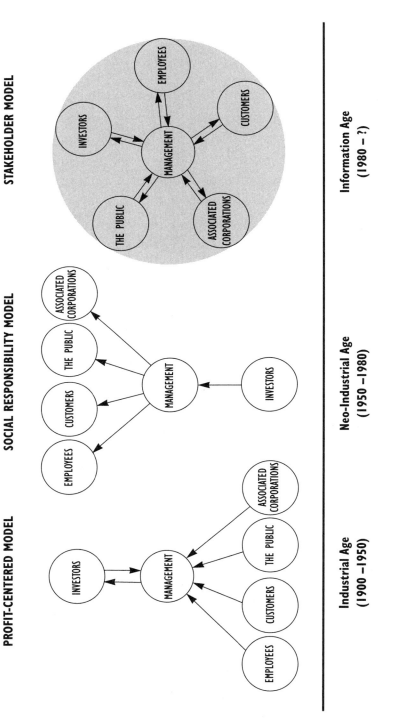

FIGURE 3.1. THE EVOLUTION OF CORPORATE COMMUNITY.

PROFIT-CENTERED MODEL

SOCIAL RESPONSIBILITY MODEL

STAKEHOLDER MODEL

Industrial Age
(1900 –1950)

Neo-Industrial Age
(1950 –1980)

Information Age
(1980 – ?)

Capitalism has great virtues, and many companies behave admirably, as we shall soon see. However, if the goal of enterprise is defined as profit making, the interests of business are opposed to the interests of society. Any philosophy devoted to "taking" contradicts the values of almost all religions, which advocate "giving" to serve others. The Reverend Billy Graham put it this way: "The biggest problem facing America is the moral situation, the scandals in business and Wall Street."

Limits of Social Responsibility

In an attempt to remedy this problem, about three decades ago American business sincerely tried to adopt the concept of "corporate social responsibility" (CSR), as also shown in Figure 3.1. Corporations voluntarily created programs to improve the treatment of their social constituencies, and they even attempted to measure this progress using "social audits."[5]

But the idea became an empty piety because it focused on "doing good" while ignoring the need to increase productivity, sales revenue, and profits. A similar fate is likely to befall today's successor to CSR—the rising popular interest in business ethics.

These concepts have been useful in educating businesspeople about their social obligations. However, social responsibility is a limited idea because it goes to the opposite extreme by advocating social service while ignoring economic realities.

The Conflict Between Business and Society

This continual conflict between profit and the social welfare has left societies bereft of what economists call a workable "theory of the firm." As Irving Kristol put it, "Corporations are highly vulnerable to criticisms of their governing structure because there is no political theory to legitimate it."[6]

The problem also extends into social institutions, with serious consequences. The role of news media is crucial in a knowledge society, yet media empires are controlled to serve financial interests. After CBS was bought by Lawrence Tisch in 1987, he fired six hundred newspeople to improve profits. Yet stars like Dan Rather were being paid several million dollars each, about as much as the savings from the layoffs. This type of logic raises puzzling questions.

Is Dan Rather really worth more than hundreds of his colleagues?

CBS was already very profitable, and the layoffs harmed CBS news coverage. Why is increasing the wealth of Tisch more important than the lives of his employees, and more important than serving the public better? Here's how a typical worker sees it, "It doesn't make sense. You can see them cutting people to get out of a bind—but just to make more profit? I don't get it."[7]

It was even harmful from strictly financial considerations. CBS's viewer ratings declined, profits plunged 68 percent, major executives went elsewhere, and affiliates switched to other networks. (David Letterman quipped on his night show, "You're watching CBS, the network that asks the question: 'Hey, where did everybody go?'") As a result, CBS was sold to Westinghouse for $6 billion, while ABC was sold to Disney for almost $20 billion.[8]

The same problem occurs in organized sports. Ask any fan or city official and they will confirm that baseball, football, and other sports are quasi-public institutions of enormous symbolic importance to their communities. Cities invest billions of dollars in building stadiums, fans provide loyal support and buy expensive season tickets, high schools and colleges invest years in training the players, and the media provide lucrative TV contracts.

Yet these groups have no rights. Owners can move teams to other cities at will. They set the price of admission and franchises to vendors. They draft young players in a form of servitude, and enjoy exclusive rights to control play in their city. The result is that this beloved public function is accorded the status of a monopoly under the sole control of owners.

It should be no surprise that a stream of disturbing incidents flows from this unchecked power. The baseball strike of 1994 so angered fans that some organized to negotiate with the owners, and 25 percent boycotted the game when play resumed in 1995; low attendance will cause the owners to lose $400 million in 1995.[9] When the owner of the Washington Redskins threatened to move the team to another location, a prominent Washingtonian had this reaction: "The Redskins aren't only a business for this region; they are a unifying institution for most of us who live and work here . . . a central force in bringing pride, cooperation, and a sense of oneness to the metropolitan area."[10]

Although some managers may try to balance profit and these social interests, they are constantly swamped with financial data, scrutiny by Wall Street analysts, and the threat of takeover. These powerful forces crowd out social concerns and their sheer inertia resists change. That's why noble mottoes such as "Our customers come first" and "Our employees are our most valuable asset" are usually mere platitudes. In an age when it is commonly understood that knowledge, satisfied customers, and a committed work force are critical to economic success, one can only marvel that we continue to treat corporations as chattel to be "owned" by investors.

Why have smart, proud citizens of the most powerful nation on Earth voluntarily yielded the power to control the major institutions of their society? Because money holds the status of a reigning theology in America. It is a sacred cow that cannot be questioned, a dogma that blinds us to a more complex reality. Profit making, the rights of ownership, and other canons of capitalist ideology constitute the de facto religion that governs our fading Industrial Age system, roughly the way medieval Christianity governed the agrarian societies of the Middle Ages.

Medieval civilization was dominated by the church: massive Gothic cathedrals provided the focus of city life; daily tasks were centered around the rhythms of mass and prayer; and society was guided by a hierarchy of priests, abbots, and bishops. Today, civilization is no less dominated by capital: massive corporate offices buildings have replaced the cathedrals; leveraged buyouts, hostile takeovers, and arcane derivatives have replaced the religious rituals; and the church's hierarchy has given way to a hierarchy of accountants, security dealers, and financiers.[11]

The Rise of Stakeholder Power

Within the past few years, however, powerful trends in corporate governance suggest that serious change is under way.

For decades, control of large corporations resided almost solely with the CEO, while the corporate board and stockholders provided a fig leaf shielding our eyes from this naked display of unilateral power. Few believed that the typical board of directors was much more than a social gathering of the CEO's associates, and the annual stockholder meeting was widely ridiculed as a farce. Only a small portion of shareholders attended; they were unorganized, poorly informed, and usually preoccupied with trivial complaints that seemed mainly intended to humble corporate executives. "It's the only forum that makes Congress look good by comparison," noted Robert Monks, a major institutional investor.

But now stockholders, employees, and other stakeholders are steadily gaining power.

Institutional shareholders—pension funds, mutual funds, insurance companies, banks—own the majority of stock at many large corporations. The California Public Employees Retirement System (CALPERS), one of the largest pension funds, began using its untested power in 1990 to influence poorly managed corporations, which brought about the fall of CEOs at GM, IBM, Sears, American Express, and other troubled firms. Today, most large corporations regularly meet with their institutional investors.[12] This relationship has been shown to improve financial performance, so large investors have become permanent players in the management of large corporations.[13]

Another new force in corporate governance is the rising power of employees, as we will see in Chapter 6. Employee stock ownership plans (ESOPs) control 12 percent of all corporate stock, and employees sit on the boards of three hundred large corporations. At some large companies, such as United Airlines, workers own a majority of shares. Further, the ESOP movement is growing 10 percent per year.

Women are also becoming more influential in corporate governance, thereby introducing a new set of "feminine" values that stress a more humane, community-oriented form of management. Women sit on most corporate boards, and one-quarter of all new corporate directors are now women. The number of businesses owned by women is growing more rapidly than those owned by men.

Other social constituencies have also gained influence in recent years. As we will see in later chapters, almost all companies now strive to build trusting long-term relations with their customers; they work closely with their suppliers and distributors, they are developing partnerships with government, and they voluntarily protect the environment.

Finally, the legal barriers are being eliminated. American law once presumed that stockholders were the sole beneficiaries of the corporation, but this is changing. "What right does someone who owns the stock for an hour have to decide a company's fate?" asked Andrew Sigler, chairman of

Champion International. "That's the law, and it's wrong." At last count, thirty states have adopted statutes that recognize the interests of corporate social constituencies, and the concept is spreading to most other states.[14]

These trends have accelerated the movement toward a broader form of governance. In 1992, fifty companies, including Levi-Strauss, the Body Shop, Stride-Rite, Reebok, and Lotus, formed the Business for Social Responsibility (BSR) alliance, and a year later membership leaped to eight hundred companies. This is only the most visible example of a broader movement that includes the World Business Academy, the Social Venture Network, and many other groups of progressive business managers and scholars.[15]

Unlike the old form of social responsibility, today's movement admits the need for financial gain. "We are here to get people to recognize that there is a link between profitable performance and responsible corporate practices," said Michael Levett, former president of BSR.[16] In 1984, investors concerned with social criteria (ethical treatment of employees, product safety, environment, etc.) owned $40 billion of corporate stock, while in 1990 that sum passed $500 billion.[17]

What all these trends share in common is that stakeholders who previously remained passive are now demanding to be heard. "There's a populist wind blowing through this country," said Ralph Whitworth, president of the United Shareholders Association. "We see less willingness to accept the status quo, whether it's in Congress or in a corporation."

How are managers going to handle this revolution of the stakeholders? By redefining a broader, more effective role as "stewards" of this emerging corporate community.

The Stakeholder Model of the Corporation

This need can be better understood if we look at the stakeholder model. As shown in Figure 3.1, this model views the corporation as a socioeconomic system composed of various constituencies: employees, customers, associated firms (suppliers, etc.), the public and its government representatives, and investors. Please note that this model differs from the social responsibility model in that stakeholders have *obligations* to the firm as well as rights. This view has long prevailed among some companies, such as those discussed in Boxes 3.1 and 3.2. Now the idea is becoming widely accepted

---

BOX 3.1. IKEA.

Sweden's IKEA has recently become the world's largest home furnishings company by forming collaborative relationships with its customers, suppliers, and employees. In 1993, the company had one hundred retail outlets around the world; it was growing at a 15 percent annual rate, and its profit margin of 8 to 10 percent was so high that all capital was obtained internally.

Active Customers. IKEA has defined an "active" role for its clients that benefits both them and the company. Strollers, free child care, and restaurants are provided to encourage parents to bring their children. Customers are given catalogues, tape measures, pens, notepaper, and detailed information to help them make informed purchases. High-quality Swedish furniture can be purchased at 20 to 50 percent below competitive prices if buyers are willing to assemble it in a hour or two. Anything can be returned at any time.

Supplier-Coproducers. IKEA furniture components are produced by a global network of two thousand suppliers located in more than fifty low-cost countries around the world; five hundred suppliers are from Eastern Europe. IKEA staff support suppliers by leasing equipment, locating partners and materials, and providing production advice. The result is low-cost, high-quality production, coordinated to meet complex, changing market demands in a timely fashion, while also creating business opportunities in undeveloped nations.

Source: Richard Normann and Rafael Ramirez, "Designing Interactive Strategy," *Harvard Business Review* (July-August 1993).

---

because managers realize that the success of their enterprise depends on gaining the support of these groups.

This essential role of social interests is clarified by my studies, which estimate the resource flows between stakeholders. The return-on-resources model and data in Tables 3.1 and 3.2 show that all stakeholders invest financial and social resources, they incur costs, and expect gains, just as investors do. These resources constitute their "stake" in the organization, which is so specific that it can be compared quite accurately to capital investments.

These data reveal how seriously limited is the traditional view of the firm that focuses on financial aspects alone. The total figures at the bottom of Table 3.2 are greater than the financial sums shown for investors by roughly a factor of ten. Thus, social concerns, which are usually regarded as

---

BOX 3.2. EXEMPLARS OF CORPORATE COMMUNITY.

Hewlett-Packard has become a major force in the computer industry by using its stated mission: "Profit is not the proper end and aim of management—it is what makes all of the proper ends and aims possible. . . . Our main task is to design, develop, and manufacture the finest electronic equipment for the advancement of humanity."

IBM continues to follow a philosophy that the founder, James Watson, Sr., stated in terms of the following goals: "obligations to stockholders," "respect for [employees]," "service to our customers," "fair deal to our suppliers," and "corporate citizenship in community affairs."

Johnson & Johnson survived the Tylenol poisoning crisis and other challenges because of a companywide "credo" that states: "Our first responsibility is to the doctors, nurses, patients, mothers, and all others who use our products and services."

NCR Corporation defines its mission as "creating value for all the constituencies with a stake in the company: consumers, NCR people, suppliers, communities, and investors. While it may appear that the various stakeholders will have conflicting demands, the points of conflict are few and the points of common interests are many."

Merck Corporation's founder, George W. Merck, defined the mission of the company in terms of service: "We try to never forget that medicine is for people. It is not for profits. The profits follow, and if we remember that, they never fail to appear."

Japanese corporations have traditionally practiced a human form of management. Akio Morita, the founder of Sony, and Konoshuke Matsushita, the founder of Matsushita Electronics, among other Japanese CEOs, describe the typical Japanese philosophy: "Profit should not be the primary goal of business. The real purpose of the enterprise is to contribute to society in return for using its resources."

Source: William E. Halal, *The New Capitalism* (New York: Wiley, 1986).

"economic externalities," are far greater than financial considerations because they comprise a vast but more subtle world of human and social realities that has eluded the Old Management.[18] Hicks Waldron, chairman of Avon Products, described this reality:

> We have 40,000 employees, 1.3 million sales representatives, a large number of suppliers, customers, and communities around the world. They have much deeper and more important stakes in our company than our shareholders.[19]

The data also show that all parties benefit. Business does not simply redistribute resources, as in a zero-sum game, but is inherently a productive institution that creates value for all its constituencies. Although the gains of various stakeholders may conflict in the short term, they are compatible in the long term. This is confirmed by various studies and common examples, which show that business creates jobs, educates people, pays taxes, and more.[20]

For example, the Body Shop is a socially oriented corporation, yet it is also very profitable. The difference is that profits are put in perspective as

TABLE 3.1. THE RETURN-ON-RESOURCES MODEL.

Constituent Group	Resources Invested (R)	Benefits Provided (B)	Costs Incurred (C)	Return on Resources [(B − C)/R]
Investors	Equity/debt capital	Dividends/ interest, capital gains	Capital losses	Return on investment
Employees	Upbringing, education, training, health	Wages & benefits, training, job satisfaction	Disabilities, meals & travel, job dissatisfaction	Return on human resources
Customers	Purchase price, search costs	Utility (consumer surplus)	Product damages, depreciation, maintenance	Return on purchases
The public	Public assets	Taxes, contributions	Government services, environmental damage	Return on public assets
Associated firms	Assets of associated firms	Sales of associated firms	Expenses of associated firms	Return on associated assets
Total corporation	Total resources	Total benefits	Total costs	Overall return on resources

Note: This model was used to conduct a computer simulation of corporate behavior, which produced the results displayed in Table 3.2. For further details of this research, see William E. Halal, "A Return-on-Resources Model of Corporate Performance," California Management Review (Spring 1977), and The New Capitalism (New York: Wiley, 1986), Ch. 6.

one goal among many. "Profits are jolly good," said Anita Roddick. "But they are a means to a larger goal." The Body Shop has built plants in poor areas, funded environmental projects, and made other efforts to combine both social and economic goals. "Now, *that's* what you do with profits!" said Roddick.[21]

This analysis leads to a precise theoretical description of the nature of the firm. *Corporate managers are dependent on stakeholders because the economic role of the firm is to combine as effectively as possible the unique resources each stakeholder contributes: the risk capital of investors; the talents, training, and efforts of employees; the continued patronage of customers; the capabilities of business partners; and the economic infrastructure provided by government.* The need for capital is essential, of course, but the contributions of other stakeholders are no less essential. Because companies are socioeconomic systems, these functions are all as essential as the diverse organs of a body.

Thus, managers should act as stewards engaged in a "social contract" to draw together this mix of resources and transform it into financial and social wealth, which they can then distribute among stakeholders to reward their contributions. The closer the integration into a cohesive community, the greater the wealth.

The good news, then, is that there does not seem to be a conflict between profit and social welfare, as we will see more fully in the next

TABLE 3.2. ANNUAL RETURN-ON-RESOURCES STATEMENT. (IN THOUSANDS OF DOLLARS)

Constituent Group	Resources Invested (R)	Benefits Provided (B)	Costs Incurred (C)	Net Return (B - C)	Return on Resources [(B – C)/R]
Investors	$ 9,993	$ 583	$ 234	$ 349	3.5%
Employees	36,520	1,691	57	1,634	4.5
Customers	10,533	4,066	2,249	1,817	17.3
The public	2,536	338	375	−37	−1.5
Associated firms	507	314	312	2	.4
Total corporation	$60,089	$6,992	$3,227	$3,765	6.3%

chapter. Yes, stakeholders have different interests that flow from their unique roles in the corporate community, but these interests can be reconciled *IF* they are organized to create a more successful enterprise. All parties could thereby benefit, including investors. Thus, a more effective goal for business would be to serve the public welfare represented by all stakeholders. Henry Ford said the same decades ago: "People believe that the only purpose of industry is profit. They are wrong. Its purpose is the general welfare."

The Coming Economic Copernican Revolution

Let me suggest an analogy that helps put these different views of corporate governance in perspective.

The profit-centered model of business is comparable to the Earth-centered model of the universe. Like the central role once attributed to the Earth, profit has been rather arbitrarily selected as the center of today's economic universe because that is the view we inherited from an Industrial Age when capital was the primary factor of production. The social interests of stakeholders were placed in successively distant orbits as being of lesser importance, even though they may in fact be as huge as the Sun.

In contrast, the social responsibility model goes to another extreme by positing an economic universe that revolves about social interests but ignores financial realities. This is roughly equivalent to a solar system that revolves about Mars, Saturn, or Venus rather than the Earth.

I think this analogy clarifies the debate that continues to confuse all of us. Adherents of the Old Management who insist on the profit-centered model are roughly comparable to those who believed in an Earth-centered universe, while advocates of a social responsibility model can be seen as "prophets" or "revolutionaries" who proclaim that the universe revolves about other planets.

The stakeholder model reconciles this confusion by showing that all such interests are equally important. Shareholder wealth, employee welfare, customer satisfaction, the public good, and other corporate interests all revolve about a common economic goal that is as central to society as the Sun is to our solar system—serving the human needs of all these diverse members of the corporate community.

If this comparison is valid, it highlights the challenge facing managers, scholars, and others involved in developing a New Management. Just as the studies of Copernicus caused astronomers, philosophers, and theologians to accept a radically different theory of the universe, the data in this chapter indicate the need for an economic equivalent of the Copernican Revolution.

PRINCIPLES OF CORPORATE COMMUNITY

Theories and data can help us see a different reality, but how can such a dramatically different view be translated into practical guides? Based on studies and the experience of progressive companies, three central principles have been found useful: community spirit, performance evaluation, and stewardship.

Create a Spirit of Community

Like any other community, a human enterprise must be created by leaders—"stewards" who instill a vision of the corporation as a community united by commonly cherished values and principles.[22] Because people in advanced nations today are hungry for this sense of belonging, there is a rising tide of interest.

The best example is offered in Boxes 3.3 and 3.4, where the close parallel between GM-Saturn's philosophy and the stakeholder model can be seen. Richard "Skip" LeFauve, the chairman of Saturn, described his goal this way: "People have been an underutilized asset in this industry. Saturn's mission is to change that by creating new relationships with the United Auto Workers, dealers, and suppliers. Saturn is more than a car, it's an idea, a whole new way of working with our customers and with one another."

To have such ideals accepted as a working part of day-to-day life, however, stakeholders must discuss, modify, and affirm these values, or they will remain a lofty set of platitudes. Levi-Strauss has taken the lead in shaping a corporate culture that actually behaves as an ethical community. Management drafted a statement outlining the values Levi-Strauss aspires to, and six thousand of the company's thirty-six thousand employees provided suggestions on replanning corporate practices.[23] A similar process was used by Johnson & Johnson some years ago.

Although this broader form of governance has advantages, institutional roles are always defined by personal beliefs. The reality is that many people feel keenly that business *should* be a strictly profit-making affair, and

BOX 3.3. THE SATURN DIVISION OF GENERAL MOTORS.

The Saturn division was created to develop progressive management methods. The company's advertising campaign says it all: "A different kind of company. A different kind of car." Although Saturn has not yet recovered its $5 billion investment, it is an unusual success by most criteria. The demand for Saturn cars is so great that a second plant is planned, and distributorships are being set up abroad. GM plans to make Saturn the first of its electric vehicles and to introduce a mid-size car. Saturn owners are among the most satisfied in the industry, quality is near perfect, dealer sales are twice the industry average, and the entire organization is energized by unusually high commitment and morale. Saturn represents a historic breakthrough because it provides a highly visible illustration of how a corporate community can produce outstanding results.

Customer Satisfaction.   The superb design, quality, and service provided to Saturn owners has attracted a large and growing number of faithful patrons. Saturn has earned this patronage by making inexpensive autos that match Japanese quality, by using a soft sales approach that avoids pressuring buyers, and by continued attention to serving the needs of Saturn owners throughout the life of the car.

Employee Commitment.   Saturn created collaborative labor-management relations in an industry noted for union conflict. Workers are organized into self-managed teams that control all aspects of their jobs, they participate in all major decisions and share in the company's financial success. In 1993 when the company earned its first profits, all 8,000 employees received bonuses. A union member said "We are the future of the American car industry."

Distributor-Partners.   Saturn's distributors obtain an exclusive territory to avoid competing with other Saturn dealers. Moreover, they are assisted in developing "electronic showrooms" that use interactive multimedia to inform customers about the car, and they offer fixed prices to avoid haggling and pressure. Franchises are renewed based on performance and service delivered to Saturn buyers.

Supplier-Partners.   The same collaborative relationship is extended to Saturn suppliers. In choosing an advertising agency to handle its $100 million account, a Saturn committee of managers, workers, union leaders, and dealers spent time developing a trusting relationship with what it calls its "communications partners." The agency's compensation is tied to Saturn's sales performance.

Other Organizations Want to "Saturnize."   The Saturn concept of management is being adopted by other GM divisions and other automakers, schools are using its philosophy, and politicians suggest it should be adopted by the U.S. Congress and the entire nation.

Source: "Here Comes Saturn," *BusinessWeek* (April 9, 1990). Gabriella Stern, "Saturn Is Deemed Successful Enough to Expand," *Wall Street Journal* (April 18, 1995).

BOX 3.4. SATURN PHILOSOPHY.

WE, THE SATURN TEAM,

IN CONCERT WITH THE UAW AND GENERAL MOTORS, BELIEVE THAT MEETING THE NEEDS OF: CUSTOMERS · SATURN MEMBERS · SUPPLIERS · DEALERS · NEIGHBORS IS FUNDAMENTAL TO FULFILLING OUR MISSION.

TO MEET OUR CUSTOMERS' NEEDS:

- Our products and services must be world leaders in value and satisfaction.

TO MEET OUR MEMBERS' NEEDS:

- We will create a sense of belonging in an environment of mutual trust, respect, and dignity.

- We believe that all people want to be involved in decisions that affect them, care about their jobs and each other, take pride in themselves and in their contributions and want to share in the success of their efforts.

- We will develop the tools, training and education for each member, recognizing individual skills and knowledge.

- We believe that creative, motivated, responsible team members who understand that change is critical to success are Saturn's most important asset.

TO MEET OUR SUPPLIERS' AND DEALERS' NEEDS:

- We will strive to create real partnerships with them.

- We will be open and fair in our dealings, reflecting trust, respect and their importance to Saturn.

- We want dealers and suppliers to feel ownership in Saturn's mission and philosophy as their own.

TO MEET THE NEEDS OF OUR NEIGHBORS, THE COMMUNITIES IN WHICH WE LIVE AND OPERATE:

- We will be good citizens, protect the environment and conserve natural resources.

- We will seek to cooperate with government at all levels and strive to be sensitive, open and candid in all our public statements.

BY CONTINUOUSLY OPERATING ACCORDING TO THIS PHILOSOPHY, WE WILL FULFILL OUR MISSION.

Reproduced by permission of the Saturn Corporation.

all the evidence in the world is not likely to sway them. It is also true that a human-centered form of business may not be useful in some industries, and it may not be acceptable for some national cultures.

For example, managers surveyed in the CIT study expressed a wide range of opinion on this point, usually in strong, emotional terms. A majority confirmed the importance of serving all interests: "Our goal is to serve all groups equally," "The trick is balancing interests. How else could one operate?" But some believe in the primacy of clients: "Our primary goal is to make sure the client is satisfied," and "The underlying reason for all our efforts is to provide the best product possible and to exceed the expectations of our customers." And a few strongly affirm the traditional view: "Profit, profit, profit—for shareholders."

These considerations remind us that changing institutional goals is uncharted territory. Subtle issues of personal values and political ideology are involved, which are poorly understood, and there is limited knowledge of the effects on economic productivity and society. A useful way to explore this domain is to gather useful information, which leads to the next topic.

Evaluate Stakeholder Performance

An old management axiom holds that one cannot manage what is not measured, and so evaluating the benefits and costs experienced by stakeholders is needed to guide decisions. Otherwise, how can managers know how well groups are benefiting? Which groups are receiving preferential treatment and which are being slighted? Where are the problem areas? What level of benefit is justified at what cost? And so on for other complex issues.

Corporations have developed systems for doing this in specific areas (such as evaluating the management of employees and customers), which we will survey in later chapters. Some broad frameworks have been used to provide a systematic evaluation of all stakeholders, but few organizations have attempted ambitious projects of this type.[24] Box 3.5 shows the main systems of this type. A prominent advance is that the 1995 Fortune list of "America's Most-Admired Companies" was heavily weighted by how well managers serve their customers, treat their workers, and behave responsibly to their communities, in addition to measures of profitability.

BOX 3.5. STAKEHOLDER EVALUATION SYSTEMS.

In addition to the return-on-resources model described in this book, the following systems have been used to evaluate corporate performance in terms of the benefits received by various stakeholders.

Fortune 500 companies have been evaluated by *Fortune* magazine since 1982 in terms of various measures that reflect the benefits realized by shareholders, employees, customers, and communities.

Stakeholder ratings are opinion surveys obtained from corporate stakeholders. Professor Robert Hays developed a method for surveying overall corporate performance using ratings from employees, clients, the local community, and government officials.

Social audits or social reports have been performed by many corporations to itemize the programs and benefits delivered to various social constituencies. For instance, the American Council of Life Insurance has published such reports for roughly four hundred insurance companies since 1972.

100 Best Companies to Work For (published by Random House since 1984) is a handbook coauthored by Robert Levering and Milton Moskowitz that rates companies in terms of their employee benefits and other social performance factors.

The balanced scorecard system was developed by professors Robert Kaplan and David Norton to translate corporate strategy into measures of overall performance to stakeholders: providing service to customers, developing skilled and motivated employees, and earning attractive shareholder returns. The system has been applied by Rockwater, Apple Computer, and Advanced Micro Devices.

Stakeholder influence has been evaluated by professor Grant Savage and his colleagues as a framework for assessing the extent to which various stakeholders can pose a strategic threat to a corporation or offer strategic advantages through cooperation.

The best way to understand stakeholder evaluation systems is to see them as an extension of financial measures. Social data are used to manage social performance, just as financial data are used to manage financial performance. Both types of information can help managers understand the attitudes of various stakeholders, forecast trends, identify critical issues, and propose strategies to resolve problems. Estimating complex social factors is difficult, of course, but what we think of as "hard" data present much the same problem. Accountants know that arbitrary assumptions underlie statements of profit and loss, and economists have equally troubling questions about measures like the GDP.

In the final analysis, managers must constantly make decisions that guide their actions in such matters, and the availability of sound, comprehensive information systems of this type can only help by replacing ignorance with knowledge. If a fraction of the enormous costs now devoted to financial measurement were applied to social measurements, we would have a powerful tool for managing the community of corporate interests.

Provide Corporate Stewardship

An inspiring vision and sound information are useful, but ultimately managers have to put these into use with groups of stakeholders who may disagree vehemently. This is difficult terrain for any leader, but it is especially wrenching for corporate managers who are mired in a perennial role conflict over profit versus social welfare.

This lack of a well-defined, defensible role is a great dilemma for today's large cadre of young professional managers who are struggling to sort out confusing issues between their jobs and their ideals. If a manager is a true professional, who is the client to be served? Only the investor, by making money? The boss, by following orders? How can managers gain the allegiance of subordinates if employees are secondary to profit? What does the professional manager do when the interests of employees, customers, and other groups conflict with making money? These tough issues have been made worse because the myth of the profit motive places managers in an impossible situation where their duties are opposed to the stakeholder groups on whom they are dependent.

The stakeholder model, however, defines a far more constructive, legitimate role that provides managers a strong sense of professional identity. From this view, managers are "servant leaders," or stewards, responsible for serving the collective welfare of the constituencies that make up their organizations.[25] They use their special expertise to help this community collaborate for their mutual benefit, and they are accountable to these groups, just as physicians and attorneys are accountable to their clients. CEO George Fisher set a bold challenge for the managers at Kodak by tying his annual compensation to performance measures that are weighted by 50 percent for stockholders, 30 percent for customers, and 20 percent for employees.[26]

Role-playing a "stakeholder meeting" can help people understand how to manage these complex interrelationships. This exercise, contained in Appendix B, asks five to ten people to simulate a company meeting to which representatives of all stakeholder groups have been invited. The impact can be profound because the abstract idea of the corporation as an extended socioeconomic community comes vividly to life, offering rich opportunities for exploring the role of corporate stewardship.

Remember that stewardship is *not* intended to "do good" in the sense of performing philanthropic deeds that give things to others, which is why concepts such as social responsibility and business ethics have had limited effect. Sound stakeholder management is a pragmatic, two-way set of collaborative working relationships between the corporate community and its members that benefits the enterprise as a whole. Because value can be distributed only to the extent it has been created, the role of corporate stewards is to ensure a match between contributions and rewards. The establishment of this reciprocity between what one creates and receives is fundamental to the health of any community.

A large body of research shows that organizations define and enforce subtle norms to set an appropriate balance between the benefits each individual or group receives versus the contributions they make. If some group is slighted, they correct this imbalance by withholding contributions to reestablish equity. This sense of equity is so precise and so strong that one idealistic CEO tried a system in which employees could simply ask the paymaster to give them any sum for their regular pay. It seemed to be an outrageous idea that would be wildly abused, but it actually worked pretty well. Very few people asked for more than small increases, and almost all realized they were fairly paid by a considerate employer.

These powerful norms of equity mean that managers cannot usually obtain more from their constituents than they consider to be reasonable. Managers must *earn* their contributions by providing corresponding benefits. Methods for evaluating stakeholder performance are useful to guide the give-and-take bargaining needed to reach agreement. But to make such complex, trusting relationships work, a new breed of manager is needed who can provide skillful leadership. As we will see in Chapter 9, good leaders today inspire others to share responsibility for the enterprise. They listen to really hear different points of view, build bridges between conflicting interests, and are generally skilled in the political art of forming coalitions.

Data from the CIT survey (see Table 3.3) indicate that this type of collaboration is occurring to some extent. The majority of managers today cooperate with stakeholders and try to serve their interests, but a third do not evaluate stakeholder performance and almost half do not seat stakeholders on their boards. One manager in the CIT survey highlighted the problem: "Our board is comprised of nine white, affluent, males with no females or minorities."

If it makes sense to cooperate with stakeholders, the logical conclusion would be to meet with them periodically. For instance, if managers really want to serve their customers better, why have responsible clients and consumer advocates remained so conspicuously absent from corporate boards? When Louis Gerstner replaced John Akers as CEO of IBM in 1993 and was exploring ways to revitalize Big Blue, a prominent analyst advised the following: "If Gerstner is sincere, he should create a new board made up of IBM customers, suppliers, partners, employees . . . a new kind of IBM that couldn't help but be more responsive because the people in charge represent the company's future . . . and clearly signal that business as usual is dead at IBM."[27]

This same concept can be used throughout the organization. Russell Ackoff has proposed an ambitious form of decentralized corporate governance in which lower-level boards set policy for each product division or major project. Membership on these miniboards can include stakeholders, support personnel, higher and lower level groups, and so on. At Hewlett-Packard, for instance, each major project is governed by a cross-functional board, and many other corporations use boards to govern individual divisions.[28]

THE EXTENSION OF DEMOCRACY

The evidence we have surveyed leads to the following conclusions:

1. Corporations lack a workable theory of governance because the profit and social responsibility models ignore the reality that business is both an economic and a social institution.

TABLE 3.3. ADOPTION OF CORPORATE COMMUNITY PRACTICES.
(SAMPLE = 426 CORPORATE MANAGERS.)

Practice	Not Practiced (0–3)	Partially Practiced (4–6)	Fully Practiced (7–10)	Mean (0–10)
The company strives to maintain cooperative working relationships with important stakeholders (for instance, investors, employees, customers, suppliers, distributors, the local community, and possibly other groups).	5%	10%	85%	8.1
The company's primary goal is to serve the interests of important stakeholders, including making money for investors.	5	7	88	8.3
In addition to its profitability, a corporation's performance is evaluated by a formal system that assesses how well important stakeholders are served.	29	20	51	5.8
The board of directors includes employees and other important stakeholders.	41	14	45	5.0
Means	19%	13%	68%	6.8

Source: William E. Halal, *Corporations in Transition* (an unpublished study n progress). Note that data in the three columns ("Not Practiced," etc.) are aggregated by collapsing portions of the questionnaire scale as shown ("0–3," etc.). See the questionnaire in Appendix C.

2. The stakeholder model resolves this conflict by treating all corporate interests as equally important constituencies that receive benefits in return for their contributions.

3. Collaboration with corporate stakeholders is occurring now as investors, workers, women, clients, the public, and other interests gain increasing power and because managers need their support.

4. A corporate community of stakeholders offers the possibility of increasing both the benefits to social constituencies and profits for investors.

Some cautionary points should be noted. This more complex system of governance could become unwieldy, time-consuming, and emotionally disruptive if managers are unable to handle the political tensions that are inevitable; as we will see in the next chapter, corporate community may be inspired by our ideal of democracy, but managers are likely to avoid this problem by using an informal system rather than some form of representative government. It is also true that the practice of human enterprise is not likely to become universal since it may not be appropriate in some industries nor desired by some people. Instead, it may become established only in large, quasi-public institutions, such as the Fortune 500 companies, and among an avant garde of progressive business leaders. Even in these cases there will always be occasions of doubtful ethical behavior. Dow Corning was lauded for its model code of ethics, but this failed to avoid the crisis that erupted over the dangers of its silicone breast implants.

These limitations notwithstanding, the transition to corporate community should prove a watershed in economics. Driven by the liberating power of information, the benefits of cooperation, and the rising aspirations of modern people, democratic ideals are being extended into daily life to form a powerful new model of business that is increasingly productive and socially beneficial.[29]

This historic change should also help resolve other nagging problems that have long resisted solution. Inflation could be better controlled because a unified corporate community would spur productivity while also constraining wage and price demands. Growth may be directed in more fruitful avenues as unmet social needs are better understood and responded to more directly. Hostile takeovers may become a thing of the past, since the firm would not be simply chattel to be bought and sold but a community governed by its constituencies. Government regulation could be minimized because business could become a relatively self-regulated system, reducing the need for external safeguards. The concept will not be limited to business, but should change government and other social institutions as well.[30]

Those who favor traditional views should note that this concept does not clash with the profit-centered model. In fact, the stakeholder model is a logical extension of Western ideals. As I stressed in the Introduction of this book, the New Management does not refute the Old Management but goes beyond it to provide more powerful ideas that absorb their older versions. Einstein's reformulation of physics did not prove that Newton was wrong; it was simply a special case of Einstein's more general theory. Likewise, the human enterprise does not imply that profit is bad; rather it is a special case of the general concept that business should serve multiple goals, one of which is profit. Corporate community can be thought of as a better way to make money, possibly even more money.

Beyond this rationale of the Old Management, however, this New Management view holds the promise of resolving the business-society conflict that has plagued capitalism for two centuries. Daniel Bell called it "the cultural contradictions of capitalism"—that destructive clash between the hard necessity of survival in a market economy and the ideals of human cooperation and social welfare that we aspire to in a democratic society.

In an age torn apart by conflict, corporate community may prove our main bulwark against civil decay. Because business is the most powerful institution in modern society, managers could take a great step forward in human affairs by developing this badly needed ability to cooperate for the benefit of everyone.

Notes

1. For a fine recent survey of views on corporate community, see Kazimierz Gozdz, *Community Building* (San Francisco: Sterling & Stone, 1995).
2. The classic work on this topic is by Robert Axelrod, *The Evolution of Cooperation* (New York: Basic Books, 1984).
3. Amitai Etzioni, "Shady Corporate Practices," *New York Times* (November 15, 1985).
4. Mark Green and John F. Berry, "Corporate Crime," a two-part report appearing in *The Nation* (June 8 and 15, 1985).
5. William E. Halal, *The New Capitalism* (New York: Wiley, 1986), Ch. 6.
6. Irving Kristol, "'Reforming' Corporate Governance," *Wall Street Journal* (May 12, 1978).
7. Matt Murray, "Amid Record Profits, Companies Continue to Lay Off Employees," *Wall Street Journal* (May 4, 1995).
8. Elizabeth Jensen, "CBS's Tisch Is Faulted," *Wall Street Journal* (May 22, 1995).
9. "Kevin McManus, "Baseball Fans: Strike Too," *Washington Post* (October 9, 1994). Allen Sanderson, "Break Up Baseball," *Washington Post* (December 9, 1994).

10. Sterling Tucker, "The Redskins: More than Just a Business," *Washington Post* (July 24, 1992).

11. This point is nicely made by James Robertson, *Future Wealth* (New York: Bootstrap Press, 1990), p. 93.

12. "An Inside Look at CALPERS' Boardroom Report Card," *BusinessWeek* (October 17, 1994).

13. See the special issue of *BusinessWeek, Relationship Investing* (March 15, 1993).

14. Steven M. H. Wallman, "The Proper Interpretation of Corporate Constituency Statutes," *Stetson Law Review* (1991), Vol. XXI, pp. 163–196.

15. A central source of information on the progressive business movement is *The New Leaders*, a periodical published by John Renesch in San Francisco, California.

16. Kara Swisher, "Getting Down to the Business of Being Socially Responsible," *Washington Post* (November 22, 1993).

17. From a scientific view, one might question which is cause and which is effect. Do human-oriented firms perform better, or is it that better-performing firms can afford to be human? It seems likely that both are true because cause and effect are circular. A human orientation improves performance, which then provides the resources to carry this approach further, and so on. See Troy Segal, "Putting Your Cash Where Your Conscious Is," *BusinessWeek* (December 24, 1990).

18. Severyn Bruyn, *The Social Economy* (New York: Wiley, 1977).

19. The special issue on corporate control, *BusinessWeek* (May 18, 1987).

20. See Thomas Donaldson and Lee E. Preston, "The Stakeholder Theory of the Corporation: Concepts, Evidence, Implications," *Academy of Management Review* (1994).

21. James O'Toole, "Go Good, Do Well," *California Management Review* (Spring 1991).

22. Amitai Etzioni, *The Spirit of Community* (New York: Crown, 1993); Juanita Brown, "Corporation as Community," in John Renesch (ed.), *New Traditions in Business* (San Francisco: Berrett-Koehler, 1992).

23. Russell Mitchell, "Managing by Values," *BusinessWeek* (August 1, 1994).

24. Social evaluations using a comprehensive system of rigorous measurements, such as dollar equivalents, have been conducted by Clark Abt Associates and Atlantic Richfield Company. See Halal, *The New Capitalism*, p. 218.

25. Robert Greenleaf, *Servant Leadership* (New York: Paulist Press, 1977), and Peter Block, *Stewardship* (San Francisco: Berrett-Koehler, 1993).

26. "Tying Executive Pay to Social Responsibility," *Business Ethics* (September/October 1995).

27. Michael Schrage, "To Reshape IBM, Gerstner Should Work from the Boardroom Down," *Washington Post* (April 2, 1993).

28. Russell Ackoff, *The Democratic Corporation* (New York: Oxford University Press, 1994); Christine Ferguson, "Hewlett-Packard's Other Board," *Wall Street Journal* (February 26, 1990).

29. Francis Moore Lappé and Paul Martin Du Bois, *The Quickening of America: Rebuilding Our Nation, Remaking Our Lives* (San Francisco: Jossey-Bass, 1994). Pat Barrentine (ed.), *When the Canary Stops Singing: Women's Perspectives on Transforming Business* (San Francisco: Berrett-Koehler, 1994).

30. For instance, hospitals, banks, and public agencies are adopting similar concepts with great success. See Nancy Nichols, "Profits with a Purpose," *Harvard Business Review* (November-December 1992); Peter Johnson, "How I turned a Critical Public into Useful Consultants," *Harvard Business Review* (January-February 1993), Ronald Grzywinski; "The New Old-Fashioned Banking," *Harvard Business Review* (May-June 1991), and Ronald Taub, *Community Capitalism* (Cambridge, Mass.: Harvard Business School Press, 1994).

4

The New Management Synthesis

Uniting Internal Markets and
Corporate Community

The two previous chapters showed that the foundation of the New Management is being built by extending enterprise and democracy into organizations. Just a few years ago, the typical large corporation was an authoritarian, top-down structure that behaved not too differently from the centrally planned economies of Communist nations. But today's large organizations are disaggregating into loosely connected clusters of autonomous business units that form "internal markets." And to gain the support of their stakeholders, managers are forming "corporate communities" that unify financial and social interests.

While these two major trends are unmistakable, they also elicit very strong, different reactions from people.

I find that "liberals" tend to consider the idea of internal markets unimaginably disruptive. I spoke to a group of sociologists who made it clear that they thought this was the "last straw" intrusion of capitalism into personal spheres of life. Folks with this orientation seem to dislike the messy, competitive nature of enterprise. The idea of corporate community is usually fine with them, however, because it favors human values.

Those with a "conservative" bent usually have the opposite reaction. They love the entrepreneurial freedom of internal markets, but abhor the thought that a corporate community would detract from the profit goal of business.

This much is fairly predictable, but if one probes a bit deeper it also seems that people have doubts about these first strong reactions. Liberals may like the idea of community, but they want to be free of the controls that community authorities must impose. I have heard fierce denunciations of authority from the very people who love the thought of corporate democracy. And conservatives may favor markets, but the dirty secret of capitalism is that most businesspeople dislike tough competition. That great capitalist, J. P. Morgan, put it best: "Businessmen hate competition. A man's competitor holds down his profits, threatens his markets, and jeopardizes the future of his family."[1]

This ambivalence at both ends of the political spectrum nicely illustrates the creative tension between these two very different concepts. People tend to favor either markets or community, and they seem to be opposed to each another. But the two are really compatible. Like enterprise and democracy in society, internal markets provide the creativity, productivity, and freedom people need to manage their complex jobs in large organizations, while corporate community provides the social cohesiveness needed to make markets work harmoniously. Both liberals and conservatives usually consider this new combination a more reasonable system for managing modern institutions than the old hierarchy. Markets and community form indispensable halves of the New Management foundation.

This chapter first shows how the Information Revolution unleashes powerful economic forces that pull organizations in these two opposing directions: complexity demands entrepreneurial freedom, while a knowledge economy requires productive collaboration. Then I show that these same revolutionary forces also lead to a "New Management Synthesis" that unites this creative tension into a more powerful organization. The New Management uses internal markets to root organizations into the economy while a corporate community orients it to society. I like to think of the organic system that results as an "organization tree." We conclude that achieving this synthesis allows managers to harness unusual power by drawing today's exploding diversity into a productive whole—an economic system of "Democratic Enterprise."

THE CREATIVE TENSION BETWEEN MARKETS AND COMMUNITY

Organizations are like all organisms in that their survival hinges on adapting to environmental change. Today, the tide of that struggle is turning as the exploding complexity of the Information Age forces the need for markets and community within organizations.

A Complex Environment Demands Entrepreneurial Freedom

This shift in our view of the world is so striking that a new field of science has emerged devoted to the study of complexity and chaos.[2] Where once managers thought their work was amenable to analysis and control, now they flounder in an unpredictable flux of what the great economist Schumpeter called "creative destruction."

Entire industries are being transformed, as in the convergence of the computer, communication, and entertainment fields. Roughly half of all jobs are being eliminated by automation, leaving masses of workers floating in temporary positions. Consumer markets are splintering into an endless assortment of unique cultural subgroups—from eco-feminists to Rush Limbaugh fans. And get ready for more competition among utilities that will make today's bruising battles between AT&T, MCI, and Sprint seem mild; all of the "Baby Bells" are likely to enter the fray, and a free market energy system is evolving in which users choose among competing power suppliers.[3]

Naturally, this upheaval has led to a reshuffling of economic structures. U.S. corporations completed more than 42,000 mergers and acquisitions between 1976 and 1993, and large organizations, such as IBM, are disaggregating into decentralized units, which in turn form alliances with other firms. The effects have been dynamic. For instance, the undisputed American lead in computers is a direct result of these flourishing business alliances among small enterprises that constantly realign talent, knowledge, and resources into productive new combinations.

Meanwhile, the constant advance of information systems is encouraging even more restructuring by making it easier and more efficient. The Internet, for example, has become famous for creative change, but this is just the beginning of an enormous explosion in electronic interaction as open-system architectures makes all types of hardware and software compatible. We may soon see the decline of Microsoft's monopoly in PC operating systems, just as IBM's monopoly of mainframes ended earlier.

The conclusion: all this electrifying communication across shifting economic markets is short-circuiting the old chain of command. As we will see in Chapter 6, the rapid growth of teleworking is producing changing assemblies of people and enterprises that constantly form and reform on the grid of global cyberspace to cut across hierarchies everywhere.[4] *Business-Week* described the result as "electronic corporations made up of individuals and groups scattered all over the world." Where the Industrial Age produced firms organized by "vertical integration," the Information Age is creating "*virtual* integration."[5] John Hagel, a partner at McKinsey & Company, put it this way:

> As the costs of using IT systems fall, we're going to see a widespread disintegration of U.S. business and the emergence of very different corporate entities.[6]

Chapter 2 showed that this historic dismantling of hierarchies can only be managed effectively by viewing modern organizations as internal market systems. Corporations and governments are becoming aggregations of small autonomous units that coalesce into near-perfect global markets—the flowering of enterprise.

A Knowledge Economy Makes Cooperation Efficient

We tend to focus on this "market half" of the New Management because it is most obvious, but the "community half" comprises an equally compelling counterforce that receives less attention. *Competition* may be increasing *between* enterprises, but *cooperation* is increasing *within* enterprises.

But what about the traditional "tough" approach to business? Why would centuries of self-interested behavior change? Because the Information Revolution is overthrowing this system as surely as the Industrial Revolution overthrew the medieval economic system. Just as the assembly line shifted the critical factor of production from labor to capital, today the computer is shifting the critical factor of production from capital to *knowledge*. Knowledge is different from capital because the marginal cost of duplicating it is trivial and its value *increases* when shared, which makes collaboration advantageous to all parties. This new economic reality is leading to the dramatic realization that cooperation with all stakeholders is now *efficient* in modern economies.[7]

The result is that the old profit-centered system is inadequate to cope with today's world. The great needs facing modern managers no longer revolve around capital but concern a vast and growing realm of more subtle social factors that are increasingly important in a knowledge-based economy. Here's how Peter Drucker defined the new role of economics:

Formal knowledge may come to occupy the place in a Knowledge Society which . . . property and income have occupied [during] the Age of Capitalism.[8]

The declining power of capital was demonstrated during the 1980s when General Motors invested $70 billion in new technology to combat the Japanese invasion of its markets. GM could have simply bought Toyota and Honda with this sum of money. Yet the company continued its slide into decline, which was signified in 1989 when the Honda Accord replaced the Chevrolet as America's most popular car. GM's total worth has now fallen from roughly $50 billion to $20 billion, so about $100 billion of value has been lost.

Such incidents illustrate that the power of capital alone is insignificant when compared with the power that Japanese competitors wielded during the 1980s—power that originated by cultivating harmonious working relations with employees, customers, suppliers, distributors, and government.[9] Charles Handy noted: "When the assets of an enterprise are primarily its people, it is time to rethink what it means to say that [shareholders] can in any sensible way 'own' the corporation."[10]

People may find it difficult to accept the use of democratic principles in organizations, but that was the original intention. During the American Revolution, Thomas Jefferson, James Madison, and other founding fathers envisioned the application of democracy to work life. Albert Gallatin, Secretary of the Treasury under Jefferson, said, "The democratic principle on which this nation was founded should not be restricted to politics but should be applied to industry as well."[11]

As Chapter 3 showed, that goal may now be realized as business evolves toward a quasi-democratic form of governance, a corporate community. Progressive firms are inventing ways to serve their clients, share power with workers, cooperate with business associates, form partnerships with government, and protect the environment—the extension of democracy.

The Organization Tree

Either internal markets or corporate community by themselves, however, lead to serious distortions. Competition alone is destructive, while cooperation alone is stifling. Profit alone undermines stakeholder support, but social responsibility alone undermines economic survival. For instance, as market forces accelerate the competition for wealth today, disturbing questions are being raised about the loss of community in modern life: Are we destined to suffer dog-eat-dog competition? Is self-interest feasible in an age when people are struggling to resolve systemic problems, such as today's crisis of the environmental commons?

So managers must strike a balance between these two powerful sets of forces that pull organizations and modern societies in opposing directions. *The marketplace fosters competition, a focus on profit, individualism, diversity, and constantly shifting relations—while community encourages cooperation, social welfare, unity, equity, and commitment.* This polarity is what Lawrence and Lorsch called "differentiation and integration."[12] It has always existed in nations, organizations, and other social systems, but now it is likely to reach new heights as competitive pressures demand higher performance of more complex organizations.

Resolving this tension between a decentralized entrepreneurial system and a cohesive corporate community will be no easy task. But the Information Revolution is not only heightening the tension between these two opposing needs, it also provides a creative spark that unifies them into a more powerful whole. Management in the Information Age seems to be marked by synthesis.

In Chapter 1, old management practices absorbed the forces of change to produce a new management. Synthesis is also seen in the foundation of the New Management: internal markets integrate small enterprises into a more dynamic organization, and corporate community unifies stakeholders into a powerful economic coalition. Box 4.1 summarizes how this New Management Synthesis is spreading throughout management: it first unifies the principles of democracy and enterprise, which then does the same for the Old and New Managements, and then for left- and right-wing politics.

This evolution of a new breed of organizations that is both entrepreneurial and collaborative can be grasped more easily with a metaphor that I find useful. The two concepts of internal markets and corporate community can be thought of as forming an "organization tree" (see Figure 4.1).

At the bottom level where daily operations take place, internal markets connect the organization to the grass roots of the economy, thereby providing revenue, information, and other nutrients that feed the tree. Note

---

BOX 4.1. MAJOR DIMENSIONS OF THE NEW MANAGEMENT SYNTHESIS.

Democracy and Enterprise. The New Management carries the ideals of democracy and free enterprise to their logical conclusion by incorporating them into everyday life. These two principles have usually been considered incompatible, which is why we have isolated them in separate compartments. Enterprise has been relegated to markets, while democracy has been restricted to politics. Today, the imperatives of information technology are extending them into all spheres of life and integrating them into a coherent whole. Markets are spreading to manage complexity, while democracy is equally essential to unify this diversity into harmonious communities.

Old and New. At an intellectual level, this synthesis of enterprise and democracy constitutes a new economic paradigm for a knowledge-based economic system. Like all paradigm shifts, however, the New Management does not refute enduring truths inherited from the past but offers a broader framework that absorbs them as a special case. That is, the old approach is not considered "wrong" or "bad" but limited, while the new approach is neither "right" nor "good" but more powerful. For example, progressive firms collaborate with stakeholders to create a broader form of governance that serves all social interests, and they also make more money.

Left and Right. A central implication of the New Management paradigm is that it resolves the perennial conflict between left- and right-wing ideologies. One of the biggest obstacles to progressive change is that liberals demand government programs to serve society, while conservatives insist on self-reliance. The New Management integrates both of these traditions into a more powerful social contract. For instance, the collaborative model of corporate governance noted above suggests corporations could becomes self-regulating enterprise systems governed by the constituencies they affect, relieving government of much of its regulatory role.

---

that a few large divisions would only constitute a tree's taproots, so it is essential that the organization be dispersed into a fine network of small internal enterprises, somewhat like a network of small feeder roots.

At the top where policy makers establish the corporate mission, collaborative governance among stakeholders exposes the organization to the light of diverse values that fuel growth and guide it to serve a useful role in society. Large, powerful trees amass enormous energy from a huge canopy of leaves. So the greater the range of diverse interests, the greater the amount and balance of this motivating energy available to drive an organization.

FIGURE 4.1. THE ORGANIZATION TREE.

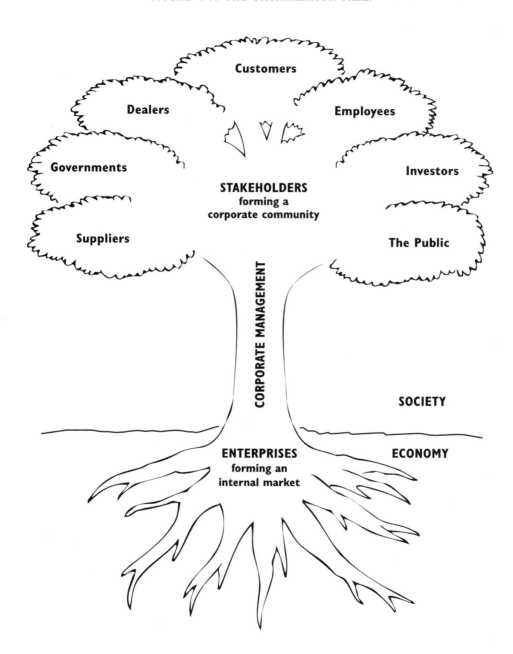

The trunk and major limbs of the tree would then represent management's role. Managers create the organizational structure, communication channels, and financial systems that support internal enterprises and stakeholders, connect them together, and coordinate their functions. Managers also act as catalysts for strategic action by providing the energizing guidance of leadership, roughly the way photosynthesis combines sunlight hitting leaves and moisture from the soil to produce growth.

We should not press this metaphor too far because all metaphors break down at some point. For instance, the neat dichotomy between "economy" and "society" is not quite accurate. In reality, social interests penetrate into economic affairs as various stakeholders exert their influence in daily operations, and some companies make a practice of inviting stakeholder participation at division levels as well as at the corporate board level. This more elaborate system suggests the image of organizations as complex organisms that grow "fractals" of the same structure at lower levels.[13]

But the organization tree is generally a useful image to help us understand today's transition from the pyramid to an organic organization.[14] Concentric circles, inverted pyramids, networks, and other popular symbols are useful, but they more closely recall the machine paradigm. Only a living organism like the ubiquitous tree can capture the organic essence of modern organizations: their ability to exhibit a life all their own, to derive power from their environment, to respond and grow to changing conditions.

GUIDES TO ACHIEVING ORGANIZATIONAL BALANCE

It is not generally known that this complementary balance between the forces of enterprise and community is a constant theme in management, and it is confirmed by a large body of evidence that suggests useful guides for managers.

Supporting Evidence for the New Management Synthesis

A wealth of research studies consistently demonstrate that two major factors correlate with effective management. One factor is usually defined as "task facilitation," "concern for work," "initiating structure," or other terms that roughly correspond to what I have called enterprise. The other is "group support," "concern for people," "consideration," or other concepts that are synonymous with community. These two factors represent a universal polarity between "hard" and "soft" science, "male" and "female" orientations, the Chinese yin and yang, and other enduring dichotomies. The evidence further shows that while either factor alone improves organizational performance, the combination of the two is far more effective.[15]

This same conclusion is reflected in a plethora of expert opinions. Russell Ackoff concurs that a blend of internal market economies and corporate democracy is badly needed today. Sumantra Ghoshal and Christopher Bartlett claim that progressive corporations now focus on developing flexible, entrepreneurial organizations directed to serving human goals. Data from the CIT study show a strong correlation between managers' scores for internal markets and corporate community.[16]

Examples of Balance

To get a better feel for the organization tree in action, let's examine how this synthesis runs through the remaining chapters of this book.

Modern marketing strives for economic success—but this is best done through a trusting client relationship that delivers genuine value. Knowledge workers must be allowed wide freedom to do their jobs—yet they must also be accountable for performance. Environmental sustainability requires corporations to become ecologically benign—which would permit the huge increases in economic growth needed by developing nations. Strategic change must be economically sound to succeed—but it must also be supported by social interests. Participation draws on the ideas of a leader—as well as the views of active followers. The Information Revolution unleashes new forces that are unifying the globe—but they also disperse global institutions into pockets of local community.

These examples illustrate the kind of balance that some of our best corporations have perfected by growing large, robust organization trees. We saw in Chapter 2 that Hewlett-Packard is a nimble confederation of small, autonomous business units—yet we also saw in Chapter 3 that it has a system of democratic governance that embraces all interests in its corporate community. AT&T has decentralized all divisions into fifty or so profit-centers—but they are evaluated and rewarded using equally weighted measures of profitability, customer satisfaction, and employee morale. Motorola has become one of the most admired corporations in the world by creating an entrepreneurial system of competing units—which are all unified about common goals of serving clients with flawless products and helping workers use their talents to succeed.

Avoiding Extremes

To maintain balance, it might not be wise to form permanent relations with any particular group of stakeholders. The fact is that democratic governance can restrict management's autonomy to some extent. It is a commitment, just as a marriage or merger is a commitment. That's why many dynamic companies, such as Nike and Dell, maintain alliances with different partners, who in turn do the same. These companies need the mutual benefits of cooperation, yet they must also avoid becoming too dependent on any one set of partners by maintaining the option of switching to others.

Thus, it may be best to keep stakeholder relationships sincere but provisional so allegiance can be moved to more appropriate partners if necessary. That explains why the concept of corporate community does not necessarily imply all of the features we usually associate with "democracy," as noted in Chapter 1. For instance, it is unlikely that we will see the corporation become a representative democracy composed of some fixed number of directors appointed by each stakeholder constituency. Rather, powerful but reasonably agreeable stakeholders should be chosen by managers to form a political coalition that can work together effectively. The corporation may become a community, but this will likely be a fluid community of frequently changing, selected members.

We could say that managers may not commit themselves to "marrying" stakeholders but simply "going steady." After all, trees drop their leaves every fall and grow a new set in the spring.

The reverse is also true: organizations cannot be so loosely connected that they are indistinguishable from the external marketplace. If an internal market permits excessive freedom, it is not an organization at all, so there would be no reason for its existence. Rather than a tree, then, it becomes more of a weed patch. As the growth of virtual relationships opens up unheard of freedom, maintaining a strong sense of corporate community will be a formidable challenge. Leaders will be tested to form a productive sense of purpose that distinguishes their organization from others and draws people toward the attractions it offers.

Balanced organizations create a strong "infrastructure" of limbs and connecting vessels to achieve this integration of markets and community, as we saw in Chapter 2. Their managers form policies that guide members' behavior, design financial incentive systems that reward contributions, create a powerful information system to share knowledge, and cultivate a corporate culture that unifies the entire organization with shared values.

However, many organizations and nations suffer severe limitations because they tend to favor one of these orientations; the roots and branches are too mismatched to support one another.[17] Americans are notorious for demanding their rights and freedoms as individuals, but they have a difficult time subordinating this freedom to form cohesive communities. On the other hand, Japanese culture stresses cooperative working relations and social harmony, but it is not very good at tolerating individual freedom. Perhaps the greatest challenge facing American managers is to instill a sense of community and self-responsibility in institutions. Conversely, Japanese managers face the difficult task of loosening social bonds somewhat to permit more fluid, individual freedom.

A Mini Case Study: The Virtual University

Universities pride themselves on being democratic "communities of scholars" with flexible systems that form a "marketplace of ideas," yet my experience is that this is largely a myth. The reality is that faculty committees have become so overgrown and preoccupied with detailed rules that they are too entangled to move, leaving administrators free to make major decisions. As a result, department budgets are allocated almost solely by the president according to some arcane formula from the dim past that now makes no sense. The arbitrary nature of this system is seen in the fact that there is usually no relationship between department performance and funding.

Thus, half of the typical university is embittered because they feel deprived while supporting others, while the half being subsidized feel complacent. Neither half is motivated by the system, and their entrepreneurial talents are constrained by this academic bureaucracy. The result is that universities do not very closely resemble their professed ideal of an entrepreneurial intellectual community because the organization tree has been engulfed by impenetrable, strangulating ivy.

Academics prefer not to get involved in resource issues because of an ethic that claims scholars should remain aloof from money. But, in fact, most professors are deeply concerned because funds are scarce in most universities, which commonly leads to intense bickering over course loads, research funds, salaries, graduate assistants, and a host of other petty financial matters. Now that corporations, governments, health care systems, and even the post-Communist bloc are restructuring, perhaps this institution can finally reconsider its old system.

There is a consensus that the "virtual university" will arrive about the year 2000, and its ability to transmit knowledge anywhere should introduce intense global competition among academics. The most prominent need is to make departments self-supporting, entrepreneurial units by requiring them to operate with some agreed-upon portion of the revenue they generate. They should then be left almost completely free to manage their own affairs. Budgets could be modified to reflect measures of academic excellence, research, publication, community service, or any other factors that the university community agrees on as its common goals. But, whatever the criteria, resources must be allocated in accordance with some commonly shared standard of performance to ensure that critical sense of equity that is essential for the formation of a genuine spirit of community.

With all of its roots and leaves in good working order, this old organization tree could blossom again in the fertile soil and light of a knowledge age.

DRAWING UNITY OUT OF DIVERSITY

It is useful to see that this synthesis of the New Management is simply part of the far greater synthesis that is now integrating the globe. The most significant force for change today is the inexorable advance of communication networks that seems destined to wire the planet into a central nervous system for a unified world.

An Age of Synthesis Is at Hand

The power of synthesis is clearly visible in the astonishing movement to steadily expand today's economic blocs into some form of global economic system. The very idea of a global economy was inconceivable just a few years ago, yet it is now a universally accepted icon, repeated everywhere as a tenet of faith in the prospect that a unified world is imminent.

Thus, a dramatically different perspective is emerging based on the principle of wholism, the integration of all views, systems, people—every-thing—into a single coherent whole.[18] I know this may sound far-fetched, but so did the notions that the Earth is round and that it revolves around the Sun. Now we are facing up to the reality that all life is connected: soci-ety to nature, citizen to nation, mind to body, person to person, human to animal, nation to nation, and so on. Vaclav Havel, president of the Czech Republic, noted that America's Declaration of Independence must be aug-mented by a new "Declaration of *Inter*dependence":

> We enjoy the achievements of modern civilization, yet our experi-ence seems chaotic, disconnected, confusing. We do not know what to do with ourselves, we understand our lives less and less. What is missing is an awareness of being anchored in the miracle of the Earth, the miracle of the universe.[19]

As Havel suggests, civilization seems to have reached a critical point at which nothing less than a new cosmology is needed, a cosmology that places the human experience in a broader context. Progressive thought now recognizes that all life is united by its essentially spiritual nature.[20] Regard-less of whether one is devoted to managing a business, working in politics, or creating art, these paths invariably converge on transcendent ideals that motivate all behavior.

Think of those existential moments in your own life, such as a death in the family or the birth of a child, a great failure or a great breakthrough in one's work or personal life. At times like these life transcends our frail human powers, and most people find themselves face to face with those ultimate issues of meaning and purpose that concern us all. Speaking for myself, I have come to see that this spiritual domain is the primary source of my energy, motivation, and ideas. Like all of us, I strive to succeed in my work, to care for my family, and to achieve other such mundane goals. But I also realize that my ability to do these things is a direct result of my state of mind, of my sense of awareness that flows from some poorly understood world of the spirit. I do not really know what it is or where it comes from, but I have little doubt that it is the most powerful force in the universe. Spirit pervades everything. Spirit *IS* wholism.

This integrating nature of the spirit helps us see that the unifying power of information noted above is mere prelude to the even greater unifying power of the spirit that is soon to come. As we will see in Chapter 6, the Information Age is almost certain to mature and fade into the past in a decade or two, just as the Agrarian and Industrial phases have done. And beyond the advance of knowledge, we are likely to discover a "Spiritual Age," in which people will strive to harness that vast but subtle power that lies everpresent, everywhere. This reminds me of the prophetic vision in that common prayer we often take for granted: "Thy Kingdom come, thy will be done, on Earth as it is in Heaven."

I conclude from this evidence that an "Age of Synthesis" is at hand. While other analysts today see paradox,[21] if we can look beyond the seeming incongruities between democracy and enterprise, left and right, small and big, local and global, among others, we should be heartened to observe that the world is moving inexorably toward a unifying wholeness. The Industrial Age was characterized by the need for analysis—the rational disaggregation of large problems into their constituent parts, which then necessitated hierarchical structures to coordinate those diverse parts. But *the Information Age is characterized by the opposite need—the synthesis of disparate nations, social diversity, and other fragmented subsystems into a balanced, integral, functioning whole.*

This process of unification does not proceed out of humankind's goodness or other utopian motives, but simply as a countervailing force that keeps today's spiraling complexity intact. Differentiation balances integration in all systems. Margaret Wheatley, in her pioneering study of the "New Science," describes a universe in which atoms, organisms, and social systems are unified by fields of energy, information, and thought.[22]

Much like synthesis in the physical domain, synthesis in the economic domain offers bold new prospects. In physics, the union of elements in a chemical reaction or in a nuclear reactor releases vast amounts of physical energy. Why should the economic world behave differently? We are about to observe how the union of economic differences releases an untapped reservoir of *economic* energy. It may even be that the union of *greater* economic differences produces equally *greater* levels of energy. If this is so, the growing diversity that is now the source of conflict among individuals and nations may prove an asset as the Information Revolution unites the enormous cultural differences that now pose one of the greatest barriers to human progress.

The Unifying Principle: *E Pluribus Unum*

Finding the leadership to guide us toward this difficult synthesis will be a huge challenge because imbalances abound in institutions, and the problem is likely to become more severe.

Many entrepreneurs and technophiles are so captivated by the revolutionary possibilities of information systems that they yearn to create a completely decentralized world that glorifies individual freedom. One said, "Cyberspace represents the triumph of the individual against dehumanizing institutions. Corporations will either radically decentralize to grant employees unheard-of autonomy or crumble altogether. Government has no . . . future."[23] At the other extreme, there also exists a large contingent of people who favor strong community bonds, government controls, and the like. President Bill Clinton and his wife seem to exemply this orientation, though they try hard to profess being "neo-democrats."

I often think that women managers may prove crucial to this challenge. Many studies suggest that women are usually more balanced and open to new ideas than men are. Women seem to be superb entrepreneurs, yet they also appreciate the need to unify organizations into supportive communities. That may be why women-owned businesses now employ 35 percent more people than the entire Fortune 500, are growing more rapidly than other firms, and have a higher success rate.

Further, women may be more forceful in bringing about change because they are dissatisfied with current management practices. After struggling to succeed for many years, female executives now realize that the present system is ineffective, unduly stressful, and empty of meaning.[24] My strong impression is that women are leading the way toward a dramatically different vision of management. They are showing us that something fundamental is seriously lacking in institutions today—the recognition that people are essentially spiritual beings with needs for meaning, purpose, fulfillment, belonging, and all of the other ideals religions have always tried to instill. They are also saying that we have ignored this reality not only to the detriment of our personal lives and society but also to the detriment of institutions themselves.

An increasing number of men are also discovering this crucial inner world of the soul, the spirit, the psyche, or whatever one chooses to call it.[25]

But women seem farther out in front because of their biological role as mothers, their special talents and interest in related emotional areas, and possibly because they have been placed historically as "outsiders," challenging the male status quo.

I do not intend this to mean that women will be our salvation, because men, racial minorities, and all other groups have equally important roles to play. In fact, today's explosion of diversity in modern workforces is likely to be a key factor driving this change. A market form of organization will be essential to accommodate this growing diversity, and some form of democratic governance will be needed to integrate such differences.

I have argued that the American heritage of democracy and enterprise can guide the creation of a New Management, and now we can see that another part of this heritage can also guide the integration of these two principles. Currency of the United States bears the motto *E Pluribus Unum*, meaning "Unity out of diversity," to remind us of that unique American spirit. Americans have immigrated from countries throughout the globe, and thus represent a wealth of racial and cultural differences united mainly by the ideals of American society. We may look like "mongrels," with our hodgepodge of mixed colors and traits, but this diversity is exactly the source of America's unusual strength.

Like the United States, institutions in a global economy will derive their strength from the same ideals of enterprise and democracy. To operate effectively across the wildly different nations of the world, managers will have to encourage a rich diversity among their constituents, and they will have to unify this diversity into a strong corporate community.

The Coming of Democratic Enterprise

Let's review the logic that leads to this conclusion that modern organizations must maintain a balance between internal markets and corporate community:

1. The Information Revolution is heightening organizational tensions as the need for enterprise and community increasingly pulls managers in opposing directions.

2. But the Information Revolution is also leading to an "Age of Synthesis" that will unify these opposing forces into more powerful organizational systems.

3. Managers must balance this creative tension to keep organizations dynamic yet unified.

As this shifting of "conceptual plates" beneath the surface of aware-ness dislodges the pillars of classical economic theory, a more powerful perspective of "*socio*economics" is emerging based on both enterprise and community, and competition and cooperation.[26] While cooperation may now be essential, rising global competition will also require us to look after our own welfare. The unavoidable fact is that a complex economy is evolving in which people must often both compete and cooperate together. GM, Ford, and Chrysler compete ferociously with Toyota, Fiat, and Renault—while they also work together as partners with these same adversaries. To manage this tension, a culture is needed that handles com-petition in a constructive way that allows people to cooperate as well.

This dynamic union between community and markets leads to the interesting conclusion that knowledge societies may no longer be "capital-ist." Peter Drucker called the emerging system of political economy a "post-capitalist society."[27] Economies are likely to be designed to serve human interests as well as those of capital, but they will not be "socialist" because business will still be governed by free markets. In fact, market systems should enjoy far greater entrepreneurial freedom and vigor than before.

As we will see in Chapter 10, the new economic system now emerging is a democratic form of free enterprise that goes beyond capitalism and socialism altogether. It could be thought of as a blend of democracy and enterprise that draws on the best features of both ideologies—a system of "Democratic Enterprise."

Notes

1. Quoted from Edward Carr, *The New Society* (Boston: Beacon Press, 1957), p. 25.
2. On the new science of complexity, see Mitchell Waldrop, *Complexity: The Emerging Science at the Edge of Order and Chaos* (New York: Simon & Schuster, 1992), and David Freedman, "Is Management Still a Science?" *Harvard Business Review* (November–December, 1992).
3. Tim Ferguson, "California Toys with Live Wires," *Wall Street Journal* (March 21, 1995).

4. See William E. Halal, "The Information Technology Revolution," *Technology Forecasting & Social Change* (August 1993), Vol. 44, pp. 69–86.

5. William Davidow and Michael Malone, *The Virtual Corporation* (New York: HarperBusiness, 1992). "The Portable Executive," *BusinessWeek* (October 10, 1988).

6. Thomas A. Stewart, "Boom Time on the New Frontier," *Fortune* (Autumn, 1993).

7. Robert Axelrod, *The Evolution of Cooperation* (New York: Basic Books, 1984).

8. Peter Drucker, "The Age of Social Transformation," *Atlantic Monthly* (November 1994).

9. Robert Ozaki, *Human Capitalism: The Japanese System as a World Model* (Tokyo: Kodansha International, 1991).

10. Carla Rapaport, "Charles Handy Sees the Future," *Fortune* (October 31, 1994).

11. Milton Derber, *The American Idea of Industrial Democracy* (Chicago: University of Illinois Press, 1970), pp. 6, 89, 374.

12. Paul Lawrence and Jay Lorsch, "Differentiation and Integration in Complex Organizations," *Harvard Business Review* (June 1964).

13. See Margaret Wheatley, *Leadership and the New Science* (San Francisco: Berrett-Koehler, 1992), p. 132.

14. For an analysis of organizational images, see Gareth Morgan, *Images of Organization* (Newbury Park, CA: Sage, 1986).

15. This conclusion was most notably reached in the classic study by E. A. Fleischman et al., *Leadership and Supervision in Industry* (Columbus: Ohio State University Press, 1955).

16. Russell Ackoff, *The Democratic Corporation* (New York: Oxford University Press, 1994). Sumantra Ghoshal and Christopher Bartlett, "Changing the Role of Top Management: Beyond Systems to People," *Harvard Business Review* (May-June 1995).

17. Gert Hofstede, *Culture's Consequences* (Newbury Park, Calif.: Sage, 1980).

18. Willis Harman, *Global Mind Change* (Indianapolis: Knowledge Systems, 1988).

19. As reported by William Raspberry, "Havel's Message of 'Forgotten Awareness,'" *Washington Post* (July 6, 1994), and Bruce Shenitz, "More Than Ourselves," *Newsweek* (July 18, 1994).

20. For instance, see Harman, *Global Mind Change*.

21. For instance, Charles Handy, *The Age of Paradox* (Cambridge, Mass.: Harvard

University Press, 1994), and John Naisbitt, *Global Paradox* (New York: Morrow, 1994), claim that paradox is the most characteristic feature of our time.

22. Wheatley, *Leadership and the New Science,* p. 68.

23. Charles McCoy, "Visionary or Cyberspace Cadet," *Washington Post* (November 14, 1994), Technology section, p. R20.

24. Betsy Morris, "Fed Up: Executive Women Confront Midlife Crisis," *Fortune* (September 18, 1995).

25. For a good treatment of this fundamental issue, see Thomas Moore, *Care of the Soul* (New York: HarperCollins, 1992).

26. For prominent works, see Amitai Etzioni, *The Moral Dimension: Toward a New Economics* (New York: Free Press, 1988).

27. Peter Drucker, *Post-Capitalist Society* (New York: Harper & Row, 1992).

Part Two

Building an
Entrepreneurial Community

This part of *The New Management* provides detailed blueprints for building an organization on the foundations of enterprise and democracy.

Chapter 5 addresses the rise of intense global competition for demanding clients who strive to improve their quality of life. We conclude that a "serving enterprise" is needed that uses technology to customize products and services, that helps employees improve quality, and that makes customers partners in the creation of value.

Chapter 6 focuses on the other organizational player who has moved to center stage—the knowledge worker. Today's economic upheaval is creating a new employment relationship in which teams of knowledge workers use information systems to manage their own small internal enterprise and are rewarded for performance.

Chapter 7 resolves the conflicting needs to protect a fragile environment while raising the living standards of billions of people. Leading corporations now regard sound ecological management as a competitive advantage, and so they are using their business skills to create an economic system that is environmentally benign.

These three chapters show that the New Management foundation can help managers perform their three major responsibilities better: internal markets and corporate community serve clients more effectively and profitably; they organize knowledge workers into a flexible, high-performing labor force; and they safeguard the environment while permitting vast increases in economic growth.

5

The Serving Enterprise

Relinquishing Our Grip on Self-Interest

Great battles are being joined in the marketplace today to decide which organizations will survive an onslaught of creative destruction. As rivals from around the world vie to meet growing demands for superior value and service, old allegiances to famous corporations of the past are being overthrown daily. Sears was replaced by Wal-Mart as America's dominant retailer, the AT&T monopoly was shattered by MCI, RCA has been eclipsed by Sony, GM Chevrolets must now compete with Hondas and Toyotas, and even IBM is fighting for its life against Microsoft and Intel.

Despite business attempts to win the hearts and minds of fickle buyers, however, excellence remains an exception in America. Surveys find that roughly half the public thinks the value they receive is poor to fair, and a third thinks it is bad and getting worse. Swapping horror stories about terrible service and shoddy products remains a popular topic of conversation.[1]

A telling incident highlights the problem. On recent a trip to Russia, I had to fly on the Russian airline, Aeroflot. Although concerned about putting myself in the hands of a foreign flight crew flying outdated aircraft in a land where nothing works, I was pleasantly surprised to find that Russian flights were better because they departed and arrived punctually. Upon returning home, however, my American flights were so late that terminals were filled with irate passengers, hopelessly watching their connecting flights, meetings, waiting friends, and other carefully made plans disintegrate. The Department of Transportation reports that 25 percent of United States flights are late. Air travel in the United States has become a recurring nightmare, as passengers struggle through a bewildering maze of prices, connecting hubs, frequent delays, and lost baggage.[2]

And what are the airlines doing to solve the problem? The airline industry seems more concerned with promoting frequent-flyer programs to discourage customers from switching to competitors. There are no net benefits because the fortunate souls who patronize the system long enough to receive free flights are in fact being subsidized through the inflated fares paid by other patrons and travel expenses paid by their own employers. The IRS estimates that employers lose $4.5 billion in excessive air fare every year because employees take unnecessary business flights to earn frequent-flyer credits. Airlines themselves lose another $2 billion as free trips displace paying customers, in addition to the cost of maintaining this complex system.[3] And because all major airlines offer the same programs now, any competitive advantage has been lost. In business terms, no value is added.

Despite the fact that almost no one benefits, the practice is spreading to hotel chains, car rental companies, and credit card companies because business cannot resist seducing buyers with the illusion of getting something free. This system may soon collapse like a chain letter, the way "Green Stamps" did a few decades ago. In 1994, the backlog of "miles" credited to frequent-flyers rose so high that airlines increased the number needed to get a free flight by 30 percent. Employers are organizing to eliminate the system, and passengers are suing airlines for discounting their earned miles.[4]

The urgent need to attract clients is understandable to anyone who has ever borne the responsibility to make a business succeed. But frequent-flyer programs are a symptom of how the Old Management often tries gimmicks to get clients rather than seriously improve service and value. In contrast, Southwest Airlines has become the most profitable firm in the industry by forsaking frills for the things that count: keeping fares below the competition, maintaining punctual schedules, offering direct flights, and encouraging employees to help passengers. One harried businessman was running to catch his Southwest flight as the plane pulled away from the gate; upon seeing the anguished look on the man's face, the pilot returned to pick him up. "It broke every rule in the book," said a Southwest manager, "But we congratulated the pilot on a job well done."[5] Now other airlines are emulating Southwest.

If it can be done, why are good service and genuine value so rare that they are celebrated as heroic? Why must customers struggle with poorly made products? Stores where you cannot find a helpful clerk? A failing educational system? Costly health care? Government bureaucracy? On the other side of the counter, why do managers tolerate such dismal performance? What can they do to regain the public's trust? And how in the world can sellers figure out what buyers really want?

This chapter draws on insights into today's changing social needs and examples of excellence to identify the principles of creative marketing in an Information Age. We will see that modern managers are challenged to focus on the needs of their clients rather than the firm—resulting in the "serving enterprise." By forming a trusting relationship with customers, the New Management can be more profitable while also serving the genuine needs of these stakeholders who are central members of the corporate community.

FROM SELLING TO SERVING

The crux of the problem in marketing today is an outmoded focus on "selling." While it seemed perfectly reasonable at one time, now this preoccupation with the interests of the enterprise is outmoded because it excludes the interests of clients. Theodore Leavitt calls it "marketing myopia."

The Wasteful Noise of Advertising

The problem is illustrated by today's barrage of advertisements. The average American is bombarded by 30,000 ads each day from TV, newspapers, and junk mail, all promoting yet another contrived bargain. Twenty million American homes are invaded during dinner each evening by 300,000 telemarketers. And ads are now appearing in schools, on shopping carts, and in every conceivable nook and cranny of life.[6] The social effects of TV advertising are so disturbing that parents consider TV an "enemy" they must fight to raise healthy children (see Box 5.1). In our urgency to sell, we have reduced the miracle of television to a sewer of commercialism that sets a squalid moral tone for the nation.

The irony is that this stampede to seize the buyers' attention is largely ineffectual; each message adds to the burgeoning maze of advertising noise,

---

BOX 5.1. MEDIA AND SOCIAL VALUES.

Advertisements, purchased by corporations, account for 80 percent of the income of newspapers and all of the income for television networks. Since these corporate sponsors are the paying clients, rather than the public, their needs influence news and entertainment itself in subtle ways. One editor of a major daily acknowledged: "We should stop kidding ourselves that we are in the newspaper business and admit that we are in the advertising business." Because of this influence, TV tends to pander to common tastes to justify the huge costs of ad time, flooding homes with violence, sex, and consumption. The American Psychological Association estimates that the average child witnesses 8,000 murders and 100,000 other acts of violence by age twelve. The Director of the Center on Aggression Research at Syracuse University summed up the effect of this powerful medium on society: "Hundreds of studies all point to this conclusion: television violence begets real-world violence."

Sources: Richard Harwood, "No Alternative to a Market," *Washington Post* (December 12, 1992); Chris Welles, "Hello Sweetheart, Get Me Advertising," *BusinessWeek* (March 3, 1993); William Raspberry, "Cut the Act," *Washington Post* (January 28, 1994).

---

turning all this costly communication into an indistinguishable blur that deadens the senses. People have been so overhyped that they either ignore it, refuse to believe it, or just plain dislike it. Recent studies find that only a small percentage of advertising recovers its costs, and even these are effective only for a matter of months. Promotions do even worse because they encourage competitors to retaliate and they lower the company's image.[7]

Special "sales" are a particular problem. At one time, a sale really meant a special situation that offered unusual value. Now the practice has been overused to the point that it is almost impossible to sell products at regular prices because people expect discounts. Thus, the public becomes confused over what constitutes a fair price, they distrust the seller, and merchants waste time and money on these futile exercises. Montgomery Ward spent 120 work days filling out 15,000 rain checks for one sale item that had run out of stock. The company's CEO acknowledged that this approach "erodes your credibility."[8] Listen to how the president of the National Auto Dealers Association views the problem in the auto industry:

> The public is tired of on-again, off-again rebate programs that confuse dealers and buyers. A child can figure out that the consumer

pays the bill. So end the phony rebate and low interest-rates, establish a single, no-nonsense price and try something revolutionary: build good, reliable cars.[9]

From an economic view, this sell-at-any-cost approach is simply too crude to solve the complex job of serving an exploding array of highly differentiated, subtle social needs. Because buyers are left to find their way through misleading claims, Americans make suboptimal purchases that waste an estimated $1 trillion out of a $4 trillion economy every year.[10] The predictable result is that people then look elsewhere for better value.

"Selling" also creates an adversarial relationship with the buyer. I am struck by the common assumption that the client is not a part of the organization, so the welfare of this impersonal figure is not of concern. Managers set the tone for this view if their main goal is making money, and this message is then conveyed to their organization. That's why clerks often treat customers as an irritating inconvenience.[11] A manager in the CIT study said, "Our philosophy seems to be 'bill, bill, bill, so we can grow rich, rich, rich,'" and another admitted, "Our clients hate us."

Consumerism Is the Other Side of Selling

While Americans are critical of shoddy goods and poor service, they also encourage the selling enterprise by responding so eagerly to the lure of quick material gratification. Americans spend 300 percent more time shopping than Europeans, and they consume roughly twice as much energy and resources.[12] All this consumerism takes effort, so people are overworked, overwrought, and overweight from pursuing higher levels of consumption that are unrelated to personal happiness.[13] Thus, consumerism is the other side of selling. They support one another.

The "selling/consumerism syndrome" is not solely the fault of managers or the public. To a large extent, this outmoded way of life persists as residual inertia from the dying forces that propelled the Industrial Age: mass production of simple consumer goods, a business focus on profit that excludes the public welfare, a throwaway culture, exploitation of what seemed a limitless environment, and the use of media to stimulate demand.

Most attempts to improve quality and service are palliative fixes because they fail to address today's economic transition—our changing assumptions about the needs of society, the goals of the enterprise, and its relationship with clients.

The Rising Demand for Value and Quality of Life

Consider the average family. Typically, both husband and wife work today, so life is a struggle to clean and maintain their home, to take care of two cars, a few TVs and VCRs, several telephones, a home computer or two, and kitchen appliances. Then they must somehow attend to laundry and dry cleaning, shop for groceries, buy clothes and items for the home, prepare meals, entertain, juggle complex finances, and figure out their taxes. Simply finding affordable child care that can be trusted is an enormous challenge, let alone putting kids through college. To cope with these demands, many people are turning their cars into mobile living and working units, equipped with cellular phones, fax machines, portable PCs, and even microwave ovens.

These needs are being enshrined in a new set of social mores that focus on handling stress and using time productively. People today often compete with one another over their demanding responsibilities—the "busier than thou" syndrome. This is not limited to the harried middle class. Some of the wealthiest, most distinguished people in the world—Bill Gates, Warren Buffett, and President Clinton—work so hard that they have to be forced to take vacations; they wear ordinary clothes and drive their own cars.[14] Thorstein Veblen's ethic of "conspicuous consumption" may have described the Industrial Age, but the Information Age is creating a new ethic that could be called "anxious achievement."

Not only are social needs more complex, people are far more discriminating because they are better educated and they have access to a wealth of product information. Caught between stagnating incomes and rising costs, buyers look over worldwide competitors to select high-quality products, competitive prices stripped of unneeded frills or fancy brand names, and thoughtful service.[15] Here's how *Fortune* put it: "The customer isn't king anymore. The customer is a dictator. Instead of choosing from what you have to offer, the new consumer tells you what he wants."[16]

Some people will continue to seek material extravagance, of course, since that is one of the celebrated features of American life, and everyone will want to ride the new information superhighways. But a survey of 2,000

Americans found that "three-fourths say they've filled most if not all of their material needs." Other polls show that 70 percent of Americans would like to lead simpler, more satisfying lives.[17] People increasingly yearn for relief from stress, financial security, less crime and violence, recreation, clean air and water, meaningful social relations, and other complex social needs that are now the goals of human progress. Thus, the mission of business today must be nothing less than to raise the quality of life.

Reversing the Buyer-Seller Relationship

Advertising and other marketing tools will remain important, of course, but there are many ways to attract clients. Just as managers now understand they must create a "learning organization" to stay apace of change, they also need to create a "serving organization" that satisfies social needs more effectively.

Paul Hawken, an author and businessman, identified this change as the reversal of that old "centrifugal" marketing, which pushed products out of factories into the hands of passive customers. In its place, a "centripetal" role is emerging that draws a deeper understanding of the client's needs and problems into the firm.[18] John Scully, former CEO of Apple Computer, put it this way:

> It used to be that marketing drove things. But marketing is really a mass-production-based concept. It's about creating something that you can push out to the whole world. Today, everything is being customized, so it's really being driven by the other side, by the customer.[19]

Wal-Mart's humbling defeat of Kmart tells it all. In 1987, Kmart dominated the discount market with its 2,223 stores, bringing in annual sales of $26 billion. Confident in its strength, Kmart focused its strategy on traditional marketing, using national TV campaigns featuring glamorous women to bolster its "image."

Meanwhile, Wal-Mart had half as many stores and was almost unknown. But instead of advertising, the company developed its now-famous logistics system. A satellite network was established to monitor sales nationwide, analyze these data to determine which products should be ordered for each store, and automatically replenish inventories by sending orders to 4,000 suppliers who were connected to Wal-Mart through computer systems. Wal-Mart was thereby able to optimize the choice of goods stocked at each store, minimize transportation and inventory costs, and pass these savings on in deep discounts. Three years later, Wal-Mart surpassed Kmart with sales of $33 billion. Sam Walton, the architect of Wal-Mart's success, knew in his bones that Americans were hungry for value and service, and he provided it.[20]

PRINCIPLES OF THE SERVING ENTERPRISE

To meet this challenge, creative entrepreneurs are reorienting all phases in the life cycle of a product or service: high-tech marketing, truthful advertising, client participation, empowered employees focused on quality, accountability for customer satisfaction, and involved leadership.

High-Tech Marketing

As the Information Revolution drives the power of IT up and its cost down, a new form of high-tech marketing is emerging to transform buyer-seller relations. As Box 5.2 shows, electronic shopping services, computerized sales systems, automated product design, and much, much more promise to reduce distribution costs, make shopping convenient, and allow people to make wiser purchases. The prospects are so enormous that they cannot be addressed fully here, but a few examples illustrate the possibilities.

Two-thirds of U.S. companies operated toll-free information lines in 1993, and this network is spreading overseas as foreign manufacturers use it to tap into the American marketplace and vice versa. The GE Answer Center, for instance, receives three million calls each year from people asking about products, seeking advice, making complaints, requesting repairs, and other information that is then analyzed for marketing purposes.[21]

IT also is creating far more efficient distribution channels. On the input end, sellers are gaining access to unprecedented amounts of valuable information that allow them to understand their diverse markets and pinpoint the sale of products to meet highly specialized needs—"niche marketing." On the output end, buyers are gaining an equally valuable source of information that evaluates various products to allow better choices—"precision shopping."

BOX 5.2. EXEMPLARS OF HIGH-TECH MARKETING.

The following companies are exemplars of how powerful IT systems can be used to deliver sophisticated products and services that serve diverse social needs effectively.

Canon Computer Systems is typical of the many companies that use large data bases to analyze customers' needs and customize marketing programs. It recently targeted potential buyers of a new color printer so accurately from its 1.3 million customers that response rates to direct mail approached an unheard of 50 percent.

Progressive Insurance provides its claim representatives an air-conditioned van equipped as a portable office so that they can work at the scene of an accident. The company now settles 80 percent of its claims within one day. "This is great, coming right out here and taking charge," said a policy holder who was in an auto accident.

MusicWriter is a high-tech distributor of sheet music. Rather than stock thousands of different songs in music stores, it sets up a computerized kiosk that simply prints out any request.

Hallmark Cards has installed computerized kiosks in stores that allow customers to design their own cards.

Anderson Windows developed a multimedia system, "Window of Knowledge," that allows salespeople and customers to design customized windows, generate price quotes, and send detailed instructions to the factory. Sales have risen and mistakes vanished.

Astra/Merck equipped its sales staff with laptop computers that access a knowledge base maintained by the company to help physicians solve complex patient problems. Said one physician: "It's distinctive. They're supporting us now. There's no selling."

Schwab Corporation offers investors a software system they can use to obtain securities prices, buy and sell, and do most other functions performed by a broker at discounted fees. Schwab's assets have skyrocketed as 800,000 new accounts have been opened, and the company's own stock has risen fivefold.

AucNet is a satellite auction system used to sell used cars wholesale in Japan. Dealers use a PC to examine photos and detailed information on cars offered for sale, and then make bids. Because the market has been extended to cover an entire nation, the larger number of buyers allows sellers to command higher prices.

Source: "The Best Way to Reach Your Buyers," *Fortune* (special issue, Autumn/Winter, 1993).

Not only are distribution channels becoming smarter, but they are also becoming shorter as middlemen are eliminated. Dell Computer became a powerful competitor to IBM when Michael Dell realized he could sell PCs through the mail—"just-in-time retailing."[22] Without the need for manufacturing shops, warehouses, retail stores, and salespeople, the cost of a Dell computer drastically undercut IBM to launch the PC clone industry.[23]

At the advanced end of the IT spectrum, interactive video shopping should enter the mainstream in the late 1990s.[24] Even now, the Home Shopping Network offers the wares of Nordstrom, Bloomingdale's, J. C. Penney, and other retail chains to 60 million homes that made up a $3 billion market as of 1993.[25] TV shows, newspapers, and other media may soon include interactive advertisements that carry the shopper into a "virtual store" where products can be examined, prices determined, and orders placed. Peapod, an electronic grocery service, allows clients to create a "virtual supermarket" customized to their unique needs by setting up standard shopping lists for reordering and comparing prices at all local stores.

Truthful, Useful Customer Relations

It may appear hopelessly naive in today's world of hard-selling, glitzy ads, but many fine companies owe their lasting success to the opposite approach: advertising and customer relations that tell the truth. L. L. Bean, Hershey Foods, Toyota, Johnson & Johnson, and countless other examples of highly successful organizations demonstrate that business can be conducted honorably, and it is usually more profitable.

In 1993 Saturn had to recall all the cars it had ever sold. Rather than proffering the typical evasions and half-truths that are normal in the auto industry, Saturn immediately announced the full details of the problem and its proposed solution. The president of the company, Richard (Skip) LeFauve, appeared on television to personally explain the situation, apologize, and tell customers to contact their dealer to arrange a free retrofit, or the company would *call them*. This candid approach turned a potential disaster into proof of Saturn's claim to a new form of management, and thereby increased public's trust in the company. (See Box 5.3.)

Saturn, Nordstrom, Toys "R" Us, Wal-Mart, Procter & Gamble (P&G),

and other companies exemplify the use of "everyday low prices" instead of contrived sales or promotions. A P&G manager said: "We want our brands to be a good value every time they are bought rather than a bargain every now and then. Our customers appreciate that"; and a Continental Airlines manager said: "Customers are all under the same constraints of price and time, which is why simplicity and consistency have great appeal."[26]

Pursuing a policy of truthful client relations is not simply a moral issue but a more powerful form of marketing. Honesty builds lasting patronage based on the confidence that the company is committed to providing value. As shown in Box 5.4, the Body Shop has enjoyed remarkable growth,

---

BOX 5.3. GM-SATURN—ON SERVING CAR OWNERS.

Saturn has used innovative management to create the highest quality cars and the highest buyer satisfaction levels in the auto industry.

A Soft Approach to Car Sales. Saturn's "soft" sales approach avoids the traditional "hard" sales job of haggling over car prices. Prices are established at a fair but comfortable margin over invoice by the manufacturer. Dealers are carefully selected and given an exclusive territory so that they do not have to compete with other Saturn dealers. Salespeople avoid pressuring customers but focus on providing information and help. As a result, customer satisfaction among Saturn buyers ranks above that of Mercedes and Lincoln buyers.

Empowered Worker Teams. The great demand for Saturn cars is attributed to the high-quality production methods that are made possible by a participative management style. Workers are organized into teams of ten people who control all aspects of their jobs: working with suppliers, selecting co-workers, setting their own work schedules, performing their own quality inspections, and even advising on the selection of suppliers, dealerships, and advertising agencies. Employee compensation is based on quality and other factors that ensure customer satisfaction.

A Company-Customer Relationship. An unusually candid approach to handling product defects, sales, and other relations with car buyers has made Saturn owners the most loyal repeat purchasers in the industry.

Spreading of the Saturn Sales Approach. The Saturn concept of marketing has proven to be such a fresh and welcomed change that GM divisions are trying its methods, and Ford and Chrysler are emulating the single-price sales system.

Sources: "Saturn: Labor's Love Lost?" *BusinessWeek* (February 8, 1993); "Saturn," *BusinessWeek* (August 17, 1992).

even though it does no advertising; it does not even have a marketing department. By offering healthful, inexpensive cosmetics while protecting nature, the company has ignited a roaring demand among satisfied customers—who then do the marketing for the firm by telling their friends. Paul Hawken described the merits of truthful customer relations:

> There is one mistake no entrepreneur can afford to make—misleading customers. They stop buying. In the tawdry world of braggadocios, the truth rings with clarity. It changes the signal-to-noise ratio. The noise is the $95 billion spent on advertising. The signal is the clear tone of honesty that comes through as compellingly as the siren of an ambulance.[27]

Client Participation

Studies have long shown that most successful new products are developed in response to suggestions by customers. Rather than studying people's needs through market surveys, progressive firms actively involve their clients in the design process. "I think the current notion of market research is going to be completely overturned," said the vice president of a marketing firm.[28] This is especially true for the new product markets and customers that make up the frontier of the emerging knowledge society. "You can't market research something that doesn't exist," said Peter Drucker.

Companies are using this concept in numerous ways to achieve excellence. GE, for example, asks its design engineers to work with customers in defining an ideal appliance. Hewlett-Packard invites buyers of its products to give presentations to engineers and managers, pointing out problems they encounter and suggesting improvements. Fisher-Price created a nursery in its corporate headquarters where parents can bring children to try out new toys; the waiting list runs into the thousands. (See Box 5.5 for more examples.)

This is just a trickle of what may become a flood of "do-it-yourself" marketing, as buyers shun the services of building contractors, repair people, retailers, and other traditional providers. Home Depot offers repair clinics that allow customers to create value by replacing contractors. Estimates suggest that the amount of work devoted to home projects is equivalent to 40 percent of the GDP. The CEO of Price Club explained why his

---

BOX 5.4. THE BODY SHOP—ON MARKETING.

The marketing aspects of the Body Shop exemplify the New Management by providing genuine value, honest dealings, and concern for human, social, and environmental well-being.

Natural Value. The Body Shop has challenged the foundations of an industry that exploited the glamour fantasies of women. Rather than sell expensive chemical cosmetics of dubious worth in designer bottles, Body Shop cosmetics are wholesome, natural products intended to promote the inherent beauty of a healthy, well-cared for body, and they are packaged in inexpensive, refillable containers.

No Advertising. Contrary to accepted practice, the Body Shop conducts no advertising, and has no marketing department because it does not try to "sell" in the ordinary sense. Rather, it provides educational information in pamphlets and posters at its stores, and relies on word of mouth among satisfied patrons to spread the message. Store personnel do not push products but are available for advice and assistance. In short, the Body Shop's philosophy is to educate rather than sell. This approach has increased sales 50 percent per year and the company has expanded to 1,400 shops in forty-six nations.

Leadership. The energizing force that guides this enterprise is Anita Roddick, the founder and CEO, who understands that women need a more reasonable approach to cosmetics. Her philosophy, "People want companies they can believe in," has been so successful that the Body Shop arouses the enthusiasm, loyalty, and commitment of political movements. When operations were to be extended to the United States, 2,500 people applied for franchises.

Source: Bo Burlingham, "This Woman Has Changed Business Forever," *Inc.* (June 1990), and personal correspondence with Anita Roddick.

---

no-frills bulk sales are so successful: "[All companies] say they provide great service, but self-service is the best kind of service."[29]

There is also a need to involve clients at the policy level by creating consumer advisory panels of typical customers who advise organizations. A more powerful approach is to appoint clients or consumer advocates to the corporate board, and it is puzzling why more corporations have not done so. If we really hope to manage organizations to serve clients, what better place to start?

BOX 5.5. EXEMPLARS OF CLIENT PARTICIPATION.

Herman Miller has design teams work at clients' offices to understand their furniture needs and produce prototypes to test on site, thereby speeding development time, reducing cost, and increasing client satisfaction. One manager said, "We bring customers in at the very beginning to become partners in design."

Black & Decker assigned a design team to work with fifty typical "do-it-yourself" homeowners around their homes, workshops, and on shopping trips to learn what they wanted in tools. This fresh understanding produced an award-winning product line, "Quantum," with interchangeable power sources, new safety features, free maintenance check-ups, and a toll-free hotline for advice.

Honda videotaped customers testing new cars and had line workers call 4,700 Honda owners to get their criticism and suggestions. The results were used to make thousands of changes over the past few years that made Honda the top-selling auto in America.

Westinghouse has developed such a close working relationship with the public utilities it serves that some managers exchange business plans and engage in joint reviews of each other's operations. "We work with the utilities in partnership arrangements to share our responsibilities," said a Westinghouse program manager.

Baxter Laboratories provides on-site inventory management of medical supplies for hospitals, sharing in both losses and gains. "This goes beyond loyalty," said a Baxter executive. "We share a common P&L. You both make money by keeping costs down."

General Electric forms cross-company teams of its own employees and those of its clients to handle tough technical problems, even sending teams to training programs together. "Working as a single entity enhanced communications," said a GE vice president.

Sources: "The Tough New Customer," *Fortune* (Autumn/Winter 1993); Rahul Jacob, "Why Some Customers Are More Equal than Others," *Fortune* (September 19, 1994).

The usual objection is that consumer advocates are likely to be critical, which would disrupt the harmony of the board. But perhaps this "harmony" *should* be disturbed to urge unresponsive firms into action. Our critics are the people we should pay closest attention to because they are keenly aware of our weaknesses. That's why they infuriate us so much. A sound enterprise listens carefully to criticism because it is valuable feedback and a source of energy that drives creative change. Most people are reluctant to complain, so brave managers hire firms like "Feedback Plus," who use professional shoppers to evaluate how well their customers are treated. "Stores that score high on our shopping service have the best sales," claims a vice president of Feedback Plus.[30]

But it is possible to become *too* close to customers. People often lack the imagination to envision major changes in lifestyles, leading companies to mimic present trends rather than radically carve out the markets of the future. The microwave oven, minivan, fax, and VCRs all bored prospective customers until they were available. Conversely, customers insisted they were mad about the New Coke, picturephones, and other products that fizzled. So it is essential to keep the buyer-seller relationship in perspective. Client-driven marketing is more than simply doing whatever clients say; it is a two-way exchange in which companies must maintain faith in their judgment about how to best serve new needs.[31]

The possibilities are endless, but they are all *variations on a central principle of the new marketing philosophy: companies are more likely to design useful, economically successful products by making the client an active partner in the enterprise.*

The Quality-and-Service Revolution

TQM has assumed mythical proportions because it is part of a "quality-and-service revolution" that is moving from business to government and all other institutions. Contrary to the prevailing prior belief that quality is "nice but costly," sound management reduces costs by building quality into superior designs, thereby eliminating the need for rework, avoiding customer returns and lost business, and permitting economies of scale.

Quality is often shrouded in complex terms, but the key factors are disarmingly simple. We saw in Chapter 2 how crucial enterprise is to making TQM work. Home Depot (Box 5.6) and Saturn show how successful firms form self-directed teams charged with the responsibility of serving clients through continuous improvement processes.

Beyond today's struggle to improve quality, a cornucopia of near-perfect customized goods should soon flow out of automated factories, as we will see in the next chapter. A good example of this "mass customization" is the way Dell Computer builds 90 percent of its PCs to order and delivers them in two days.[32]

BOX 5.6. HOME DEPOT.

This chain of about four hundred lumber-hardware-home-supply stores was paid the ultimate compliment by the CEO of Wal-Mart: "They're running the best retail organization in America today." Home Depot's earnings have grown an average of 43 percent over the past ten years, highest in the Fortune Service 500, and return on investment averaged 46 percent per year. Here's why:

Customer Value and Service. Rather than sales or promotions, customers are offered everyday low prices that consistently underprice their competitors, and service is outstanding. The CEO describes his philosophy this way: "Every customer has to be treated like your mother, father, sister, or brother." A client said, "I've never had such a positive service experience."

Evaluation of Client Satisfaction. Intensive evaluations of client needs and satisfaction are obtained from 5,000 interviews annually. In response to these analyses, the company started free clinics that teach customers plumbing and construction.

Employee Support. Shoppers are assisted in solving problems by employees who are trained in product knowledge and home repairs, and who are instructed to spend time helping people in a courteous manner. To ensure this level of service, pay is set well above the market rates, employees are offered company stock at a discount, and managers can earn bonuses of 50 percent.

Leadership. All of this is inspired and directed by the leadership of CEO Bernard Marcus and president Arthur Blank, who are constantly available at stores. The two hold a companywide meeting every Sunday, "Breakfast with Bernie and Arthur," that is broadcast over closed-circuit TV to all 45,000 employees. Home Depot's seven outside directors are each required to visit twelve stores per quarter.

Sources: "Beyond Quality and Value," *Fortune* (Autumn/Winter 1993); "The Man Who Walked Out on Ross Perot," *Forbes* (November 22, 1993).

Employee Rewards Linked to Client Satisfaction

It is also necessary to measure how well these goals are accomplished. Sales and profit are important, but they focus on the needs of the *organization* rather than the needs of the *client*. Financial performance is the *result* of client satisfaction, so the primary focus should be on evaluating this crucial factor.[33] One manager in the CIT survey expressed it well: "Customer feedback is the key to sound business; revenues are a lagging indicator." Sears was the subject of national scorn in 1992 because workers in its auto repair shops, under pressure to increase sales, were gouging clients; now the company is using client satisfaction evaluations.

McDonald's and L. L. Bean use periodic surveys to evaluate customer satisfaction. Marriott and Western Union make unannounced inspections of outlets. Giant Foods and Avis have employees and executives patronize their stores incognito to observe how they are treated. Ford invites car owners to meet engineers and dealers to discuss problems with their cars. State Farm and Toyota measure customer "loyalty" and "retention rates."[34]

An old management axiom that holds that organizations get what they reward, so it is also essential to base employee pay at least partly on evaluations of client satisfaction. GTE's system allocates 35 percent of employee and manager pay in accordance with client satisfaction ratings. Xerox bases 30 percent on client surveys. Chrysler has begun to pay bonuses to its dealers with high client satisfaction scores.[35]

As some of these examples suggest, it is best to reward an entire team or business unit, rather than individuals. Group rewards are easier to manage and they promote unit cohesion. We will say more about the management of teams in Chapter 6.

Involved Leadership

Organizations that deliver products of lasting value with genuine service are usually blessed with the leadership needed to bring a serving enterprise to life. Only executives can provide the vision and personal example that focuses a large organization on serving its clients. Home Depot would not be the same without Bernard Marcus and Arthur Blank. The Body Shop is inspired by Anita Roddick. Sam Walton created Wal-Mart.

Xerox executives spend one day each month taking complaints from customers. The president of Hyatt Hotels occasionally works as a bellhop. Skip LeFauve invited all 700,000 Saturn owners to attend a barbecue at its plant; 28,000 people showed up, making it the "Woodstock" of the auto industry. "It's a good way to say thank you and foster a closer relationship," said Saturn's marketing manager.

Harley-Davidson has organized 700 Harley Owners Groups (HOG Clubs) that hold an annual rally; the highlight occurs when the company's CEO, Rich Teerlink, roars in on his own gleaming top-of-the-line Harley. When Teerlink first started this approach, the company was almost bankrupt.

The stock has since gone from $1.20 per share to $26, and buyers have to wait years to get a Harley.

Herb Kelleher, the CEO of Southwest Airlines, is a clowning genius who sets such a friendly tone with clients that Southwest personnel often joke mercilessly with passengers. One flight heard this announcement over the PA system: "Good morning ladies and gentlemen. If you wish to smoke, please go to our lounge on the wing where you can enjoy our feature film, *Gone with the Wind.*"[36]

A small Oregon restaurant chain highlights the importance of leadership by illustrating all of the principles discussed in this chapter. After struggling to improve service, the CEO established a policy that all patrons must enjoy a pleasant dining experience. Just as Avis claims "We Try Harder" and Federal Express promises "Absolutely, Positively, Overnight," this company's primary goal was "Your Enjoyment Guaranteed. Always." As the CEO put it, "My company exists to make other people happy."

He then changed operations to ensure that this guarantee was fulfilled. Employees were told to do anything necessary to satisfy a customer—offer free drinks, meals, or special attention—and they were trained to do so effectively. Customer satisfaction was evaluated using a monthly phone survey and by measuring the number of complaints, and the total cost of resolving them was tallied. The company found that many customers had been unhappy but reluctant to complain, so they had simply voted with their feet and gone elsewhere. Under the new guarantee, the costs of correcting complaints rose, making the problems that were formerly hidden visible.

Where most managers would be aghast at seeing costs rise, this CEO recognized that such costs are symptoms of deeper problems, and as such are valuable information. As the CEO said: "Every dollar paid out is a signal that the company must change." As these system failures were found and corrected, costs dropped to modest levels, clients became delighted at the service, employees took pleasure in their work and were better paid, sales increased, and profits doubled.[37]

MAKING THE CLIENT A PARTNER

But why should we go through all this trouble, cost, risk, and personal discomfort to satisfy demanding people? L. L. Bean worked hard to become customer-focused and was rewarded by a wave of merchandise returns valued at $82 million. Let's face it. Many clients are impossible to satisfy at all, much less at a profit. The CEO of Southwest Airlines writes to customers who abuse employees, asking them to fly on another airline.

It's also hard to change the habits of people who have raised the narcissistic pursuit of self-interest to an art form. Admonitions to serve clients have to fight the influence of an American culture that urges employees to "Look Out for No 1." The reality is that genuine service requires discipline and hard work. A field of study has emerged to understand the rigors of "emotional labor" performed by service personnel, and an industry has sprung up to train employees in dealing with quarrelsome people. Flight attendants must be friendly, nurses are expected to show sympathy, and teachers must be supportive, even when they may feel upset.[38]

And how can employees please customers when they must struggle against bureaucracy, authoritarian supervisors, and other common management problems that hinder service and quality? The serving enterprise is a part of the New Management, so it is necessary to change the entire management system, as other chapters will show.

Seeing Problems as Opportunities

There is little choice but to overcome such objections because they now conflict with reality. Managers have been told endlessly that they must be primarily concerned with selling and financial goals, yet that belief is being challenged as a new breed of clients, complex social problems, and global competitors demand a shift to serving the needs of the client. Table 5.1 shows that these concepts are now widely practiced.

Each lost customer takes two to three others away after complaining to an average of nine friends, and it costs five times as much to recruit a new customer as to retain an existing one.[39] Each lost client costs an automaker $400,000 over a lifetime and a grocery store $25,000 every five years. Improving the customer retention rate by 2 percent will typically increase profits 10 percent. Driven by such economic realities, an executive described the reaction: "It's not like we sat here and said, 'Let's change the way we sell.' We had no choice."[40]

This enlightened form of marketing also offers important long-term

TABLE 5.1. ADOPTION OF SERVING-ENTERPRISE PRACTICES.
(SAMPLE = 426 CORPORATE MANAGERS.)

Practice	Not Practiced (0–3)	Partially Practiced (4–6)	Fully Practiced (7–10)	Mean (0–10)
In addition to sales levels, customer satisfaction is evaluated by surveys and interviews, monitoring complaints, and other formal systems.	17%	15%	68%	7.1
The views of customers are solicited by product designers, managers, or other personnel when making decisions about products and services.	13	20	67	7.0
Customers can use a toll-free line for information and to have problems corrected.	31	7	62	6.1
Advertising is designed to provide useful information rather than inflated claims.	12	15	73	7.3
A significant portion of operating managers' pay is based on customer satisfaction.	46	26	28	4.1
Means	24%	17%	59%	6.4

Source: William E. Halal, *Corporations in Transition* (an unpublished study in progress). Note that data in the first three columns ("Not Practiced," etc.) are aggregated by collapsing portions of the questionnaire scale as shown ("0–3," etc.). See the questionnaire in Appendix C.

benefits. A working partnership with clients better positions the organization to understand complex new social needs in order to convert these problems into business opportunities.

The auto industry, for instance, could enter a fresh cycle of growth by finding a better way to satisfy the public's travel needs. The Japanese made great inroads into American markets by realizing that a car is more than a stylish piece of machinery. Rather, they viewed a car as a *transportation system* involving fuel efficiency, maintenance, safety, and insurance—all of which have become vitally important to car owners. An average auto cost about $17,000 in 1993, but these additional factors cost another $40,000 over a typical product life of ten years, making the ownership of an automobile a major investment of roughly $60,000.[41]

The amount of money spent on auto repair and maintenance alone is about as great as that spent on the purchase of new vehicles. Roughly two-thirds of this sum is wasted because of improper diagnosis, poor workmanship, and fraud.[42] Businesspeople should see that this problem is actually an opportunity crying out for a solution. By learning how to maintain autos better, dealers could save customers thousands of dollars per year while minimizing the time and aggravation involved in car ownership— creating a virgin market that roughly equals the entire new car market. Similar opportunities are possible in reducing the fuel, safety, and insurance costs of this system.

As Hamel and Prahalad point out, all industries must redefine their mission to meet the needs of tomorrow.[43] Sweden now produces 95 percent of its homes in factories, and the Japanese are moving toward automated construction of high-quality housing modules that can be assembled quickly into an infinite variety of pleasing, inexpensive homes. Will the American building industry suffer a replay of the Japanese invasion of U.S. auto markets? Which companies will develop the first reasonably priced, convenient telecomputer? Automatic language translation? Mechanical hearts and other vital organs? Personal tutoring systems? Optical computers? And an endless array of other revolutionary new products that will make today's microwave ovens and PCs look primitive?

Other institutions will be forced to surmount similar challenges in the years ahead. Medicine must move beyond curing illness to develop convenient, inexpensive ways to help each individual find a healthy style of living. Education must use IT to make learning a continual part of everyday life in a fast-paced technological age. And government must regulate this entire system in a way that assists people while minimizing taxes and regulations. These goals constitute a vast frontier of progress precisely because the world is swamped with so many difficult social problems that can be converted into opportunities. A few years ago I noticed a small sign in a shop window that quietly announced the secret of sound business that successful entrepreneurs have always known:

> Business success is not for the greedy. On the contrary, lasting success results from giving more and charging less. The possibilities are infinite.

Yielding Self-Interest

This discussion of modern marketing leads to four main conclusions:

1. A global economy of fierce competition and demanding clients requires that customers' interests become paramount.

2. Appeals through "selling" have become largely ineffectual because they merely add to the noise of advertising.

3. Managers must create a "serving enterprise" that uses information technology and involved employees to form a working partnership with clients that serves their genuine needs.

4. This concept of a serving enterprise can help managers reorient their organizations so as to convert today's social problems into profitable opportunities for improving the quality of life.

Although economics has been called "the dismal science" because it has generally assumed scarcity, economic life can be abundant when approached with faith in the creative nature of a bountiful world. The key to this pivotal change is to see that a serving enterprise combines the two powerful forces of internal markets and corporate community, as we noted in Chapter 4. Inventive managers organize operations into entrepreneurial teams that serve clients better, thereby uniting financial and social goals. By giving thoughtful consideration to others, it may be returned to us manyfold. "Cast your bread upon the waters," as the Bible expressed it.

Putting the welfare of clients foremost does not mean managers and employees must become self-sacrificing martyrs, although they do have to give of themselves. As we stressed in Chapter 3, the idea is to develop a working *relationship* based on mutual rights and responsibilities. Like any partnership, both partners have to give, including the client. Part of the New Management would be to help clients learn how to use the product or service wisely, to hold reasonable expectations, and seek resolution of problems before withdrawing patronage or pressing a lawsuit.

Individuals and organizations must handle these issues in their own ways, and many will opt for conventional methods. Despite the growth of a soft sales approach, for instance, some car dealers continue to thrive on overstated ads and sales pressure. The fact is that many buyers are reluctant to give up the thrill of haggling over prices.[44] We are reminded again that the New Management cannot be used as doctrine if it hopes to meet the diverse needs facing organizations.

Because a diversity of approaches is possible, tough choices must be made that hinge on our personal values and willingness to change. Do we really have to accept this challenge of yielding our self-interest? I know that I have trouble subjugating my interests. If it is true that serving others is more effective, what prevents us from doing it? What would we give up? What would we gain? What will happen if we do not change?

I must admit that I do not have good answers to these questions, but I do know that the trends noted above are going to severely test us all during the difficult years ahead.

Notes

1. "Pul-eeze! Will Somebody Help Me?" *Time* (February 2, 1987). Amanda Bennett, "Making the Grade with the Customer," *Wall Street Journal* (November 12, 1990).
2. "Is Herb Kelleher America's Best CEO?" *Fortune* (May 2, 1994).
3. Rex Toh et al., "Frequent-Flier Games: The Problem of Employee Abuse," *The Executive* (February 1993).
4. "15 Firms Target Workers' Frequent-Flyer Awards," *Washington Post* (May 9, 1994). "Frequent Flyer Changes Rile Passengers," *Washington Post* (February 2, 1995). For a good analysis see Jeff Blyskal, "The Frequent Flyer Fallacy," *Worth* (May 1994).
5. "20 Companies on a Roll," *Fortune* (Autumn/Winter 1995).
6. Don Oldenburg, "Don't Just Hang Up," *Washington Post* (January 14, 1993).
7. Magid M. Abraham and Leonard M. Lodish, "Getting the Most Out of Advertising and Promotion," *Harvard Business Review* (May-June 1990), pp. 50–60; John Philip Jones, "The Double Jeopardy of Sales Promotions," *Harvard Business Review* (September-October 1990).
8. Paul Farhi, "The Everlasting Sale," *Washington Post* (June 20, 1993). Francine Schwadel, "The 'Sale' Is Fading as a Retailing Tactic," *Wall Street Journal* (March 1, 1989).
9. In "Letters to the Editor," *BusinessWeek* (July 3, 1989).

10. James H. Snider, "Consumers in the Information Age," *The Futurist* (January-February 1993).

11. A survey of 260 marketing executives found that "profitability" was rated as their highest priority, "quality" was third, "better communications with customers" was fifth, and "customer satisfaction" was not mentioned. "Marketing Priorities," *Research Bulletin No. 205* (New York: The Conference Board, 1987).

12. See James Patterson and Peter Kim, *The Day America Told the Truth: What People Really Believe About Everything That Really Matters* (Englewood Cliffs, N.J.: Prentice-Hall, 1992).

13. Juliet Schor, *The Overworked American: The Unexpected Decline of Leisure* (New York: Basic Books, 1992).

14. Richard Todd, "Po' Boys on Parade," *Worth* (September 1993).

15. See the special issue *Value Marketing, BusinessWeek* (November 11, 1991).

16. *Meet the New Consumer,* special issue of *Fortune* (Autumn/Winter 1993), pp. 6–7.

17. "Most Consumers Shun Luxuries," *Wall Street Journal* (September 19, 1989). Duane Elgin, *Voluntary Simplicity* (New York: Morrow, 1993).

18. Paul Hawken, "Truth or Consequences," *Inc.* (August 1987).

19. Quoted from Rich Karlgaard, "An Interview with John Scully," *Forbes* (December 1992).

20. Christina Duff and Bob Ortega, "How Wal-Mart Outdid a Once-Touted Kmart," *Wall Street Journal* (March 21, 1995).

21. *Conference Board Monthly Briefings* (February 1987).

22. Gretchen Morgenson, "The Fall of the Mall," *Forbes* (May 24, 1993).

23. Alice LaPlante, "It's Wired Willy Loman," *Forbes ASAP* (June 1994).

24. Patricia Sellers, "The Best Way to Reach Your Buyers," *Fortune* (Autumn/Winter 1993).

25. "Retailing Will Never Be the Same," *BusinessWeek* (July 26, 1993).

26. Patricia Sellers, "Keeping the Customers You Already Have," and Rahul Jacob, "Beyond Quality & Value," both in *Fortune* (Autumn/Winter 1993).

27. Hawken, "Truth or Consequences."

28. Michael Schrage, "Customers May Be Your Best Collaborators," *Wall Street Journal* (February 27, 1989); "The 'Bloodbath' in Market Research," *BusinessWeek* (February 11, 1991).

29. Ronald Henkoff, "Why Every Red-Blooded Consumer Owns a Truck," *Fortune* (May 29, 1995).

30. Kevin Helliker, "Smile: That Cranky Shopper May Be a Store Spy," *Wall Street Journal* (November 30, 1994).

31. Justin Martin, "Ignore Your Customer," *Fortune* (May 1, 1995).

32. B. Joseph Pine et al., "Making Mass Customization Work," *Harvard Business Review* (September-October 1993).

33. There is controversy over this point. Some authorities claim that client satisfaction does not correlate well with retention, so it important to distinguish client satisfaction from loyalty. See Frederick Reichheld, "Loyalty-Based Management," *Harvard Business Review* (March-April 1993), and Leonard Berry et al., "Improving Service Quality," *Academy of Management Executive* (May 1994).

34. "King Customer," *BusinessWeek* (March 12, 1990). Rahul Jacob, "Why Some Customers Are More Equal than Others," *Fortune* (September 19, 1994).

35. These examples are noted in "Smart Selling," *BusinessWeek* (August 3, 1992); "King Customer," *BusinessWeek* (March 12, 1990).

36. Kenneth Labich, "Is Herb Kelleher America's Best CEO?" *Fortune* (May 2, 1994).

37. Timothy W. Firnstahl, "My Employees Are My Service Guarantee," *Harvard Business Review* (July-August 1989).

38. See Arlie Hochschild, *The Managed Heart* (Los Angeles: University of California Press, 1983), and Blake Ashforth and Ronald Humphrey, "Emotional Labor in Service Roles," *Academy of Management Review* (January 1993), pp. 88–115.

39. J. C. Szabo, "Service = Survival," *Nation's Business* (March 1989).

40. "Smart Selling," *BusinessWeek* (August 3, 1992), p. 47. Emily Thornton, "Revolution in Japanese Retailing," *Fortune* (February 7, 1994).

41. Halal, *The New Capitalism* (New York: Wiley, 1986), Ch. 3.

42. See Halal, *The New Capitalism*, Ch. 3.

43. Gary Hamel and C. K. Prahalad, *Competing for the Future* (Cambridge, Mass.: Harvard Business School Press, 1994).

44. Douglas Lavin, "Youwannadeal?" *Wall Street Journal* (July 8, 1994).

6

Knowledge Entrepreneurs

*A Working Contract of Rights
and Responsibilities*

Not long ago, work life was a pretty straightforward affair. You found a job, did what you were told, and were paid a salary.

But recently this system began coming apart. Layoffs have shattered the bonds of employee-employer loyalty. Wages have been falling for two decades. Union membership has dropped to a fraction of its former levels. And one-third of the labor force has become lost in a "contingent" status of part-time or temporary work.

At the same time, other changes have begun introducing more enlightened work practices. Employees are encouraged to participate in major decisions. Many now own their companies. They enjoy broader rights to control their work. The labor force is becoming diverse. And most jobs are far more interesting than they once were.

These crosscurrents in the employment relationship flow out of a turbulent passage in our concept of work. The paternalistic system in which "bosses" supervised "employees" in running the machinery of an Industrial Age is yielding to a complex world of knowledge work where more is asked of us. Organizations today need the intellect, involvement, and creative ideas of everyone who works in them. The confusing changes noted above are searching steps toward redefining work life.

This chapter sketches out the work roles most people will occupy in a decade or so. In a world governed by knowledge, change, and complexity, people will increasingly work in a self-directed capacity to solve intellectual problems. Most workers will be part of a self-managed team that collaborates with other teams and organizations, all operating freely over the global grid of information networks. As I outlined in Chapter 2, managers will have to organize these people into Information Age equivalents of the entrepreneur—knowledge entrepreneurs—who enjoy the freedom and rewards of being self-employed, while also bearing the responsibilities and risks that are involved.

REDEFINING THE EMPLOYMENT RELATIONSHIP

This transition poses daunting conflicts as people are wrestled out of their old roles, but it also promises to realize the human potential that has lain dormant throughout history. For instance, knowledge workers must be treated as self-employed professionals because their work is inherently complex, innovative, and requires deep personal involvement, so it cannot be "supervised." That's why all professions invariably develop an ethic of self-control.

The Labor-Management Conflict Intensifies

These adjustments are not going to be made by simply "empowering people" in some vague sense. How does one "empower" 100,000 employees of a typical Fortune 500 company to join in major decisions? Can any group larger than a few hundred people reach consensus quickly enough to survive, or would it resemble the U.S. Congress? Even the famed Mondragon system of Spain suffered a breakdown as a result of growing bureaucracy.

Consider the concept of employee stock ownership plans (ESOPs), which is often considered the way to salvation. ESOPs are spreading through the airline industry because they offer employees pride of ownership, a partial defense against hostile takeovers, tax deductions, and other advantages. In 1985 Eastern Airlines became the first large American company to be employee-owned, and four employees gained seats on the board of directors. I vividly recall the excitement of seeing Eastern pilots, flight attendants, and ticket agents appearing in TV commercials announcing the superior service on *their* airline. Yet severe labor-management conflict soon led this great airline to bankruptcy.[1] A worker expressed the yawning gap between promise and reality: "I worked here before [the ESOP] and I worked here afterward. I don't see any change. Things go on exactly as before."

This is a chronic problem in ESOPs. The evidence shows that employee ownership itself is rarely advantageous; rather, it is the *self-management* that ESOPs allow in small firms that is most useful. However, any system involving more than a few hundred members is simply too big for open decision-making among all concerned. A large meeting could hold everyone, but groups of more than twenty to fifty people can rarely work together well, and so a formal management hierarchy of some type is unavoidable. Also, resources are always scarce, which leads to the economic reality of making tough decisions that will not please all parties. As we saw in Chapter 3, a more fundamental problem is that employees represent but one stakeholder, so ESOPs cannot provide the broader governance needed to form a corporate community. That may explain why the pattern of employee ownership in America has been limited to a minority of stock in almost all corporations where it is used.

The list of such obstacles to a human workplace is long, usually leading ESOPs back to the very system they were designed to avoid. It will be interesting to see if the fate of Eastern Airlines is visited on the newest big ESOP, United Airlines.

Most of the other innovations in employee relations have experienced similar disappointments. Scholars such as Abraham Maslow, Douglas McGregor, and Rensis Likert demonstrated the virtues of participative management in the 1950s, yet very little changed until the 1990s, and some of this is questionable. The demoralizing effects of downsizing, TQM, and reengineering are so notorious they are usually considered to be euphemisms for "layoffs"; one of the hottest training seminars for managers in 1995 was "How to Fire Employees."[2]

These problems may escalate because advanced nations such as the United States are passing through a chronically depressed phase of economic development. There are minor highs and lows, of course, caused by the normal four-year business cycle. But superimposed over these short-term oscillations is the trough of a sixty-year Kondratieff cycle that should continue throughout the 1990s. The Great Depression was caused by the previous trough that occurred in the 1930s. And global competition is intensifying as Latin America, Asia, and other developing nations that pay their workers $1 per hour take work away from modern labor forces that cost $20 per hour. Not only are jobs going to low-wage countries, their workers are coming here. Just as a global economy now allows capital to seek its highest returns around the world, poor people from Eastern Europe, China, Mexico, and other developing nations are flowing across borders searching for higher wages.[3]

Thus, relentless labor competition is likely to produce further economic pressures on employment. Knowledge workers may remain largely immune to these pressures because their valuable skills are in short supply. But unskilled workers who must compete in a global market for blue- and white-collar jobs will suffer increasing demands for low wages and high productivity.[4]

These pressures are growing at a time when workers need higher incomes. Because the cost of living has soared, surveys show that 75 percent of college students are primarily interested in "being well-off financially."[5] Little wonder when the price of a middle-class home in New York, Paris, or Tokyo starts at half a million dollars. It does not take long to discover that one cannot afford a reasonably comfortable lifestyle with an income of less than $50,000 per year.

This review of employment relations does not dispute the important progress that has been made. Employees have gained many benefits, and employers have gained increased responsibility for performance. It does, however, caution managers against letting overly optimistic intentions and unreasonable expectations turn into disappointing failures. The labor-management conflict that persisted throughout industrialization remains alive today. Both parties remain stuck in an adversarial posture because we lack an institutional system for sorting out this complex relationship.

Rise of the Knowledge Workforce

In roughly the same way the Great Depression prepared the ground for the booming service economy that flourished between the 1950s and the 1980s, today's recession should lead to a robust knowledge economy starting during the decade of 2000–2010. The painful symptoms of economic decline—high employee turnover, low wages, and restructuring—are unfortunate preludes in the process of "creative destruction" that clears the economic landscape for this coming burst of growth.

The first priority is to put the industrial past behind by automating as much routine work as possible. Many people resist automation because it eliminates jobs, and others fear technology generally. Automation is certainly traumatic, but better jobs are created by opening up new frontiers. That's why the historic trend continually moves in this direction, as shown in Figure 6.1.

Blue-collar work has declined from its high point, when half of the labor force worked in factories, to roughly 20 percent in 1995. Automation should continue to the point where 10 percent or less of the workforce will perform blue-collar work in a decade or two, just as agriculture, which once claimed two-thirds of all workers, now employs only 3 percent of the workforce. The Service Economy began about 1950, when the number of white-collar workers first exceeded the number of blue-collar workers. As we learn to use powerful new information technologies better, office automation should also decrease the number of white-collar workers from its present 40 percent to about 20 to 30 percent over the next decade or two. The remaining 60 to 70 percent or so of the workforce may then be composed of knowledge workers: skilled manufacturing teams, information system designers, managers, professionals, educators, scientists, and the like.[6]

This process represents a natural cycle in economic development that is disruptive, to be sure. Nonetheless, work is slowly but inexorably moving from physical labor, to social relations, to creating knowledge, thereby boosting productivity, living standards, and the quality of life to unprecedented levels.

Some economists contend that service work is so inherently personal that it cannot be automated. But ATMs, electronic shopping, computerized communications, educational television, and other advances are proving otherwise. AT&T used computer systems to reduce its force of phone operators from 250,000 in 1956 to 50,000 today, and the number is still falling.[7] Imagine the impact on universities when courses featuring "star" professors can be broadcast around the globe. As Figure 6.1 also suggests, this process should in time lead to a focus on the "mental/spiritual" domain, as we noted in Chapter 4, but that is another story.

FIGURE 6.1. THE EVOLUTION OF WORK.

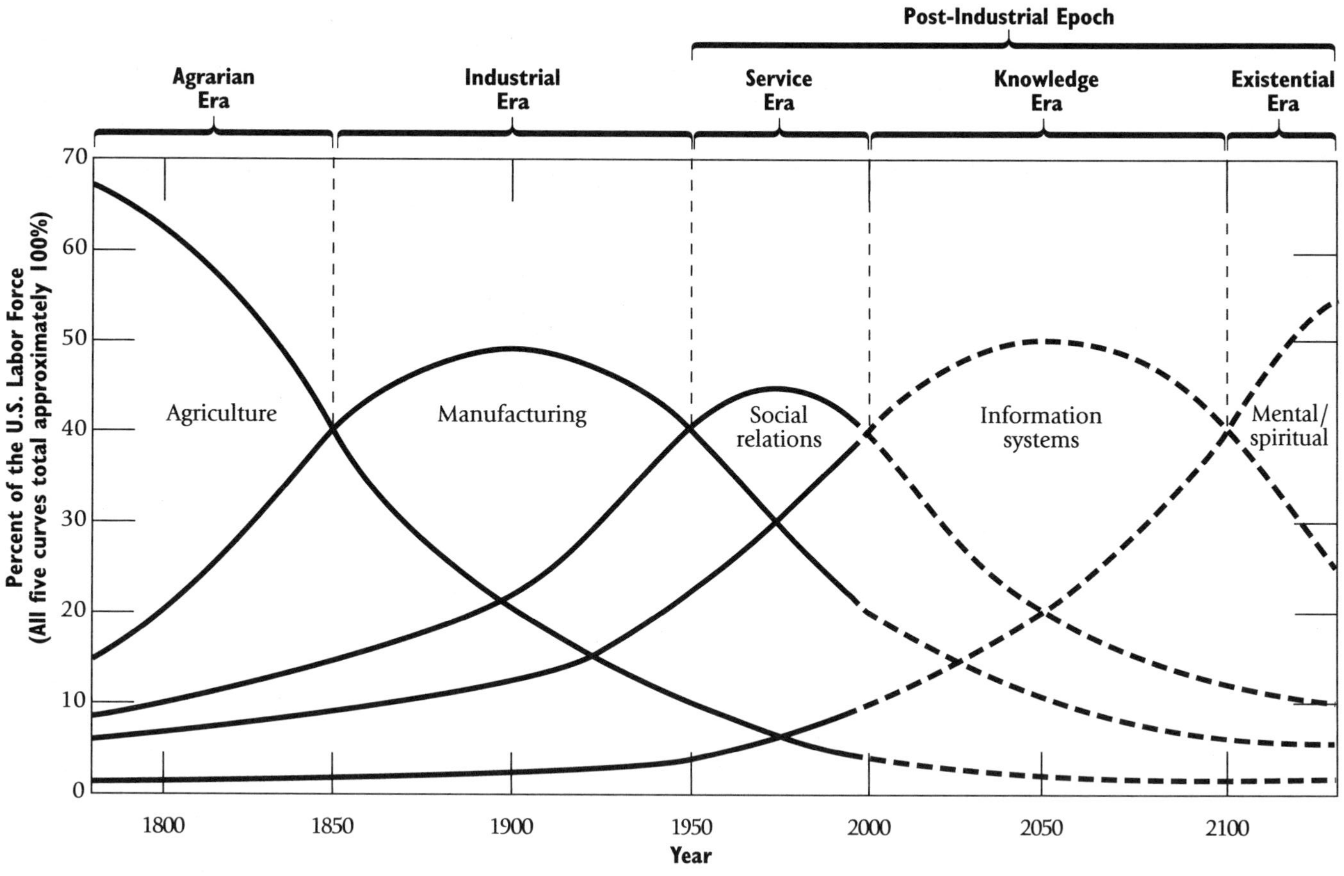

PRINCIPLES OF KNOWLEDGE WORK

Naturally, knowledge work will dramatically change organizations. American business invested $1 trillion in office automation during the 1980s, but saw little gain because the technology was simply laid over outmoded organization structures. Paul Strassmann, who was chief information officer at Xerox and at the U.S. Department of Defense (DoD), noted: "For thirty years America brought in computers to speed up the kind of work that just accentuates bureaucracy."

The payoff began in the 1990s as managers learned how to redesign organizations.[8] Although scholars and consultants have struggled to define the emerging principles of work, I am most impressed by the remarkable pragmatism and diversity all about us, as illustrated in Box 6.1. It is truly amazing to see, time and time again, how the myriad variations people can devise almost defy any model. Although the concepts offered here reflect the New Management themes of internal markets and corporate community, they are general guides rather than firm principles.

Use Information Systems to Create Small Self-Managed Units

The focus is on breaking large organizations down into small, self-managed units. The large manufacturing plant is giving way to small "focused factories" that produce a variety of small products or subassemblies of large products (such as autos). The same concept is breaking large white-collar organizations into small offices that provide some well-defined service. This move from economies of scale to small, autonomous units minimizes bureaucracy, encourages unit cohesion, and permits flexibility for change.

Intelligent information systems then integrate all operations into a working whole. Within factories, computer-integrated manufacturing (CIM), uses distributed networks of powerful PCs to assist all phases of work, from computer-aided product design (CAD), to manufacturing (CAM), to inventory control, to distribution. In offices, local area networks (LANs) or groupware systems are doing the same, allowing people to "telework" from any location. The result was nicely summed up by Ramchandran Jaikumar: "The behemoth is gone. The efficient factory is now an aggregation of small cells of electronically linked and controlled flexible manufacturing systems."[9]

BOX 6.1. EXEMPLARS OF KNOWLEDGE WORK.

IBM, Motorola, GE, and Hewlett-Packard have developed assembly plants that use teams of skilled workers to produce dozens of different products simultaneously. These operations are coordinated by computer systems that receive orders electronically; they then specify all parts needed to assemble each unit, transport the parts to an assembly line, assist line workers in their operations, and ship finished goods, often within hours of receiving the order. "Our vision is simultaneous manufacturing," said one manager. "To make products even as the customer talks. We're getting close."

Aetna Life & Casualty plodded along for decades processing policy applications through the hands of sixty different staffs. After redesigning the system so that one employee performs all steps using a PC, the number of employees dropped from 3,000 to 700 and customers get their policy in two days instead of thirty.

Lockheed created a focused factory to fabricate aircraft parts. Automated machinery was rearranged into an integrated, self-contained unit, reducing movement from 2,500 feet before the change to no more than 150 feet afterward, and allowing a small team to manage the entire facility. The time needed to design and manufacturing parts dropped from fifty-two days to two days.

National Bicycle Company uses an assembly line operated by computerized robots to produce 11,231,862 variations of bicycles, each designed to meet a customer's specifications, at 10 percent above normal costs. The sales manager describe their goal: "Our idea was to make a separate model for every customer."

Coors Brewing opened a new facility that handles twice the output of its other plants by using an integrated information system to coordinate all operations of its 350 workers from the front office to the shop floor. It has become the lowest-cost, safest, most productive brewery in the industry.

Travelers Insurance has automated two-thirds of its office work, so the bulk of employees are no longer clerks but professional nurses who supervise accounts. They use medical data bases and expert systems to determine whether a second or third opinion is needed in any given case, question unreasonable costs or procedures, and coordinate between clients and medical staff. Ultimately, the company expects to have two thousand nurses working in this capacity.

Boeing used nine IBM mainframes, a Cray supercomputer, and 1,500 workstations to build a massive interactive computer network that coordinates the design, testing, and construction of its new 777 aircraft in three dimensions. Like a giant CAD/CAM system, it can access all details of three million parts, operate them at will, and check all interfaces. The system reduced the time required to build the plane by 90 percent and produced unheard of accuracy.

Sources: "Rethinking Work," *BusinessWeek* (October 17, 1994); "The Digital Factory," *Fortune* (November 14, 1994); The Productivity Payoff," *Fortune* (June 27, 1994).

Each unit is then managed by a self-directed team of knowledge workers who are given almost total control—from product design, to manufacturing, to sales, to service, to disposal. Computerization permits such flexibility that products can be customized to suit individual needs; thus close liaison with the client initiates the manufacturing cycle by specifying product design. Suppliers and distributors can be integrated into operations using on-line computer systems to automatically move merchandise. And ecological concerns increasingly require prior planning during product design and manufacturing.

Teams are held accountable by allocating budgets, pay, bonuses, and other resources in proportion to performance, and they are then allowed to run their affairs as they think best. They typically choose their co-workers and leaders, select their operating systems and tools, and work with suppliers and other units, usually doing a better job than formally appointed supervisors. Self-directed teams are particularly good at disciplining their own members. "Sometimes we have to tell our co-workers who aren't carrying their load that this is hurting us," said one woman.

Although every unit should ideally be managed by a self-directed team, good teams cannot be much larger than about twenty people. Larger units may be broken down into several teams that assume responsibility for some more limited function. And, obviously, teams must coordinate their work with other teams to create a coherent, collaborative organization.

The New Employment Contract

These changes present a Herculean challenge, of course, because they require new concepts to redefine the employment relationship. Note, for instance, that there has been no mention of the traditional "job" in this discussion. In 1994, *Fortune* magazine announced "The End of the Job":

> The job is vanishing like a species that has outlived its time. . . . The conditions that created jobs—mass production and the large organization—are disappearing. [Managers] will have to rethink almost everything they do.[10]

Along with the move to self-managed teams, organizations are moving away from the old concept of "pay-for-position," in which workers were traditionally paid for fulfilling specified duties: arriving at work punctually, being cooperative with others, and other behaviors covered in the typical annual performance evaluation. This system maintained a sense of orderliness, but it had little to do with productivity, and it was highly subjective. It is now being replaced by a more business-like arrangement in which employees are simply paid for the output they produce—"pay-for-performance." Roughly three-quarters of American workplaces now use some type of "variable pay system": incentive rates, merit bonuses, profit sharing, and other plans. "Performance pay is growing like wildfire," said one executive.[11]

These trends appear to be moving toward a "new employment contract" that links employee *rights* with *responsibilities*. This is the same "participative management" that was advocated for decades, but we now see that it would be unworkable without unifying these two functions into a balanced system. *If employees enjoy freedom in their work, good pay, and other rights without being accountable for results, the organization may not survive; conversely if they bear the burden of responsibilities without commensurate powers and benefits, they will be neither willing nor able to carry out their duties.*

We should note that the new employment contract embodies the same logic that forms the foundation for internal market structures discussed in Chapter 2: workers are paid an agreed-upon sum for an agreed-upon result, and they are free to perform their work as they see fit. This can be thought of as an extension of an internal market system. Where internal markets concern the structure of enterprises within an organization, the employment contract concerns the structure of teams within enterprises, somewhat like an "internal *labor* market."

The new employment contract offers the same advantages as do internal market systems: organizations are assured of performance, workers enjoy opportunities to earn and control their work, the system lends itself to complexity and change, and so on. But it incurs the disadvantages of market systems as well: the level of disorder is higher, there is a risk of occasional failures, and so on.

Many thoughtful people insist that work systems based on financial incentives are inherently flawed because only self-initiated work motivated by personal goals can be effective and elevating. In plain English, this view holds that money does not motivate, nor should it. This logic is appealing, but it flies in the face of common experience and the opinions of almost all business executives. The fallacy in this view comes from seeing money and higher-order interests as mutually exclusive. A wealth of research evidence shows they are both necessary.[12]

Motivation surveys consistently show that money alone would cause serious disenchantment with work, as the critics contend, but the surest way to devastate an organization is to not pay people equitably. The new employment contract resolves the money issue by ensuring that people are paid fairly for their contributions, and it then encourages them to channel all their talents into the creative management of their work. What more could one ask for?

Myriad variations in work practices and pay systems exist that may grow even more diverse, as the examples in Box 6.2 illustrate. Some people like incentive plans, while others prefer salaries. Some plans focus on individuals, others on teams, and still others on companywide plans; many organizations use all three levels of incentives. The difficulty of managing thousands of individual arrangements is one of the factors that make self-managed teams so attractive. Teams are also useful because they build cohesion, whereas individual pay-for-performance systems often flounder because they are seen as forcing people to compete for a limited pool of funds.

In schools, for instance, merit pay faces an uphill fight because individual performance evaluations pit teachers against their colleagues. A better solution would be to unite all teachers, administrators, and parents into a single self-managed enterprise that serves students better, thereby attracting more resources to be shared equitably among members of the team.

Whatever the pay system and the organization, the central idea is to ensure a sense of equity between the contributions each individual makes versus the rewards they receive, as noted in Chapter 3. Since equity is such a crucial but subjective matter, the optimal pay system can only be determined by the people involved. Box 6.2 shows that a wide variety of systems can be perfectly workable.

It is important to note that the concept of self-managed teams lends itself to various other arrangements, as shown in Chapter 2. Teams may be internal consultants serving internal and external clients, they can be external business groups serving internal clients, and members of teams may also be interchanged. Because teams are self-managed, they can organize their work style to include job sharing, rotation of assignments, using

BOX 6.2. EXEMPLARS OF PAY-FOR-PERFORMANCE.

Springfield Manufacturing educates employees on all phases of management, gives them access to financial information, encourages teams to make decisions for their units, and provides stock ownership and profit-sharing plans. "When an employee joins this company," says Jack Stack, president, "We make it clear that his/her job is not to turn metal or answer the phone, it is to boost profits."

Nucor Steel is widely regarded as "the closest thing to a perfect company in the steel industry." Minimills are run by teams of technicians who have almost complete control over all operations and receive bonuses that can double their incomes. In 1994, John Doherty, who heads the Nucor mill in Norfolk, Nebraska, earned an additional $80,000 in cash and $40,000 in stock. "We're running our own businesses, and we'd better perform," he observed.

The auto industry introduced profit-sharing bonuses in 1984. Since then, GM, Ford, and Chrysler have paid hundreds of million of dollars each year to 600,000 employees, averaging about $750 each. In 1994, Chrysler paid its employees an average bonus of $4,000.

AT&T bases the incomes of 80,000 middle managers and 30,000 technical people on profits at three levels: teams, business units, and the company as a whole. Team members can receive 5 to 10 percent bonuses for their team's performance, business unit managers can receive an additional 10 percent, and all managers receive another 7.5 percent if the company hits its performance targets.

General Mills fixes management salaries below industry standards and then rewards managers for excellent performance. For instance, the Yoplait yogurt team did so well that a half-dozen managers collected an additional $30,000 to $50,000 in bonus money. The product manager explained: "If you do a great job, you get a bigger reward."

Marshall Industries replaced an incentive system with fixed salaries and a companywide bonus. Now sales are up and people prefer the predictability. The star salesperson gave up her $400,000 paycheck for less than half that sum, but is satisfied because the plan is less stressful. "At first I thought, 'God, do I really want to do this?' But you can't put a dollar value on the benefits I have."

Munger, Tolles & Olsen, a Los Angeles law firm, asks all fifty-three partners to rate each other's performance every year, and the averages are posted in rank order. The compensation committee reviews the data, talks to each partner, and allocates pay that can vary as much as five times the lowest sum. "The standard by which we assess each other is well understood," said one partner.

Sources: Shawn Tully, "Your Paycheck Gets Exciting," *Fortune* (November 1, 1993); Jacyln Fierman, "The Perilous World of Fair Pay," *Fortune* (June 13, 1994).

temporary workers, or any other arrangements they prefer. It is then an easy step to visualize an organization as a changing assembly of teams and individuals, held together by information networks, common values, and other aspects of infrastructure, thereby composing a "virtual organization."

In such protean organizations, the challenge will be to strike a balance between the advantages of creative flexibility and the difficulty of uniting people who are working in cyberspace, as noted in Chapter 4. Both are essential, and the need for these opposing qualities is likely to grow. Tumultuous change will demand continual adaptation, yet diverse economic actors working around the globe must remain integrated into a coherent whole.

This fundamental transition to knowledge-based work is so vast in its implications that we probably cannot really anticipate where it will lead. But the new employment contract seems a reasonable direction, and it fits in nicely with other important facets of work today, to which we now turn our attention.

Teleworking

As Chapter 1 showed, the drive to make IT systems cheap, powerful, and convenient is producing a revolution in work that will enter the mainstream soon. Roughly forty million Americans were engaged in various forms of teleworking in 1994, and that number is growing 50 percent per year as the cost of ever more powerful information systems drops by a factor of ten every few years.[13]

People will always need personal contact, and there are problems working in an "electronic cottage," to be sure. But teleworking offers convenient ways to augment face-to-face meetings as information systems become user-friendly and inexpensive. Rather than permanent employees working 9 to 5 within the same building, then, this mode of "electronically mediated work" will transcend previous restrictions of time and place. In a world of such vast possibilities, the idea of having employees dutifully report to their supervisor becomes positively quaint. Under the new employment contract, however, things look more reasonable. With accountability established, teams can use IT capabilities to work wherever and whenever they think best. Box 6.3 describes signs of speeding traffic along the information superhighway.

BOX 6.3. GROWTH OF TELEWORKING.

Decreasing IT Costs. IT costs are dropping by a factor of ten every few years, making far wider usage feasible. A teleconferencing system that cost $1 million in 1982 could be bought for about $50,000 in 1994, and transmission time has gone from $2,000 per hour to $100. The coming "telecomputer," which will combine the functions of today's PC, TV, and telephone, is likely to sell for roughly $1,000 — or possibly less — by about the year 2000.

Telecommuting. Nine million Americans were telecommuting full time in 1994, but the number leaps to 40 million if part-time telecommuters and self-employed people are included. Bell Atlantic has its 16,000 managers telecommuting at least part-time, and plans to add its 50,000 employees. The federal government is increasing its program from 3,000 to 60,000 employees who are expected to be telecommuting by 1997. Companies such as Chiat/Day are turning their offices into meeting rooms for occasional gatherings because everyone uses portable computers to work together from their homes and in the field. Roughly 60 percent of all office products are sold to lawyers, stock brokers, and other entrepreneurial people who work at home, while traveling, and from other locations. "Think of any job, and someone's doing it from home," said the editor of *Home Office Computing.*

Teleconferencing. Various forms of teleconferencing are growing at 40 to 60 percent per year, and this communication method should be commonly used before the year 2000. Companies such as Boeing, 3M, and Hewlett-Packard use interactive teleconferencing across several organizations, reducing the time required to complete a typical project by 90 percent. As of 1994, there were about 30 million PCs in the United States, wired together by 6,000 local networks that are operated by 300 types of groupware, such as Lotus Notes. Internet is expected to have 100 million users around the world by the late 1990s. The installation of telecommunication and fiber optic networks is growing at 50 percent per year to connect all electronic systems into one great digital soup.

All Functions. IT use now covers the entire span of business and social activity: electronic banking, shopping, education, publishing, medicine, and other functions are being added to this list daily. Small rural towns like Aurora, Nebraska, have access to the information superhighway through fiber optic cables that permit video conferencing. "We're another suburb of Chicago now," boasts the mayor. Thus, all forms of social interaction can, in principle, be replaced by electronic equivalents.

Sources: William Halal, "Teleworking" (Washington, D.C.: Information Strategies Group Report, 1992); "The Information Technology Revolution," *Technological Forecasting and Social Change* (August 1993).

Working at home now becomes a feasible option. At one time, a home office was an embarrassment because it implied the lack of a regular job, but now it has become trendy. Pick up any magazine and you will see photos of lavish home offices equipped with the latest information systems, beckoning the high-pressured executive to unwind in a tranquil setting and release the creative intellectual within. "The biggest benefit is that I can maintain a full schedule while also being involved in my family," said one consultant.

But there are costs. "You can't leave because it's always there," said a saleswoman. Employees working at home often worry that they are not noticed being productive, and supervisors get uneasy not being able to supervise. A manager at Bell Atlantic says some telecommuters are "afraid to go to the bathroom for fear of missing a phone call from the office."

This does not mean that we will become hermits slaving away alone in our homes. The growth of electronic communications is unlikely to *replace* direct interaction because people will always seek opportunities for contact with others at work, at school, and in other settings. However, information systems will become a viable *alternative* to the real thing as IT grows more convenient, so we will use these systems to augment personal contacts. Travel is becoming ever more time consuming, environmentally damaging, wasteful of energy, and hectic; all this increases incentives to use IT part of the time while maintaining social relations through occasional direct contact.

A survey conducted in 1987 found that 56 percent of respondents would continue to go to the office every day if given the choice of working at home electronically, 36 percent would split their time between home and office, and only 7 percent would work at home exclusively.[14] Recent studies I have conducted show a similar mix of acceptance, but with a somewhat stronger leaning more toward combining office and home work.

This is the direction professional groups are moving in, particularly salespeople, consultants, and others who must work in the field. In 1993 Compaq Computer automated its routine saleswork by offering clients toll-free information lines for inquiries, and then shifted its entire sales force into home offices to make them more effective as traveling consultants. Each salesperson was provided state-of-the-art IT systems (high-powered PC notebook, fax, copier, cellular phone, access to centralized account listings) and other needed support. Revenues doubled while the sales force dropped by one-third. IBM is making similar changes. So many managers are now routinely connected to their offices using portable IT systems while traveling that they have been defined as a new breed of "perpetual motion executive."[15]

Plans are also under way to achieve a happy compromise between working at the office and working at home. Employers want to spare their people long trips to offices in urban centers, yet managers often feel uncomfortable allowing employees to work at home. One solution is the "telework center"—a satellite office containing IT equipment that enables employees to work in their neighborhoods. The U.S. government established such centers around the Washington, D.C., area, and Pacific Bell has been operating centers in California for years.[16] Similar centers are being experimented with in European countries and Japan. If this trend continues, the conflict between working at home and working at the office could be resolved by an intermediate solution—working in a satellite office *near* home.

Contingency Work

A related trend involves the many people who are joining the "contingent work force" of part-time employees, temporaries, and other marginal groups. The contingency work force comprised one-third of American workers in 1994 and is growing so rapidly it should include roughly half by 2000. "A tremendous shift to contingency work is under way," observed an economist.[17]

This is not a temporary solution to the lack of regular jobs, but a major shift to an independent, more mature mode of "self-employment." Contingency workers are becoming true knowledge entrepreneurs who take charge of their careers by packaging themselves as self-employed contractors able to move from company to company, consultants working for various firms, and individuals starting their own businesses.[18] About 20 percent of all professionals now work as "temps," including lawyers, doctors, and even executives. "The temporary executive is now a permanent fixture in American corporate life," claimed an executive recruiter.[19]

Self-employment is attractive to many people and it provides important professional services to large organizations. Many individuals prefer the freedom, challenge, rewards, and excitement of being on one's own. After all, what better way to fully satisfy those higher-order longings? Despite the low pay and benefits of marginal continency workers, studies find the average pay of self-employed people is 40 percent higher than that of their employed counterparts.

And companies like working with small suppliers because they minimize costs and bureaucracy and are usually more competent. AT&T buys goods and services from 100,000 small companies. "Small firms have an advantage," said AT&T's director of procurement. An entire infrastructure of home equipment, professional associations, and other services is springing up to support small entrepreneurs. One firm called "HQ Inc." leases office space, secretarial services, meeting rooms, and anything else fledgling CEOs might need at 152 locations. "We provide instant credibility for startups," said the president of HQ in New York City.[20]

IT also encourages an easy-flowing exchange of people between these two sectors. Large companies are increasingly trolling through information services to find small suppliers, and vice versa. A company representative described his experience finding specialized consultants over the Internet: "I can get fifty responses in a few minutes." Telecommuting at home often leads to taking the leap into starting one's own business and, conversely, selling one's services to a large company often leads to a regular job.

A useful way to grasp this upheaval in work is to see that employment has now spread out along a continuum. At one end is the traditional full-time job, while at the other end is the self-employed entrepreneur. The new employment contract lies at the middle of this continuum, offering a loose association with the employer but also the autonomy of the entrepreneur, something like "in-sourcing" rather than "out-sourcing." In this strategic position, it acts as a gatekeeper, allowing the speedy passage of employees to and fro to suit their needs as well as those of organizations. With the death of company loyalty to workers, employers can no longer offer secure employment, but they can assist people in moving along this continuum.[21]

What will it feel like to work this way? Box 6.4 presents a hypothetical scenario that projects current trends into the year 2000 to convey the feel and flavor of a typical knowledge worker's daily life. Vera Pace is a member of a

BOX 6.4. WORK 2000: A DAY IN THE WORK LIFE OF VERA PACE, ASIAN REPRESENTATIVE, BIOTRONICS, INC.

Vera was awakened by the persistent beep of her personal assistant, Vera-2, lying on the night table. She asked who it was and heard Azmi Ibrahim's undulating voice announcing that he had a serious problem at the bioplant in Sarawak. "The Malay Union of Pipefitters has struck the factory, and nothing is getting done," he wailed. "They are offended at being forced to work on a Moslem holiday."

She asked Azmi to arrange a meeting with the union leaders at 10:00 A.M. over the hotel's video conferencing system, and she started preparing for the day. Vera asked her assistant, Vera-2, to reschedule her breakfast meeting with Henri Latour for lunch instead and to transmit the Biotronics proposal for him to look over in the meantime. "This project with the French is a great opportunity to enter the Thai market," she mused.

At ten o'clock promptly, Azmi was patched through while Vera sat at the desk in her room at the Hong Kong Hilton. "Good morning Ms. Pace," he intoned formally. Looking up at the wall monitor, Vera attributed his unusually diplomatic mood to the three union leaders seated with him at the Biotronics plant in Sarawak, Malaysia. "Please allow me to introduce Mister Seri Anwar, chief of the Malay Pipe Fitters Union, and his associates," he said while bowing slightly.

Although Azmi spoke good English, the three union leaders relied on the automatic translation system to convert their Malay. "Blessed be Allah," they said in greeting to Vera, who returned the salutation in English, as she had learned to do.

"Mister Anwar," Vera continued, "please explain the cause of your unhappiness and I will do what I can." After an hour of discussion, it was agreed to release the workforce for the three-day holiday with half pay and to jointly plan a schedule that would avoid Moslem traditions in the future. Vera and the union chief then signed the electronic agreement on the screen using pen entry systems at both ends of the video conference. When the good-byes were automatically translated from English to Malay and from Malay back into English, the screen dimmed.

Vera still had an hour before meeting with Henri, so she called up her New York office to tell her team, the Plant Development Unit of Biotronics, about the incident. Her colleagues were out, so she told Vera-2 to locate them and to transmit a brief report of the union agreement culled from the video conference the machine had been monitoring. She then made a few calls to sort out plans for five other projects her team was working on, such as the joint venture with Henri Latour of Companie Biogenetique Orientale in France. Finally, she called her youngsters in Portland to make sure they were using their new IBM Personal Tutor to go over the lessons assigned by their teacher. Sure enough, they had been goofing off on Virtual Reality.

team that develops biofactories for its parent company, Biotronics, and for other organizations as well. If you have trouble imagining yourself in this setting, think of people living a mere hundred years ago. What would they have thought to witness today's world of TV, jet flight, and supermarkets? The world of Vera Pace may be equally unsettling, but it will be no less real very soon.

WORK LIFE IN THE INFORMATION AGE

This restructuring of work life is not without its problems. New technologies must automate old processes, work must be reorganized into self-contained clusters of activities performed by teams, performance goals and incentive plans must be defined, and organizational architectures need to be established to support this system. The social problems of self-management can be especially knotty. Jon Hart, president of Overly Manufacturing, summed up how he experienced the change: "It's like Pandora's box. You open up the door and everything comes out."

Some union leaders claim that teamwork amounts to a system of "management by stress," intended to push workers to maximum productivity, so they are trying to reverse this trend.[22] Yes, people can be exploited, but rather than oppose these inevitable changes, unions should look after the interests of labor constructively. As one union leader put it: "The union's job is to prevent management from speeding up the line. There's nothing inherent in work-team systems that has to be stressful."[23]

There is also a dawning realization that these changes are not a one-shot thing, but a more demanding new way of work life with no end. The comfortable days of coasting along in a hierarchy, typified by the old Broadway musical "How to Succeed in Business Without Really Trying," are over. "In ten years, anybody who runs a business on the old model isn't going to be in business," said the owner of a manufacturing firm.[24]

We should also caution that a large class of unskilled workers may be unable to compete in the demanding new world of knowledge work. Even with good educations and remedial social programs (a generous assumption), some sectors of society are likely to become chronically marginalized, leading to unemployment, crime, and other disorders. In *The Bell Curve*, his controversial work on intelligence, Charles Murray described the prospect of life being governed by a "cognitive elite":

The twenty-first century will open on a world in which cognitive ability is the decisive dividing force in determining where an individual will end up. Unchecked, these trends will lead toward something resembling a caste system.[25]

This threat is real but not inevitable because our growing power to spread knowledge should allow anyone to be educated effectively, and human nature is far more malleable than we commonly think. We should also bear in mind that sophisticated information systems can increasingly support people in doing tasks that would otherwise beyond their abilities—some call it "just-in-time training."[26] The real issue is finding the political will and the personal discipline to address such problems.

Working with Flexibility

Table 6.1 shows how widely this new work role is practiced now, and the idea should continue to spread simply out of the hard necessity of coping with an avalanche of change. One manager expressed the prospects succinctly: "This will be common practice for just about any firm in the near future." This more sharply focused business arrangement should provide people in an Information Age the entrepreneurial freedom and resources to work as they choose, while also providing organizations the freedom and productivity they need to compete.

Organizations are destined to confront more turbulence in the next ten years than we have ever experienced, which will require an exceptional degree of flexibility. Self-managed work teams will be essential to create organic structures composed of interchangeable modules that can be added to meet a rush of demand, dropped during a downturn, revised to obtain a different mix of skills, and so on.

People increasingly need the same flexibility to cope with the hectic nature of modern life. Now that the two-career family is the norm, both men and women must choose their time and place of work in order to balance the demands of job, family, education, and who knows what else. Jake Mascotte, CEO of Continental Airlines, noted: "So much of business is still structured like fourth grade." In 1990, Continental began encouraging telecommuting, stopped tracking absences, and instituted other family-friendly practices. Productivity rose and turnover fell.[27]

TABLE 6.1. ADOPTION OF KNOWLEDGE ENTREPRENEUR PRACTICES.
(SAMPLE = 426 CORPORATE MANAGERS.)

Practice	Not Practiced (0–3)	Partially Practiced (4–6)	Fully Practiced (7–10)	Mean (0–10)
A significant portion of employee pay is based on performance incentive systems.	39%	25%	36%	4.9
Employee attitude surveys are conducted periodically.	41	16	43	5.1
Employees are encouraged to develop their creative ideas into new ventures.	23	27	50	6.0
Employees are organized into self-managed teams that choose their leaders, work methods, equipment, hours, co-workers, and most other aspects of their work.	67	20	13	2.7
Employees can use information systems to "telework" from home, in the field, and other locations.	57	21	22	3.5
Means	45%	22%	33%	4.4

Source: William E. Halal, *Corporations in Transition* (an unpublished study in progress). Note that data in the first three columns ("Not Practiced," etc.) are aggregated by collapsing portions of the questionnaire scale as shown ("0–3," etc.). See the questionnaire in Appendix C.

Flexibility will also be indispensable in handling the unique needs of older people, young people, minorities, the handicapped, and countless other groups of workers who would otherwise pose special problems. And despite much talk of empowered workers seeking self-fulfillment, the fact is that many people do not really want to take on such responsibility; the nice thing about the new employment contract is that teams can manage their affairs in whatever style they prefer: a full-fledged democracy, some sort of spiritual unity, or old-fashioned authoritarian leadership. The extensive skills of those who focus on behavioral issues (human resource management, organizational learning, project management, and the like) will be invaluable for making this diversity work effectively, and for helping teams work together to form complete corporate communities.

Most of the complex trappings we think of as indispensable parts of a job may disappear. The proportion of employers offering medical benefits has dropped from 84 percent in 1982 to 56 percent in 1995. Annual reviews, supervisors, step grades, training programs, and so on are all declining in use. Why should anyone want to engage in this ancillary busywork when their real interest is to get their task done effectively? Listen to how author William Bridges described the simplifying advantages of being freed from our old notion of a "job":

> What would happen to our present policies on leave of absence, vacation, retirement, etc.? Leave from what? Vacation from what? Retirement from what?[28]

Accepting Self-Responsibility

These are the main features that should mark work life in the year 2000 or so:

1. The natural evolution of economies is likely to make a new phase of knowledge work common in a decade or so.

2. The old employment relationship in which people were paid for holding a "position" is dying because it is too confining for a turbulent economy, leaving employees without secure work roles.

3. Knowledge workers should ideally be organized into self-managed teams that are free to control almost all aspects of their operations and are rewarded for team performance.

4. This system should permit both employers and employees to use alternatives such as teleworking and contingency work to gain the flexibility needed to cope with a dynamic economy.

Like most academics, I spend about half of my time working in a self-employed status at home and with a variety of organizations, and I find that it requires great self-discipline. Indeed, that is both the greatest advance as well as the greatest challenge of the new employment contract. It requires managers to treat workers as fully competent adults, and workers in turn must accept the responsibility for carrying out their tasks diligently. Although the demands are hard, I cannot imagine working any other way.

Despite the daunting nature of these challenges and the failures that are certain to come, the new employment contract seems likely to roll on. For all the pitfalls of performance pay, for instance, most managers believe in the concept because it represents an important future direction. "We don't think the alternative—paying everyone the same—is better," said John Hillins, vice president for corporate compensation at Honeywell.

Organizations are being transformed by the Information Revolution into a fine web of small, automated systems, managed in real time by changing assemblies of self-employed teams, with such complete information available that their behavior becomes transparent. It's not going to be easy, but this historic transition promises to eliminate the drudgery long associated with work, thereby freeing people for the more sophisticated tasks that now form the principle challenges facing a knowledge-based economy.

Notes

1. Alex Gibney, "Paradise Tossed," *Washington Monthly* (June 1986).
2. Andrea Gerlin, "Seminars Teach Managers Finer Points of Firing," *Wall Street Journal* (April 26, 1995).
3. Lars-Erik Nelson, "Unwelcome Guests," *Washington Post* (August 14, 1995). William B. Johnston, "Global Work Force 2000: The New World Labor Market," *Harvard Business Review* (March-April 1991).
4. This point is effectively made by Robert Reich in *The Work of Nations* (New York: Knopf, 1991).
5. See the annual survey of the American Council of Education, UCLA.
6. A sound analysis of these trends is provided by Nuala Beck, *Shifting Gears: Thriving in the New Economy* (New York: Harper Collins, 1995).
7. G. Pascal Zachary, "Service Productivity Is Rising Fast," *Wall Street Journal* (June 8, 1995).
8. See the special report "The Technology Payoff," *BusinessWeek* (June 14, 1994), and Myron Magnet, "Good News for the Service Economy," *Fortune* (May 3, 1994).
9. Ramchandran Jaikumar, "Postindustrial Manufacturing," *Harvard Business Review* (November-December 1986).
10. William Bridges, "The End of the Job," *Fortune* (September 19, 1994).
11. Jay Mathews, "Do Job Reviews Work?" *Washington Post* (March 20, 1994). The Conference Board Briefing (July-August 1989), and "Bonus Pay," *BusinessWeek* (November 14, 1994).

12. For instance, the well-known studies by Frederick Herzberg showed that pay, benefits, and other "extrinsic" factors were necessary to prevent people from feeling dissatisfied with their work, while challenge, creativity, and other "intrinsic" factors were also necessary to provide active motivation.

13. See William E. Halal, "The Information Technology Revolution," *Technology Forecasting & Social Change* (1993), Vol. 44, pp. 69–86.

14. "Home or Office?" *Wall Street Journal* (March 31, 1987).

15. Michael Malone, "Perpetual Motion Executives," *Forbes ASAP* (January 1994).

16. Mitch Betts, "'Telework' Hubs Sprout in Suburban America," *Computer World* (July 22, 1991).

17. Jaclyn Fierman, "The Contingency Work Force," *Fortune* (January 24, 1994). Peter Kilborn, "New Jobs Lack the Old Security," *New York Times* (March 15, 1993).

18. For a fine account of this perspective see Cliff Hakim, *We Are All Self-Employed* (San Francisco: Berrett-Koehler, 1994), and Kenneth Labich, "Take Control of Your Career," *Fortune* (May 1992).

19. "Part-Timers Are In," *Conference Board's Monthly Briefings* (March 1988); "And Now, 'Temp' Managers," *Newsweek* (September 26, 1988).

20. Liz Spayd, "Growing Ranks of Self-Employed Reshape Economy," *Washington Post* (April 4, 1994); Brian O'Reilly, "The New Face of Small Business," *Fortune* (May 2, 1994).

21. Brian O'Reilly, "The New Deal," *Fortune* (June 13, 1994).

22. See Mike Parker and Jane Slaughter, "Management by Stress," *Technology Review* (October 1988); "UAW Delegates Dispute 'Jointness,'" *Washington Post* (June 24, 1989); and "Workers Aren't Anxious, They're Proud," *Washington Post* (October 29, 1988).

23. John Hoerr, "Is Teamwork a Management Plot?" *BusinessWeek* (February 20, 1989).

24. Marc Levinson, "Playing with Fire," *Newsweek* (June 21, 1993).

25. Charles Murray, *The Bell Curve: Intelligence and Class Structure in American Life* (New York: The Free Press, 1994).

26. Lewis J. Perelman, *School's Out* (New York: Avon, 1992). Tim Ferguson, "Help! How Best to Avail the Labor Force," *The Wall Street Journal* (May 16, 1995).

27. "Work & Family," *BusinessWeek* (June 28, 1993).

28. Bridges, "The End of the Job."

7

Intelligent Growth

Balancing Ecological Health
and Economic Progress

It is tempting to think that Mother Nature will be safe now that an environmental ethic has swept around the world. Even business firms are competing to prove how "green" they are. But recent events suggest that the problems remain formidable. The "Big Green" initiative in California was defeated soundly in 1994, and an antienvironment backlash is under way in other parts of the United States.[1]

These reactions represent more than resistance by growth advocates. In a wholistic world, they are another part of the whole, telling us that environmentalism is not easily reconciled with protecting jobs, improving living standards, avoiding government intrusion, and other issues that concern most people.

The "McDonald's Clamshell Decision" offers a good example of the complexity involved. Environmentalists demanded that the company use paper packages rather than the plastic "clamshells," which, it was claimed, cause pollution and do not decompose well. But the company had spent millions of dollars developing a biodegradable plastic package. Furthermore, studies published in *Science* concluded that plastic is *less* environmentally harmful than paper when all factors are considered, such as the loss of trees and the energy needed to make paper packages. Yet the public pressure became so intense when droves of children were organized to write letters of protest, that McDonald's relented and switched to paper, against the better judgment of its managers.[2]

Thus the call for environmental protection may be long overdue, but it is not simply a moral issue. A sweeping transformation of the entire techno-economic system is involved that produces complex conflicts between equally valid but opposing interests. The concept of "sustainability" has become widely accepted because it is now clear to all that the environment must be sustainable indefinitely. But this point of view fails to recognize the enormous demands posed by billions of deprived people who are just starting to industrialize. Some broader vision is required that reconciles the urgent need to protect the Earth with the equally urgent need to vastly improve human life.

This chapter describes an economic perspective now emerging that offers the promise of resolving this dilemma. It may seem too good to be true, but an "ecological-economic transformation" is under way as progressive corporations around the world use the power of information technology (IT), the creativity of enterprise, and the collaborative ideals of democracy to devise an intelligent form of growth that is both productive and ecologically benign. In place of the begrudging compliance with regulations that marked the past, most business leaders now understand that there can be no future without a sound ecological system, and so they are turning their formidable problem-solving talents to this goal in earnest. Matthew Kiernan, CEO of a Swiss-based global corporation, put it this way:

> We are currently witnessing the beginning of nothing less than a global industrial restructuring [in which] a company's environmental performance will be increasingly central to its competitiveness and survival.[3]

RECONCILING ECONOMICS AND ENVIRONMENT

Although an ideological battle over the environment has continued for decades, polls show that the great majority of people from all walks of life and all nations now understand the imperative need to safeguard the environment.[4]

Rise of the Environmental Ethic

The urgency of sound environmental management became starkly clear when the collapse of Communism revealed what can happen if nature is ignored. Shoddy practices had so undermined the ecological system of the entire Soviet Union that one trillion dollars may be needed to restore it to health. This highly symbolic failure, combined with similar incidents in the West, such as the Exxon oil spill in Valdez, Alaska, drove home the wisdom of ecological protection. In 1993, 81 percent of business executives thought protecting the environment was necessary and reasonable.[5]

To be sure, much of this newfound motivation is the result of stern social pressures. Consumers are so concerned about the environment that 80 percent are willing to pay more for ecologically safe goods. The U.S. government has passed demanding legislation, and the Environmental Protection Agency (EPA) increased indictments of illegal practices dramatically to enforce these laws. Many corporations have been fined millions of dollars, and offending executives spent 550 months in jail during 1993.[6]

The most obvious justification for environmental protection is that pollutants cause disease. Cancer rates are rising 1 percent per year and now account for roughly one-third of all deaths in modern nations; as a result, people living today suffer twice the risk of cancer that their grandparents did. The incidence of brain cancer has doubled during the past two decades.[7] Although this is partly due to people smoking, living longer, and other social factors, cancer rates are highest in industrialized areas, suggesting that a major cause may be the presence of chemicals, combustion exhausts, and other pollutants.[8] It is estimated that the thinning of the ozone layer alone will cause 200,000 deaths over the next few decades. "The problem is more serious than we believed," said William K. Reilly, former head of the EPA.[9]

But the problem goes beyond practical concerns. People now grasp the profound reality that the Earth is a unified global organism supporting an intricate web of life. To put it in symbolic terms, the planet is a great living being in its own right. And if all life is intimately connected, then humans share a familylike relationship with other species. That's why psychologists find acute signs of distress over the destruction of nature. "I am amazed at the number of people who break down in tears when they think about what we're doing to the Earth," says Theodore Roszak.[10]

Many claim that ecological awareness today represents a historic shift in consciousness, comparable to the religious consciousness of old and the technological consciousness of the Industrial Age. Willis Harman defines it as a "global mind change," a fundamentally different philosophy that views the entire Earth as a sacred creation imbued with spiritual meaning.[11]

The Coming Leap in Global Industrialization

It's wonderful that so many people now feel a compelling need to protect nature, but they often fail to recognize other unavoidable realities. Apart from the satiated West, most of the world's population is starved for the same material comforts now enjoyed by a few prosperous nations such as the United States. Try telling the Mexicans, Indians, or Chinese that material growth is a bad idea. Despite the fact that pollution has made lung disease the leading cause of death in China, the nation is determined to pursue economic growth as rapidly as possible.[12]

Moreover, the number of people in undeveloped nations is five times greater than in developed nations and is almost certain to double. Thus, the stark reality is that industrial output is likely to increase by roughly a factor of five to ten over the next few decades. The industrialization of China alone should double the load on the environment, and India may double it again.[13]

In short, the rapid industrialization of the globe seems almost unstoppable. The world faces an unprecedented challenge of creating some new and as yet unknown techno-economic system that can manage such a great leap in economic growth on a planet already suffering from severe environmental stress.

Between Two Groups of True Believers

Beyond general agreement on protecting the environment, opinions divide sharply when tough questions are raised about how to handle this imminent burst in industrialization.

The idea of sustainability advocated by environmentalists is a useful concept, but it does not address this huge problem. Somewhat like the equally popular appeal of "corporate social responsibility," sustainability focuses on an *ecological* goal while ignoring the economic goal—a massive increase in industrial growth is needed. "Sustainability has become devalued to the point where it is now just a cliché," noted one analyst.[14]

Sustainability alone would be realized admirably if we returned to the agrarian past, but how many of us are willing to give up our comfortable lifestyles? I often wonder, when hearing people lecture an audience about the evils of industrialization, Didn't they take a jet airplane to attend this meeting? They must drive cars? Don't they shop at supermarkets? The fact is that we all depend on modern technology and industry for the necessities of modern life.

A similar myopia prevails at the other end of the political spectrum. Many conservatives still celebrate the virtues of unbounded economic growth, and some even insist that population growth—the key factor driving the despoliation of the planet—should not be curbed because people are the "ultimate resource."[15] With billions suffering from poverty, famine, and other symptoms of overpopulation, one can only marvel at such faith.

Thus, the primary obstacle to environmental progress today is a clash between two groups of true believers who obscure the complex nature of the problem: one side is intent on protecting the environment at great cost to human welfare, while the other side is intent on growth at great cost to the environment.

A few years ago, big business was unreasonable in its opposition to the environment, but now many environmentalists can be just as unreasonable. Some environmentalists are themselves critical of the movement. John Heritage blamed the "go-for-the-throat" attitude of his colleagues for today's anti-environment backlash, and Gregg Easterbrook had a similar criticism: "Through the next few years, conventional environmental viewpoints will collapse, done in by their own disjunction from the realities of the natural world. In their place will emerge a new middle path I call 'eco-realism.'"[16]

An obvious example of the lack of communication is the continual attacks on prominent corporations. Business could improve, certainly; however, 92 percent of corporate executives now understand that the environment must be one of their top priorities, and many have voluntarily taken the lead on critical issues.[17] When data on the ozone problem was announced, Du Pont immediately accelerated its plans to phase out all harmful gases. The chairman of Dow Chemical was the first CEO to call for full-environmental pricing of all products, a bold step toward using economic incentives to curb pollution (see Box 7.1).[18] Yet environmentalists persist in condemning these companies, often handcuffing themselves to corporate facilities under TV coverage. Are these attacks justified? Do they serve any useful purpose?

This clash between the Luddite mentality of environmental purists and the zealotry of unlimited growth advocates has squandered the lead America once held in the exploding environmental industry. Germany and Japan now dominate the market for product recycling, solar cells, high-efficiency appliances, pollution control equipment, and other booming fields.[19]

BOX 7.1. THE GREENING OF DOW CHEMICAL.

Although Dow Chemical may have a poor image where environmental matters are concerned, in fact the company has been a model of corporate enlightenment on environmental management.

A Long History of Environmental Protection. The founder, Herbert Dow, had a reputation for despising waste and pollution, and pioneered in developing many of today's environmental protection technologies during the 1920s. Later, in 1972, CEO Carl Gerstacker said: "Solving pollution problems is good business as well as good citizenship. So let's get at it with energy and enthusiasm."

First Environmental Advisory Council. In 1991, Dow became the first American company to form a council of outside authorities to provide advice on environmental matters. The council is headed by David T. Buzzelli, Vice President for the Environment, Health, and Safety, and includes roughly a dozen independent authorities from government, academe, and journalism.

Leadership on Full Environmental Pricing. In 1992, Chairman Frank Popoff, took the bold step of calling for full-cost environmental pricing on all products. By including the costs attributable to pollution prevention over a product's full life cycle, market forces would be harnessed to protect the environment.

Sources: Laura M. Petty, "Is the Greening of Corporate America Real?" (Unpublished paper, George Washington University, 1991); Martha Hamilton, "Dow to Name Advisers on Environment," *Washington Post* (October 16, 1991); Martha Hamilton, "Making a Product's Cost Reflect Pollution's Costs," *Washington Post* (November 29, 1992).

The Ecological-Economic Transformation

Curbing wasteful lifestyles and business practices is urgent, but moralizing against economic growth ignores the vast dimensions of the task. Even now we see a rising tide of industrialization doom wildlife species to extinction, destroy forests, turn farmland into desert, wipe out fishing stocks, foul our air and water, and cause severe disease[20]—while the underdeveloped nations are likely to magnify these problems manyfold over the next few decades.

The only feasible solution is to devise a more sophisticated way of life that is both economically comfortable and ecologically benign—an "ecological-economic transformation," or "eco-economic transformation." There are few easy answers because this enormous task will require serious compromise as we trade off the costs and gains of various solutions. Expenditures for environmental protection in the United States rose from 0.8 percent of GDP in 1972 to 2.4 percent in 1992, about $200 billion, causing total declines of several percentage points in productivity, economic growth, and per capita income.[21]

For instance, the problem of auto emissions is not likely to be resolved easily. The world's fleet of 500 million cars, which even now has made driving in major cities almost unbearable, is expected to double to a billion vehicles by 2010. Leading American states, such as California, have mandated electric cars to reduce auto exhausts, but this approach has its drawbacks. The added cost and limited range of electrics will limit their use, old batteries with toxic chemicals may soon litter the Golden State, and pollution is likely to move to power plants that provide the electricity. Indeed, a study conducted by the Environmental Protection Agency found that electric cars could *increase* pollutant levels.[22]

We could simply recycle everything, people say, and solve the problem. Well, it's not that simple. The systemic nature of the recycling problem became apparent when cities found themselves holding bulging warehouses of old newspaper because present recycling programs are having trouble covering costs.

Integrating Economic Progress and Ecological Health

Fortunately, a wave of innovation is under way as business managers, environmentalists, government officials, and consumers struggle to protect nature while also serving human needs. These "green economic practices" go beyond the old war between business and the environment because the two can reinforce one another if approached properly. Just as the quality revolution revealed that we can have both high-quality goods and lower prices, the eco-economic transformation is based on the careful integration of environmental and economic goals.

Having accepted the economic reasons for change, pragmatic business corporations have moved ahead on the issue. Indeed, there is a refreshing tone of bold innovation because sound environmental management can avoid litigation, reduce operating costs, attract customers, and be in accord with social values. Environmental protection is now regarded by progressive managers around the world as a new economic frontier offering huge opportunities. Stephen Schmidheiny, a Swiss businessman, expressed it best: "Sustainable development makes good business sense because it can create competitive advantages and new opportunities. But it requires far-reaching shifts in corporate attitudes and new ways of doing business."[23]

PRINCIPLES OF ENVIRONMENTAL MANAGEMENT

Managing this leap in growth prudently requires dramatic changes in all phases of management, so many authorities have developed concepts to help understand this complex undertaking: the "three Ps" ("Pollution Prevention at a Profit"); "three Rs" ("Recycling, Reclamation, and Remanufacturing"); and progressive phases of environmental management ("Reactive, Receptive, Constructive, and Proactive").[24] My studies show that this field can be described in terms of the five principles discussed in the sections that follow.

Internalize Environmental Costs and Benefits

Possibly the single most effective action we can take is to internalize environmental costs. People may favor ecological protection in the abstract, but their actions are guided by economic costs and benefits. One of the reasons auto congestion is so heavy is that $300 billion of public funds subsidize auto travel. In cities such as Singapore—where the cost of environmental "externalities" are passed on to drivers, or "internalized"—the problem almost solves itself as people decide that other alternatives are cheaper.

The concept is being adopted widely. A good example is provided by the 1990 Clean Air Act: by allowing firms to sell pollution rights to one another, companies balance the costs and gains of various cleanup facilities against the cost of pollution rights to arrive at optimal decisions. Early estimates were that this would cost $600 to $1,600 per ton of pollutants removed, but the actual cost was $150 per ton. "Once you give people a choice and they have an incentive, they find a way to do it," said an EPA administrator.[25]

Other examples abound. Power companies in thirty states are paying the public to avoid using energy, thereby supplying half of future energy growth through "negawatts." Governments around the world are using various methods to estimate the costs polluters must pay to compensate for environmental damage, as when the U.S. government fined Exxon $1 billion for the Valdez oil spill. Cities are beginning to charge people for picking up their trash. Some firms are basing managers' pay partly on environmental performance.[26]

Extend Prevention Throughout the Product Cycle

Pollution prevention is no longer limited to cleaning up waste but is now regarded as a constant activity extending throughout the product cycle. As the examples in Box 7.2 suggest, companies now design products with materials that minimize environmental impact, they develop manufacturing processes that are energy efficient and nonpolluting, simplify consumer packaging to avoid waste, refill used containers, repair products to extend their life, and recycle the final discarded product.[27]

The significance of this new perspective can be assessed by comparing it to progress in other fields. Just as TQM now emphasizes more robust product designs and continual improvement, and just as health care is changing focus from curing illness to prevention and wellness, environmental protection is best achieved early in the product cycle.

Close the Manufacturing Cycle

When a product's useful life comes to an end, another principle comes into play: close the manufacturing cycle by using waste as the source of raw materials.

The large-scale recovery of useable resources from waste is improving to the point where business often prefers recycling materials because it is

---

BOX 7.2. ENVIRONMENTAL PROTECTION THROUGHOUT THE PRODUCT CYCLE.

Product Design. Products ranging from lightbulbs to entire homes are being redesigned to reduce energy consumption, avoid toxic materials, and facilitate repair and reuse. Amory Lovins claims that such changes have saved four times as much energy as that obtained from new energy sources over the past decade, and he expects we could save 90 percent of present electricity use.

Production. The Minnesota Mining and Manufacturing Company (3M) has become famous for its "Pollution Prevention Pays" program. By choosing less-polluting materials, devising more efficient manufacturing processes, and recycling waste materials, the company has converted an otherwise massive pollutant stream into savings of $1 billion over the past decades. Herman Miller, Inc., the famous furniture maker, saves two to three million dollars every year by recovering manufacturing wastes, recycling scrap materials, reducing packaging, and refurbishing old furniture. The company expects to be a waste-free system by 1995.

Recycling Used Products. European manufacturers are actively planning to reclaim all discarded products. The companies will reuse old containers, repair selected product parts for reuse, and recycle the remaining materials. Laws have been passed requiring this plan for consumer goods, and they are being extended to include appliances and even automobiles.

Sources: William Bryant Logan, "The Futurists," *Worth* (December-January 1993); Francis Cairncross, "How Europe's Companies Reposition to Recycle," *Harvard Business Review* (March-April, 1992).

---

cheaper. "The enthusiasm out there for recycling is overwhelming," said Dean Buntrock, chairman of Waste Management, Inc., the primary recycling corporation in America.[28] Major portions of aluminum, copper, steel, glass, paper, and other products are produced from recycled materials now, especially in Japan, where half of all waste is recycled.

To facilitate recycling, manufacturers such as BMW, IBM, Xerox, and HP are rapidly introducing a technique called "design for disassembly" (DFD). BMW estimates that 20 million European cars will be recycled by the end of this decade. GM, Ford, and Chrysler have built a joint laboratory for developing DFD methods. American autos are now built of 75 percent recycled materials, and BMW's are approaching 95 percent. Many managers claim all products will be recycled in about ten years.[29]

Thus manufacturing is moving to a position that regards pollutants as not inherently bad, but simply resources that are in the wrong place. The task then becomes one of converting waste into useful resources. By developing sophisticated recovery methods, the level of recycled materials should approach 100 percent in time, turning today's overflowing garbage dumps into veritable mines of valuable material deposits.

Obtain Accurate Information on Environmental Impacts

In order to guide such complex matters, effective information systems are needed that will allow managers to assess the trade-offs between environmental and economic costs. Sound decisions depend on accurate information.

Studies by Alcan, a large Canadian maker of aluminum windows, show that construction only consumes 1 to 2 percent of the total energy costs incurred during a window's typical life. The rest is passed through the window, so attention should focus on better insulated designs. Procter & Gamble and many other companies have conducted such life cycle analyses (LCAs) and found them equally useful. "If you don't use sound science to make these decisions, you'll make environmentally bad choices," said a P&G vice president. Sophisticated software programs are being developed that conveniently conduct LCAs on typical PCs.[30]

Companies are also evaluating the environmental impacts of their practices. Various forms of "ecological audits," "green accounting," and "social indicators" are being developed, including the translation of environmental impacts into dollar equivalents. And a "green GDP" is being developed that will bring environmental damage, renewable resources, and other nonmarket costs and benefits into national economic accounts.[31]

Develop Collaborative Working Relations

Because ecological problems are wide-ranging issues that span different institutions and nations, they can only be handled by interested parties working together, and it is in the interests of all parties to do so.

The Environmental Defense Fund has joined with McDonald's, General Motors, and other major corporations to advise these companies on improving their environmental policies. Roughly one-third of major corporations had organized permanent environmental advisory councils as of 1993. The U.S. government has formed the Green Lights Program to assist companies in developing business practices that are ecologically sound and profitable.

THE POWER OF ECONOMIC REALITY

The hopeful feature of the principles of environmental management is that they are eminently practical, so they reinforce the interests of average people rather than requiring heroic altruism that cannot often be sustained. Table 7.1 shows they are being adopted, albeit slowly, and Peter Coors, CEO of Coors Brewing, known for his conservative views, expressed the hard-core business perspective in these terms:

> Environmental performance is a dependable path to profitability. Find pollution or waste and you've found inefficiency . . . fundamentally, all pollution is lost profit. By striving to eliminate it, we can together grow a more efficient, competitive economy.[32]

TABLE 7.1. ADOPTION OF INTELLIGENT GROWTH PRACTICES.
(SAMPLE = 426 CORPORATE MANAGERS.)

Practice	Not Practiced (0–3)	Partially Practiced (4–6)	Fully Practiced (7–10)	Mean (0–10)
Environmental impacts are studied as they affect product design, manufacturing processes, packaging, waste treatment, recycling, and other aspects of operations.	30%	24%	46%	5.4
Environmental costs and benefits are incorporated into management decisions.	34	26	40	5.1
The company solicits advice from an environmental advisory committee and/or various environmental groups.	49	22	29	4.0
Means	38%	24%	38%	4.9

Source: William E. Halal, *Corporations in Transition* (an unpublished study in progress). Note that data in the first three columns ("Not Practiced," etc.) are aggregated by collapsing portions of the questionnaire scale as shown ("0–3," etc.). See the questionnaire in Appendix C.

Obviously, this approach lacks the love of nature that motivates environmentalists and some other companies. As shown in Box 7.3, the Body Shop not only strives to operate by the above principles, but it goes beyond them to conduct public interest campaigns that protect the environment. However, it seems unlikely that more than a minority is capable of such admirable conduct.

That is precisely why the view of ordinary businesspeople like Peter Coors is so promising: it makes sense in hard economic terms. This fundamental conclusion reminds us once again that markets can be compatible with social values, as argued in Chapter 4.

Recent surveys of hundreds of environmental business investments found average annual returns running from 63 percent to 204 percent. The researcher concluded: "Pollution prevention is one of the fundamental shifts taking place in business throughout the world. Every company can increase its profits and productivity by reducing pollutants."[33] Other studies

---

BOX 7.3. THE BODY SHOP—ON ENVIRONMENT.

A central part of the Body Shop's unusual success is its focus on safeguarding the environment. When Anita Roddick started the company her approach seemed a radical idea; now it has altered the mainstream of business in the UK as British companies rush to advertise their ecological awareness.

Natural Products. The shops are bright, aromatic, individualized settings filled with colorful posters and literature describing products made of natural sources from around the world: a mud shampoo from Morocco with special properties, a grape skin toner, a peppermint foot lotion. The result is a tantalizing array of ethnic cosmetics that delivers value and stresses human safety.

Ecological Protection. Everything the company does is designed to minimize its environmental impact. Products are biodegradable and come in refillable containers. Three independently verified environmental impact audits have been conducted, and a "Values Report" is under way to assess the Body Shop's environmental and social performance.

Environmental Campaigns. The company campaigns to protect the environment. It spent hundreds of thousands of dollars to help indigenous tribes in Brazil save their rain forests, operated public campaigns to promote "Refill, Re-Use, and Recycle," and collected 70,000 signatures and $57,000 to protect sea otters.

Source: Bo Burlingham, "This Woman Has Changed Business Forever," *Inc.* (June 1990).

find that chemical plants using pollution-prevention technology typically recover their investment in six months or less and then go on to save huge sums every year after. An environmental think tank concluded, "The pollution prevention ethic is firmly taking root in American business."[34] Box 7.4 describes successful projects under way.

The economic advantages are enormous. As of 1991, the environmental management industry in America consisted of 70,000 businesses employing 1 million workers and generating $130 billion in sales. Considering the normal economic multiplier, the total impact likely produces 3.5 million jobs, $270 billion in sales, and $76 billion in federal taxes. If Americans could conserve energy as efficiently as the Japanese, we could save $200 billion per year, which would eliminate the federal budget deficit.[35]

Achieving this societal transformation will be a mean feat that is sure to test fervent environmentalists and staunch growth advocates alike. Neither a pure allegiance to the environment nor to growth will be possible; instead, a more intelligent, balanced synthesis is needed that goes beyond sustainability. Gunter Pauli, CEO of Ecover, a European corporation, put it this way: "The era of Left Greens [environmentalists] is over. The era of Right Capitalists [growth advocates] is over. The two sides are converging."[36]

The concept of "sustainable *development*" is closer to reality, but it is also somewhat misleading because the word "development" is really a euphemism that avoids the negative connotations of "growth." I find the concept of "intelligent growth" or "smart growth" more useful because it acknowledges the need for growth, but in a more sophisticated manner based on the use of knowledge to make choices that protect nature and serve society as well.

These distinctions may appear to be quibbling over words, but they can be crucial because they often lead to different types of action. For instance, much attention is being devoted to defining sustainability in precise terms so it can be implemented, and many people are convinced that only by abandoning the free enterprise system can we create an equitable enough distribution of resources and reasonable enough lifestyles to solve the environmental problem.[37]

Such a scenario may be possible, but it is hard to even vaguely envision what it would look like. The fall of Communism has affirmed that free enterprise is the only viable way to manage today's complex world.

BOX 7.4. ENVIRONMENTAL BUSINESS PROJECTS.

The Super Refrigerator. Twenty-five power companies put up a $30 million reward for the development of an ecologically safe refrigerator. The competition was won by a Whirlpool team that produced a design benefiting all parties. The utilities will avoid the need to build new power plants, Whirlpool will gain a lead in the market, buyers will save $500 in operating costs of each unit, the nation will save $250 million per year, and the environment will be spared damage to the ozone layer.

The Green Car. Automakers are forming R&D programs to produce a "Green Car" that will be nonpolluting and energy efficient. An annual race has been held for years among solar-powered cars—the Sunrayce Competition. In 1992, GM, Lockheed, and Pacific Gas & Electric formed a consortium (CALSTART) to produce an electric car for California. Mazda has an operable hydrogen-fueled car that produces no pollutants. The Clinton administration has announced a consortium of U.S. carmakers that will develop a "Clean Car" that burns hydrogen in a fuel cell.

The "Garbage House." The National Association of Home Builders has erected an attractive, comfortable house in Maryland that is constructed completely out of recycled materials. The steel frame is made from junked cars, insulation is from old polystyrene packages, and the ceiling tiles are made from newspapers.

Molten Metal Technologies. This company is commercializing a new process to recycle metal into useful gases, metal alloys, ceramics, and other valuable products. Maurice Strong, a businessman and environmentalist, said: "I've seen a lot of environmental technologies, but I've never seen anything as exciting as this."

Green Chemistry. Novo Nordisk in Denmark is using natural enzymes to replace chemicals used for industrial purposes. The company has developed forty processes for making penicillin, cleaning agents, pesticides, and a growing range of other products. "We're finding natural solutions to industrial problems," said the CEO.

The "Fling" Camera. Kodak developed a throwaway camera, the "Fling," which so outraged people that sales slumped even though it served a real need. The company then began recycling it in 1990, causing unit sales to hit 22 million in 1992. "I see sales quadrupling within three years," said a Kmart manager.

Interactive Manufacturing–Ecological Systems. The town of Kalunborg, Denmark, has integrated several companies into an ecologically supportive complex of manufacturing and environmental systems. A power generating plant, oil refinery, biotechnology plant, plasterboard factory, sulfuric acid producer, cement company, and local farms are all designed to share the same water, energy, and ecological infrastructure in the most economically productive and ecologically benign manner.

Sources: James Teece, "The Great Refrigerator Race," *BusinessWeek* (July 15, 1993); "Handle with Care," *New York Times* (April 11, 1990); "The Hottest Thing Since the Flashbulb," *Business-Week* (September 7, 1992).

Likewise, achieving sustainability is far too complex to be entrusted to some government agency, a group of scientists, or other elites. Like other complex undertakings—achieving success in a career, a corporate strategy, or a national goal—it can only be pursued by incrementally moving in a general direction as our understanding improves. Thus, an ecologically sustainable future cannot be planned, but must emerge out of free markets guided by democratic institutions to continually balance the needs of the Earth and its inhabitants.

Finding our way will be easier if we bear in mind the principles of the New Management. The Information Revolution should make it possible to draw on democracy and enterprise to create an intelligent form of growth that protects the environment. Corporations and governments should involve their constituencies in creating a green economic infrastructure and then allow internal market forces to sort out conflicting claims into optimal decisions. The task will be daunting, but information systems should improve our ability to monitor environmental conditions, understand the trade-offs, internalize costs, educate people, embrace nonpolluting modes of "teleworking" and "teleliving," and generally shape a more conserving society.

The concept of corporate community described in Chapter 3 helps put the role of environmental management in perspective. Protecting ecological systems is a fundamental priority because it affects not only the general public but all stakeholders as well. After all, the environment is the ultimate corporate stakeholder.

Reconciling the Obstacles Within

The following conclusions stand out as a guide to the major changes that are needed:

1. The world is very likely to experience a five- to tenfold increase in economic growth over the long term.

2. A complete transformation in technological, economic, and social systems is needed to make societies ecologically benign.

3. Business will have to develop systems for green manufacturing, recovery of discarded products, and full environmental costing.

4. Government must bear the responsibility for monitoring the environment, passing protective laws, and internalizing costs.

5. The public must adopt a more temperate style of living that is compatible with ecological health.

This transformation will inevitably alter the way modern societies are structured, but the truly difficult obstacles lie within us as individuals. The change to an ecologically healthy economy will require an inner change in our personal values. Can people in advanced nations, especially the United States, tame their extravagant consumption habits? How many business-people will be able to see beyond their immediate financial performance? Can environmentalists accept the need for economic growth, especially as it races through the undeveloped world?

It is sure to be a difficult struggle for average Americans to accept limits on their indulgent lifestyles. Is it reasonable for many families of two or three people to live in 5,000-square-foot homes, consuming enough resources to sustain several families in other parts of the world? Isn't a second home used for a few weekends a year wasteful? Can we tolerate a throwaway culture in which everything—from cigarette lighters to autos—is disposable, without bearing environmental costs? (I know the first reaction of my family when faced with anything outmoded is to just toss it out—then I retrieve it from the trash.)

Although business has made great advances, one of the themes that emerged from the CIT survey is a lack of awareness of how pervasive the problem really is. Most manufacturing managers are working on environmental protection, but time and again, others claimed it did not apply to their white-collar organization because they "did not manufacture anything." Yet they operated buildings that had to be constructed, lighted, heated, and cooled. They employed people who drove cars to work, used electrical equipment, and discarded paper. One manager noted: "I am amazed to see lights left on during long vacations and reams of paper trashed without being recycled."

Oddly enough, environmentalists may prove the most resistant. Sharon Newsome, vice president of the National Wildlife Federation, noted: "I wondered if the environmental community was capable of [compromise]?

I've come to the conclusion we're not. Taking on your enemies is more fun."[38] If we Americans cannot agree among ourselves, how can we expect the Mexicans, Indians, Chinese, and members of other nations to agree with us on the urgency of disciplining their birth rates and their newfound appetites for consumption?

Resolving these conflicts involves accepting the reality that life is more complex than any single perspective. For instance, despite the fact that the weather has been unseasonably hot in recent years, scientific evidence for global warming remains controversial because the temperature rise that has occurred since 1900 lies within the normal range of temperature cycles. One wonders how much of today's concern happens to be a result of political fashion? George Will notes that a decade or two ago we were deluged with similar fears over global *cooling*.[39]

It seems to me that it is necessary in these personal, overwhelmingly complex matters to go beyond management and technology by carefully attending to the subtle interactions between life and its environment. A new form of "biologic" is needed that appreciates these subtle ecological considerations, that recognizes the unique character of each natural system, senses each one's state of ecological health, learns how to draw what we need with minimal disruption, and develops appropriate means for doing so.[40] If we can cultivate a society attuned to the needs of other species, we may then learn to coexist with them in harmony.

A small accomplishment in my life had a great impact on my understanding. I love to be surrounded by nature, and so I have cultivated a garden that envelops my home in profuse greenery. It's not practical in any economic sense, and it requires considerable time and resources to maintain. But I built a compost system that helps make gardening convenient. Rather than having to bag leaves, grass, and the tons of other organic matter any garden produces and then having it hauled miles away to some dump, I just toss it into my compost bin. Throughout the year I can then extract rich black soil from the bottom that nourishes my garden with better nutrients than costly and damaging chemicals.

It's a modest success, of course, but I've found that this humble system is not only convenient, it is also spiritually refreshing. There is something about closing the cycle of nature that strikes me as proper, in keeping with the rhythm of seasons. Tending a garden with grace is my small but cherished offering to the propagation of life on a healthy Earth.

If we can become attuned to the larger garden composed of the vast ecological diversity that surrounds civilization, there is no good reason why we cannot develop a benign global economy that allows us to live in harmony with the Earth. We would then find a way to build clean factories, turn farms and parks into chemical-free natural settings, reforest denuded deserts and cities, downsize our homes and public buildings, harness the power of IT to replace needless travel, and employ countless other ways of maintaining a bountiful, healthy environment.

These difficult changes should be easier if we see that they constitute an historic innovation, somewhat comparable to the invention of democracy. Where democracy created a sustainable social order based on the sacred rights of people, the eco-economic transformation should form a sustainable economic order based on the sacred rights of Nature. Recognizing that all life is sacred does not mean we cannot harvest plants and animals to serve human needs. It means that we should do so sparingly, with reverence for the passing of their lives into ours, like a sacrament.

Notes

1. See Carl Deal, *The Greenpeace Guide to Anti-Environmental Organizations* (Berkeley, Calif.: Odonian Press, 1993).
2. George C. Lodge and Jeffrey F. Rayport, "Knee-deep and Rising: America's Recycling Crisis," *Harvard Business Review* (September-October 1991). Art Kleiner, "What Does It Mean to Be Green?" *Harvard Business Review* (July-August 1991).
3. Matthew J. Kiernan, "The Eco-Industrial Revolution," *Business in the Contemporary World* (Autumn 1992), p. 133.
4. Pollster George Gallup summed up the results of his surveys on environmentalism in a talk given at the National Press Club in Washington, D.C., on May 4, 1992: "The state of the environment is no longer an exotic, elitist issue [but] a truly global concern, reaching all levels of society and nations around the world."
5. Mark Starik, "When Business Goes for the Green," *GW Magazine* (Summer 1993).
6. Starik, "When Business Goes for the Green."

7. David Brown, "Cancer Risk Up Sharply in This Era," *Washington Post* (February 9, 1994).

8. Eliot Marshall, "Experts Clash Over Cancer Data," *Science* (November 1990), pp. 900–902; Susan Okie, "Cancer Rates in Industrial Countries Rise," *Washington Post* (December 9, 1990).

9. Michael Weisskopf, "Skin Cancer Risk Increases," *Washington Post* (October 23, 1991).

10. Theodore Roszak, Voice of the Earth: An Exploration of Ecopyschology (New York: Simon & Schuster, 1992); Terrence O'Connor, "Therapy for a Dying Planet," *Networker* (September/October 1989).

11. Willis Harman, *Global Mind Change* (Indianapolis: Knowledge Systems, 1988).

12. He Bochuan, *China on the Edge* (China Books, 1991); Vaclav Smil, *China's Environmental Crisis* (Armonk, New York: Sharpe, 1993); and Sheryl WuDunn, "Chinese Suffer from Rising Pollution," *New York Times* (February 28, 1993).

13. See the "Bruntland Report" by the World Commission of Environment and Development, in *Our Common Future* (New York: Oxford University Press, 1987), and Jim MacNeill, Pieter Winsemius, and Taizo Yakushiji, *Beyond Interdependence: The Meshing of the World's Economy and the Earth's Ecology* (New York: Oxford University Press, 1991). Many older studies have predicted a tenfold increase in industrial consumption, such as Herbert Robinson, "Can the World Stand Higher Productivity and Incomes?" *The Futurist* (October, 1977), and Jay Forrester, "Counterintuitive Behavior of Social Systems," *Technology Review* (January 1971).

14. Johan Holmberg, *Making Development Sustainable* (London: Earthscan, 1992).

15. One of the most articulate proponents of this view is Julian Simon, of the University of Maryland. For one of his recent statements, see "The Unreported Revolution in Population Economics," *The Public Interest* (Fall 1990), pp. 89–100.

16. See the views of Wallace Kaufman, former president of two environmental groups, *No Turning Back* (New York: Basic Books, 1994). John Heritage, "When Environmentalists Go for the Throat," *Washington Post* (June 2, 1995). Gregg Easterbrook, *A Moment on the Earth* (New York: Viking, 1995).

17. *The Corporate Response to the Environmental Challenge* (Amsterdam: McKinsey & Company, 1991). Pieter Winsemius and Ulrich Guntram, "Responding to the Environmental Challenge," *Business Horizons* (March-April 1992).

18. Boyce Rensberger, "Decline of Ozone-Harming Chemicals Suggests Atmosphere May Heal Itself," *Washington Post* (August 26, 1993). "Quick, Save the Ozone," *BusinessWeek* (May 17, 1993).

19. Curtis Moore and Alan Miller, *Green Gold: Japan, Germany, the United States, and the Race for Environmental Technology* (Boston: Beacon Press, 1994).

20. For an assessment of the environmental problem see Lester Brown, *State of the World* (New York: W.W. Norton, 1993), and Donella Meadows et al., *Beyond the Limits* (Post Mills, Vt.: Chelsea Green, 1992).

21. Bruce Bartlett, "The High Cost of Turning Green," *Wall Street Journal* (September 14, 1994). Noah Walley and Bradley Whitehead, "It's Not Easy Being Green," *Harvard Business Review* (May-June 1994).

22. Oscar Suris, "Electric Cars Also Pollute Air, ERA Study Says," *Wall Street Journal* (April 5, 1994).

23. Stephan Schmidheiny, *Changing Course: A Global Business Perspective on Development and the Environment* (Cambridge, Mass.: MIT Press, 1992), p. xii.

24. These examples are from William K. Reilly, "Environment, Inc.," *Business Horizons* (March-April 1992), pp. 9–11; Joseph F. Coates, "Waste Not," *American Way* (November 1, 1992); and Winsemius and Guntram, "Responding to the Environmental Challenge," pp. 12–20.

25. Martha Hamilton, "Selling Pollution Rights Cuts the Cost of Cleaner Air," *Washington Post* (August 24, 1994).

26. Paul Klebnikov, "Demand-Siders," *Forbes* (October 26, 1992). Robert Repetto et al., *Green Fees* (Washington, D.C.: World Resources Institute, 1992). Emily Smith et al., "The Greening of Corporate America," *BusinessWeek* (April 23, 1990).

27. See Jim Jackson (ed.), *Clean Production Strategies* (Boca Raton, Fla.: Lewis, 1993).

28. Brian Bremner, "Recycling," *BusinessWeek* (March 5, 1990).

29. Gene Bylinsky, "Manufacturing for Reuse," *Fortune* (February 6, 1995).

30. "The Green Machine," *Enterprise* (October 1994).

31. Hazel Henderson, *Paradigms in Progress* (Indianapolis: Knowledge Systems, 1991). Herman E. Daly and John B. Cobb, Jr., *For the Common Good* (Boston, Mass.: Beacon Press, 1989).

32. Peter Coors, "The New Corporate Environmentalism," *BusinessWeek* (May 11, 1992).

33. Joseph Romm, *Lean and Clean Management* (New York: Kodansha, 1994).

34. Martha Hamilton, "Firms Saving Money by Preventing Pollution," *Washington Post* (June 17, 1992).

35. Timothy Wirth, "Easy Being Green," *Washington Post* (October 4, 1992).

36. "Gunter Pauli Cleans Up," *Fast Company* (November 1993).

37. Willis Harman, for instance, is a leading spokeperson of this view, which is well described in "Global Dilemmas and the Plausibility of Whole System Change," *Technological Forecasting & Social Change* (May 1995).

38. Daniel Glick, "Barbarians Inside the Gate," *Newsweek* (November 1, 1993).

39. George Will, "Chicken Littles," *Washington Post* (May 31, 1992).

40. The concept of "biologic" was coined by David Wann; see his *Biologic: Designing with Nature to Protect the Environment* (Boulder, Colo.: Johnson Books, 1994).

Part Three

●

Leading in the
New Economic Order

In this final part of the book, we turn our attention to how the New Management helps managers carry out their role as leaders: providing guidance in a world of constant change, empowered people, and a global economy.

Chapter 8 shows that creating strategic change requires uniting the organization with the forces that cause change. An internal market roots the organization into its economic environment, while a corporate community draws on the diverse values of stakeholders to integrate business with society. Modern managers use this organic form of organization to produce continuous change through the ebb and flow of external forces.

Chapter 9 explores how the coming shift to empowered workers, demanding clients, and temporary business partners requires managers to find collaborative solutions in the face of strongly held differences. Leading without formal power can be best accomplished by drawing on the leader's inner resources: really listening for the meaning in other's views, living with problems and crises, and expanding awareness to heighten one's inner wisdom.

The final chapter examines the implications of a decentralized global economy that is emerging as the old structures of big business and big government give way to shifting networks of small enterprises spanning the world. To thrive in this unstructured arena, managers will have to work across vast cultural differences to form pockets of entrepreneurial community at the local level.

8

Continuous Change

Rooting the Organization into Its Environment

All agree that coping with change is critical now that the Information Revolution is roaring upon us, yet attempts to manage change do not succeed very often. Look at the failed promise of nuclear power "too cheap to meter," the AT&T PicturePhone, the Great Society, and many other formidable undertakings. If we hope to manage a complex future, it is best to have no illusions. Strategic change is an unusually difficult undertaking. Consider two roughly similar attempts to produce major social change in the USA and the former USSR that took very different, unexpected paths.

The health care system in the United States is suffering from skyrocketing costs, a large uninsured population, and mediocre performance.[1] Eli Ginsberg, an authority on health care, says that "the system is likely to be derailed some time this decade," and former Surgeon General C. Everett Koop claims that "there is something terribly wrong. We need a complete change."[2] Then why did attempts to reform the system fail when President Clinton aroused the nation to act? Here is a sophisticated nation that planned the success of World War II and landed men on the Moon, yet it seems unable to change a health care mess that is likely to grow far worse.

Contrast this with the transition of communism to capitalism. The Soviet Union's system was so fiercely supported by generations of faithful adherents that it dominated half the globe. In fact, Western nations feared it was more powerful than democracy because an authoritarian state does not have to please a fickle public. Yet suddenly this formidable structure began a conversion to the market system Russians considered their nemesis for seventy years.

There is no better way to understand change than by probing the meaning of these two contrasting experiences. Was Mikhail Gorbachev a more skillful change agent than Clinton? Gorbachev hardly intended to bring down Communism; he simply wanted to improve it. Did Gorbachev have greater support? As Chapter 10 will show, most Soviets did not want to end Communism, whereas, when Clinton proposed health care reform in 1993, more than 60 percent of the public supported him and he had solid backing from the media and congress. True, the Soviet system was starting to fail, but so was American health care when Clinton became president.

I think these examples illustrate that the primary requirement for effective strategic change does not lie in the leaders, their followers, or the system itself. Then what *did* drive the change from communism to capitalism, and what *prevented* the change of American health care? It was the economic and social environment that surrounded each of these systems. A more complex global economy is being born that demands organic markets rather than the mechanistic bureaucracies of the past. This imperative forced the Soviets to replace their planned economy with a market system, and it caused Americans to reject the Clinton health care plan because it was seen finally as more big government.[3]

Thus, effective strategic change requires far more than a skillful leader able to arouse his or her constituents to redesign their organization. Executives certainly attempt to bring about change, and some brilliant leaders shine at this task. However, the reality is that their power is limited because strategic change can only occur when it is supported by the environment. Skillful methods, sound forecasts, clever strategies, competent workers, and brilliant leadership are needed, to be sure—but ultimately the irresistible movement of external forces determines which efforts succeed and which fail. *The true source of strategic change lies in the larger environment, and managers are servants of this master.*

This may shock managers because it implies that they are not really in control of their organization's destiny, but the implications are more subtle. The key to creating change is to work closely with these external powers in order to harness their energy. Japanese corporations thrived in the 1980s because they understood that modern consumers were hungry for value, quality, and service; they are in trouble now because they have not been able to align themselves with the new reality of fast-moving, free enterprise. The Saturn division of GM stands out because it honors the new attitudes of workers, car owners, and other forces in its environment. The Body Shop is a huge success, but this is largely a result of having chosen the right time to tap the vast social changes favoring a healthy ecological system.

This chapter describes a perspective of "continuous change" based on the symbiosis between organizations and their technical, economic, and social environment. Just as all organisms adapt to their environment to survive, organizations must also adapt to their environment. This analogy helps us see that the Old Management approaches to change—strategic planning, top-down restructuring, and bottom-up learning—have proved disappointing because they unwittingly isolated organizations from this external reality.

But suppose we could direct our efforts outward to build external relationships that convert the powerful but chaotic forces in the environment to useful purposes?

That is exactly how the New Management derives its special advantage in creating strategic change. Just as nations rely on enterprise and democracy to change, these same two imperatives help organizations change. Small enterprises in an internal market constantly adapt to economic trends, while democratic governance brings the changing views of stakeholders into management decisions. Rather than fight the environment, the New Management uses it as a constant source of energy and information.

OLD APPROACHES TO A NEW CHALLENGE

After decades of debate, the future arrived in the 1990s when managers realized that major structural change was inevitable. The Conference Board noted: "In today's business environment, ignoring the need for change places a company at peril," and *BusinessWeek* issued a special edition in 1992 on "Reinventing America."[4]

Not only has change become a major concern, it has become what Peter Vaill calls "permanent white water."[5] Production engineering was crucial early in this century when manufacturing systems were being developed; marketing dominated the 1950's and 1960s to stimulate consumer demand; and finance has thrived in the recent period of mergers and acquisitions. As the century ends, however, the challenge of adapting to a continually changing future is bringing strategic change to the fore. As Table 8.1 shows, the focus has moved from production management, to marketing management, to financial management, and now to *strategic* management.

TABLE 8.1. THE EVOLUTION OF STRATEGIC MANAGEMENT.

Period	Main Need	Management Focus
1900–1930	Manufacturing efficiency	Production management
1930–1960	Create demand	Marketing management
1960–1990	Mergers and acquisitions	Financial management
1990– ?	Continuous change	Strategic management

The idea of strategic management has become very popular for this reason, but most views of this field seem limited by concepts of the Old Management. Textbooks and managers themselves usually discuss strategic *management* in essentially the same terms as the process of strategic *planning*—which became outmoded a decade ago.

Strategic Planning: The Approach That Failed Communism

When strategic planning was at its peak of popularity, I conducted a survey among Fortune 500 companies and found that most of them had developed sophisticated, corporatewide planning systems to cope with an onslaught of social turbulence.[6] Under direction from the CEO, large corporate planning staffs coordinated a complex process that shepherded all operating units through an annual planning cycle. The only problem was that this rarely produced strategic *change*. Yes, managers were deeply engrossed in formulating impressive strategic plans, but they were not usually implemented, for a host of reasons. One manager in my CIT survey said: "Rarely are strategies turned into reality."

The first round of the planning cycle was usually stimulating, but interest sagged as its complexity escalated into an elaborate and pointless annual event. Operating managers soon found themselves spending huge amounts of time filling out forms and attending meetings. The result was that strategic planning became a bureaucratic routine. *Fortune* summed it up in 1982 to mark the end of strategic planning's influence: "The process ends up having the perverse effect of desensitizing people to strategic issues."[7] The disenchantment was so bad that most companies cut back their planning efforts, and many abandoned the practice completely.

In retrospect, it is now clear that changing large organizations is so difficult that it cannot be "planned" in this sense. Indeed, conventional planning itself is the problem. If companies are managed from the top down, planning adds more bureaucracy because it is simply grafted on to the hierarchy. As the failure of centrally planned economies shows, any type of central planning is too slow to respond to rapid change, it drives out creative thought in favor of worn-out routines, undermines motivation, and produces other bureaucratic symptoms.[8] I recall visiting IBM before the company's fall from grace and marvelling at how cumbersome their planning system was, almost like "socialism."

Strategic planning is still needed to cope with change, as we shall see, but it is now conducted in an informal manner to minimize these problems. Most importantly, it is initiated by operating managers rather than imposed as a companywide process.

Revolution from the Top: Shock Therapy for Corporations

Another school of thought contends that strategic management avoids these problems by focusing on the actual *implementation* of strategic change, rather than on the planning process.

This approach may advocate instilling "strategic thinking" and a "readiness for change" throughout the firm, but the reality is that it remains flawed by a reliance on power. Without replacing the hierarchy with some form of decentralized system, this is usually a top-down process initiated by a small group of corporate executives: they usually establish an urgently felt need for change, define a guiding vision, communicate it to the rank and file, and ensure that it is accomplished.[9] Widespread participation may be involved, but this is usually avoided because it is time-consuming and disruptive. Managers in our survey often told the same story: "Strategy is centralized," "Not enough is done at low levels," and "Employees have no knowledge of what is going on."

For example, the way Jack Welch restructured GE is telling because it was a "revolution," in the words of Noel Tichy, one of the "revolutionaries." Welch and other executives planned the change, somewhat like a plot. As in any revolution, they seized the levers of power—allocation of resources, corporate communication systems, training programs, and so on—and turned them to their agenda. In a symbolic event, Welch and his followers burned the GE Blue Books (policy manuals) to announce the end of the old system.[10] GE is a better organization now, but the way it was changed bears a striking resemblance to the overthrow of a government.

Not only does one wonder about the legitimacy of forced change, there are questions about its effectiveness. As we noted in Chapter 2, TQM, downsizing, reengineering, and other strategies are usually forced on corporations, leaving behind a trail of organizational damage. Some analysts have noted the close similarity between these forced attempts to get "lean and mean" and dieting to lose weight. Neither works, but we seem determined to keep trying. Why does this "management anorexia" go on?

The common belief seems to be that change is now essential to survive, and so CEOs impose it in ways they believe will overcome the inevitable resistance and get over the pain quickly. It is roughly akin to the "shock therapy" used on socialist economies. Jack Welch noted that the role of corporate leaders is to create "shock" and then lead the company into recovery.[11]

This approach may succeed if the leaders are brilliant, as in the case of Jack Welch and many other unusually capable CEOs. But it is risky because it is driven by the limited vision of a few people. The fact is that most leaders are fairly ordinary, and often flawed, human beings, so they can easily lead their followers over a cliff. Countless attempts at strategic change have failed with varying degrees of damage because CEOs thought they knew best. American health reform died because the Clintons tried to impose their solution. "The bill was the product of an ivory tower," said Senator Charles Grassley. Former CEO William Agee almost destroyed Morrison Knudsen Corporation by imposing a misguided strategy until he was ousted by a revolt of the board of directors.[12]

Such examples are not uncommon because they are among the intrinsic disadvantages of top-down change. For every organization that is revitalized by a great leader, many others are held hostage by mediocre leaders. The future presents such complexity that no single group of people can plan it effectively.

We will continue to see more of this type of change because it appeals to those holding a tough, expedient view of management. However, corporate shock therapy is all shock and little therapy. Economic shock therapy may be justified to convert socialized economies into market systems, but most corporations remain centrally controlled hierarchies after all the dust settles.

That is the most serious fault of this approach. It is a temporary solution that relies on executives to periodically introduce top-down change, rather than create an organic system that is inherently adaptive. Top-down change is roughly comparable to forcing the old USSR through a course of shock therapy—only to restructure the system into a more efficient form of central planning.

Learning at the Bottom: A Replay of Organizational Development

At the risk of seeming difficult to please, let's examine a bottom-up approach to change, "organizational learning" (OL). OL focuses on helping teams create a shared vision, engage in honest dialogue on how to achieve this goal, and solve organizational problems.[13] The intent is to learn how to cut through the misunderstanding and confusion that prevents working together.

Who would not agree that we need to learn how to work together better, especially in a competitive world? However, such intense personal interaction can only be done in small groups. Like the limits of participation discussed in Chapter 6, these group process methods are great for unifying teams of about twenty people, and possibly units containing a few hundred people. But they can rarely address the complex structural problems of large organizations.

I was deeply impressed by a similar movement that swept through the 1960s. "Organizational development" (OD) also used group process methods to vitalize organizations by altering personal values and working relationships. During the heyday of OD, most managers tried this approach, and the results were often dramatic as people rediscovered their humanity and vowed to foster harmony.

These were fleeting effects, unfortunately, because the hard reality of work life reasserted itself, usually causing the system to return to the *status quo ante,* often with a vengeance. It became clear that a large organization is more than the good intentions of its members. If there is one thing that management science has demonstrated through decades of study, it is that organizations are not simply collections of people. They transcend individuals because they are so much larger, more powerful, intricate, mythical, and enduring that it takes a heroic act to change them, like Welch's revolution at GE. That is why people often feel trapped in their institutions. The pressures of competition, the labyrinth of communication channels, persistent differences in values, complex departmental roles, lasting heritages of failure and success, and other structural features of work life impose exacting demands all their own.

My main impression is that OL represents the rebirth of OD. The focus on catharsis of pent-up emotions, authentic expression of differences, and on achieving a unifying vitality are strikingly similar. Even the names are alike. I do think these group process methods are needed to build effective work teams. However, I also suspect that OL practitioners are likely to realize in time that something else is lacking—the design of sophisticated organizational structures that can make such behavior a widespread, enduring way of life. OL claims to offer insights from systems thinking, but that appears to be a minor goal, and it does not recognize the dominant need to transform organizations into entrepreneurial, democratic systems. After struggling to change the way his employees worked, one frustrated manager finally got the point: "It isn't the people, it's the system."

It is interesting to note that OL represents the opposite of corporate shock therapy. Shock therapy uses power to force change from the top, while OL uses team learning to encourage change from the bottom. The limits of shock therapy were noted above, but consider the limits of OL. Relying on OL to produce strategic change is roughly analogous to transforming the old Soviet economy by helping groups of Russians learn to work together—hoping that they will discover how to create a complex market economy.

PRINCIPLES OF CONTINUOUS CHANGE

If centralized planning, top-down change, and bottom-up learning do not provide an effective form of strategic management, what will? Institutions are like people writ large. They have a hard time understanding themselves. They don't know what they want, or how to get it. They often can't bring themselves to take actions they know are in their best interests, and so they await external events to move them. What unusual force can overcome this inertia?

The reader will not be surprised to find that I propose a different approach to strategic change. As the following sections will show, effective managers today combine internal markets and a corporate community within an intelligent infrastructure to harness the power of the environment.

An Organization Tree Harnesses the Power of the Environment

A little reflection will acknowledge that any institution is an inseparable part of the larger environment. Indeed, it is meaningless to think of change otherwise because any organism exists in a reciprocal symbiosis with its surroundings. All materials, energy, information, and everything else an organization depends on for its existence flow from the dynamic life of the economy, technological progress, society, and nature itself. Like individuals, institutions atrophy if isolated from life, and today organizations are immobilized by Old Management structures that shield them from the vital energies swirling all about.

The case of the automobile industry offers an object lesson. Disaster befell the big three American carmakers in the 1980s because they lost touch with environmental forces beyond their power: rising global competition, the ecological crisis, demands for quality, and the like. In a very real sense, the crisis of the auto industry was life's way of forcing these companies to reestablish contact with the changing world about them. They are recovering now only because they have yielded a misplaced arrogance to adapt to these external forces.

From a strategic perspective, the power of the New Management is that it is precisely designed to harness these forces of the environment. Only markets can tap the vitalizing energy of economic life, and democracy is essential to convert social differences into legitimate governance.

As we saw in Chapter 2, MCI, Johnson & Johnson, Hewlett-Packard, ABB, and many other dynamic companies are energized by entrepreneurial systems that continually probe the environment for opportunities. There is simply no substitute for the power of enterprise. Small, *free* enterprise forms the very essence of economic creativity, and most large, mechanistic organizations are dying because they stifle this energy.

As Chapter 3 also showed, GM-Saturn, the Body Shop, Home Depot, IKEA, and a growing number of other companies have harnessed another source of power by drawing on the ideas and vision of their stakeholders. This power of human values, cooperation and other democratic principles differs from that of enterprise, but it is equally energizing. They complement one another.

We also showed in Chapter 4 that these two principles form an "organization tree," which is reproduced here for your convenience. At the bottom, internal enterprises connect the organization to the grass roots of the economy, thereby providing revenue, information, and other nutrients that feed the tree. At the top, democratic governance among stakeholders exposes this entrepreneurial community to the light of diverse values that fuel growth and guide it to serve a useful role in society.

An Intelligent Infrastructure for the Entrepreneurial Community

As we saw in Chapters 2 and 3, this entrepreneurial community needs an "intelligent infrastructure" to help it create new knowledge and learn how to act strategically. OL tries to do this, but serious organizational learning is more than the sum of individual learning in teams; it is the learning of an entire corporate *system* to produce a higher form of intelligence. But how can we increase an *organization*'s ability to learn? By using information technology to create a total learning system.

It will soon be possible to combine high-performing information networks and dynamic organization structures to produce an unusual capacity to amass raw information, distill it into useful new knowledge, store this intelligence in common knowledge bases, and retrieve it from any part of the network.[14] The organization tree would provide the management system, and a distributed network of PCs would provide the

THE ORGANIZATION TREE.

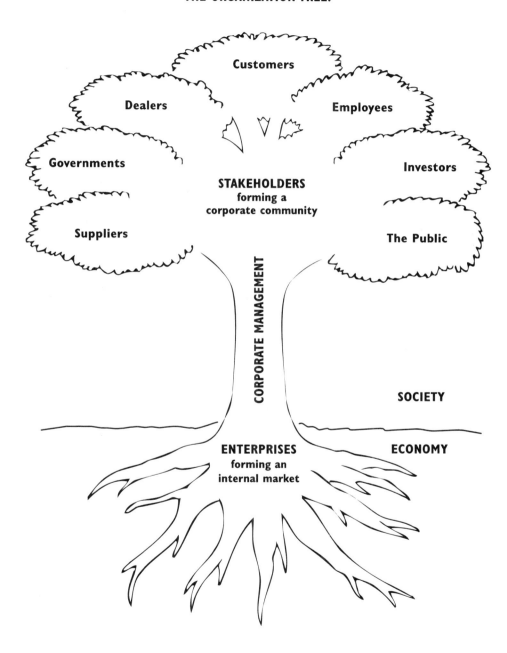

Customers

Dealers

Employees

Governments

Investors

STAKEHOLDERS
forming a
corporate community

Suppliers

The Public

CORPORATE MANAGEMENT

SOCIETY

ENTERPRISES
forming an
internal market

ECONOMY

information system. Microsoft's "Cairo," Novell's "Tuxedo," and other PC networks are now being developed for this purpose.

These systems should serve as the backbone of the intelligent organization, constituting a central nervous system that leverages ordinary learning into powerful new strategies for guiding a complex institution. If we carry this line of thought further, each individual or team becomes a node in the information network, which then forms a sort of "corporate brain" possessing powers of mass intelligence. A manager at Sun Microsystems described the concept this way: "The network is the computer."[15]

McGraw-Hill developed an early prototype that illustrates this concept nicely. The company works in industries that produce various forms of knowledge: publishing, information services, and so on. The CEO created a corporatewide information network, performance incentives, and training programs to engage all units in an "intellectual community," somewhat like a university or research lab. The central element in this system was a computerized knowledge base that pooled information gathered by the units; they could then draw on that information to serve their clients better. The system was aptly called an "information turbine" because it converted raw data into a stream of knowledge that "powered" the organization.

The ability to create this type of intelligent organization would have vast importance for creating effective strategic change. In an Industrial Age, competitive advantage went to companies that produced valuable goods effectively, but in an Information Age it will go to those who can produce valuable forms of *strategic knowledge* quickly and constantly.

An Organic Form of Strategic Management

The utility of these concepts lies in the insight they offer for creating an organic form of strategic management: an organization that combines the entrepreneurial creativity of internal markets, the political support of corporate stakeholders, and the knowledge-generating power of an intelligent infrastructure.

This organic approach is so dynamic that it transcends the change methods of the Old Management discussed above, but this does not mean that those methods have no use. On the contrary, as we noted in Chapter 1, the Old Management can play an effective role by being incorporated into the New Management. Here's how Andrew Grove, CEO of Intel, describes the role of planning in a flexible organization capable of rapid change:

> Let chaos reign, then reign in chaos. Does this mean you shouldn't plan? Not at all. . . . You plan by shaping a flexible organization capable of responding to unpredictable events.[16]

Consider how an organic form of management can overcome the drawbacks we described above for strategic planning, top-down change, and bottom-up learning.

Strategic planning will always be indispensable because it represents the problem-solving logic all organizations need to survive. As Michael Porter put it, "The questions that good planning seeks to answer . . . will never lose their relevance."[17] The need is to free planning so it is performed voluntarily by entrepreneurs throughout the organization, rather than centrally planned by bureaucrats. At GE, the former citadel of strategic planning, strategy formulation now consists of business units developing a one-page outline of critical issues and possible strategies for the next two years. Andrew Grove describes this approach as a natural part of everyday business: "People form strategy day in and day out as they respond, by virtue of the products they promote, the price concessions they make, the distribution channels they choose."[18]

This organic quality is seen in the intuitive, unpredictable way that managers make strategic decisions.[19] Formal planning methods may use a linear, rational process, but that is not how decision makers actually think. One manager told me that "strategic planning is what goes on inside the CEO's head." Strategic decisions are so complex that managers may take years to define the problem and reach a solution. They seek information and ideas from a variety of sources, continually cycle through the problem in a rather haphazard way until it begins to take shape, and finally reach a decision when all the pieces fit together into a coherent whole. Amar Bhide's study of strategic decision making among entrepreneurs found that only 28 percent develop a complete plan, 26 percent sketch out a rough plan, 5 percent work up financial projections alone, and 41 percent have no plan at all. Bhide concluded:

> Too much analysis can be harmful; by the time an opportunity is investigated fully, it may no longer exist. . . . The entrepreneur only does as much planning as seems useful and makes subjective judgements when necessary.[20]

This shows that strategic planning is as natural as ordinary learning, the search behavior of wild creatures struggling to survive, and all other forms of adaptive change. An effective organization helps its managers improve their own idiosyncratic approaches by developing intelligent information systems, internal markets, and a strong corporate community. These elements of the New Management assist operating managers by providing useful knowledge, entrepreneurial freedom, colleagues who can help, and the support of stakeholders who must make a venture succeed.

Likewise, top-down change is essential to redefine the corporate infrastructure, the corporate mission, and other broad elements of planning that are needed to guide business units. The difference is that this planning should be done democratically by some process that includes stakeholders and operating managers so that it is energized by the diverse views that every organization must reconcile. Box 8.1 describes how a public power company resolved crises by involving stakeholders in policy decisions. Listen to how the CEO, Peter Johnson, described the advantages:

> By inviting the public to participate, our adversaries helped us make better decisions. We gained authority and legitimacy, avoided costly lawsuits and political challenges, and arrived at creative solutions to seemingly intractable problems. Having seen our victories, I am convinced that public involvement is a tool that today's managers must understand. With external stakeholders now exerting substantial influence in every sector, conflict is inevitable. The only choice is whether to dodge the controversy or learn how to harness it.

Bottom-up learning is also essential to create effective teams, but it should be done by small autonomous business units as part of their strategy formulation to succeed in a market system. Box 8.2 describes the transformation at Xerox from a hierarchical structure into a loose association of self-managed, entrepreneurial business teams. Here's what the CEO, Paul Allaire, has to say about this approach to strategic change:

We have embarked on a process to [become] more entrepreneurial, more innovative, and more responsive to the marketplace. I envision a time when this company will consist of many small work groups . . . tied directly to the customer [with] the capability to design their own work processes and to adapt continuously as business conditions change.[21]

Note the common element that makes all of the above approaches effective. In each case, a method is used because all parties to a small enterprise chose it as a more useful way to manage their own affairs.

BOX 8.1. STRATEGIC CHANGE USING STAKEHOLDER POWER.

The Bonneville Power Administration (BPA) was once managed in a traditional way, which the agency head described: "I viewed conflict with people outside the company as an annoyance. Those of us on the inside knew we were capable of making good decisions and made every effort to explain our reasoning. We were essentially telling people that we knew what was best for them. Meanwhile they were telling us that the father-knows-best approach is unacceptable." Here's what happened later:

The Formation of Working Relations. BPA began an ambitious program to engage its critics in direct discussions. Managers invited input from anyone; they held public hearings, adopted suggestions (such as moving transmission lines), released internal reports and "issue alerts" to the media on upcoming decisions, and even met with environmental "crazies." After these demonstrations of sincerity, frank, tension-free discussions could be held on any topic.

Saving the Aluminum Industry. When the Washington Public Power Supply System (WPPSS) failed, energy rates leaped eightfold, threatening the local aluminum industry, which depended on cheap power. BPA formed a committee representing utilities, local governments, the aluminum companies, labor unions, and private citizens. After dozens of meetings, attended by a total of 4,600 people, a consensus was reached that saved the industry, jobs, and the local economy, and established newfound legitimacy for BPA.

Reconciliation on Nuclear Power. When construction of two nuclear plants stalled due to political opposition, losses totaling hundreds of millions of dollars had to be absorbed by public and private utilities. BPA held meetings with both groups, which at first greeted them with "hoots and hollers," but finally reached a settlement that satisfied all parties.

Source: Peter Johnson, "How I Turned a Critical Public into Useful Consultants," *Harvard Business Review* (January-February 1993).

Whether it is a unit manager planning his or her internal enterprise, the board of directors guiding a corporation, or a small work team managing its operations, good strategic management is an entrepreneurial, collaborative process of problem solving that may at times involve the use of strategic planning, top-down change, organizational learning, or any other approach.

Most organizations are moving toward this organic form of strategic management as unit managers are freed to pursue their own strategies, assisted by a corporate planning process and committed executives (see Table 8.2). We also find wide variation in the way different individuals and organizations go about it. Some feel the need to define a creative mission; others forecast the environment; many focus on resolving critical issues;

BOX 8.2. STRATEGIC CHANGE USING MARKET POWER.

CEO Paul Allaire set out to transform Xerox from a traditional hierarchy producing copiers into an entrepreneurial, market-driven system dedicated to the creation, storage, and transmittal of reports, financial records, and all other types of "documents." He described the task this way: "The change we are making will alter completely the way this company is managed."

Managing the Change Process. A "Future Architecture Team" of Xerox's best managers and employees was organized to plan the transition. They surveyed the field for concepts and examples, studied various alternative structures, and passed their recommendations on for discussion and implementation.

Nine Independent Business Divisions. The major change was to move from a staff-driven structure to a product-driven structure in order to respond quickly to the flurry of new technologies being spewed out by the Information Revolution. Nine business divisions have been organized as profit centers that produce products for different markets. These divisions, in turn, have dozens of smaller business teams to serve particular customer needs. Additionally, over a dozen other new products are being developed by small Xerox subsidiaries.

Performance Incentives. To motivate entrepreneurship, a plan has been set up that rewards 2,000 people with annual bonuses based on their performance at team, division, and corporate levels. Allaire explains the logic: "We want people to think in terms of their individual units, but also in terms of the company as a whole."

Sources: Robert Howard, "The CEO as Organizational Architect," *Harvard Business Review* (September-October 1992); "Redesigning the Corporation," *Enterprise* (January 1994).

still others simply turn their intuition free to think creatively; some strive to design new products and ventures; and others prefer training and education.[22] No single approach is best because the optimum type of planning should be chosen by the unit to suit its special needs.

Whatever the approach, the central idea is to create a fluid, organic form of strategic problem solving to be used freely by all units from the corporate boardroom to the blue-collar workbenches. *If managers hope to thrive in a world of constant, massive change, strategic management will have to be built on the New Management foundation of internal markets and corporate community to create an organic organization.* The outcome would combine the power of both top-down leadership and widespread participation, constant learning in entrepreneurial units, and voluntary planning everywhere.

This approach offers no panaceas, certainly. Transforming institutions into this type of system is itself a challenge, and helping people manage themselves in a democratic, entrepreneurial way is always difficult. These

TABLE 8.2. ADOPTION OF CONTINUOUS CHANGE PRACTICES.
(SAMPLE = 426 CORPORATE MANAGERS.)

Practice	Not Practiced (0–3)	Partially Practiced (4–6)	Fully Practiced (7–10)	Mean (0–10)
A formal strategic planning process is conducted periodically to determine how corporate strategy should respond to technological advances, economic conditions, social attitudes, and other critical issues.	11%	20%	69%	7.2
Unit managers are free to pursue their own strategies for their units.	18	32	50	6.0
Top management encourages major structural changes when they are needed.	12	16	72	7.3
Means	14%	23%	63%	6.8

Source: William E. Halal, *Corporations in Transition* (an unpublished study in progress). Note that data in the first three columns ("Not Practiced," etc.) are aggregated by collapsing portions of the questionnaire scale as shown ("0–3," etc.). See the questionnaire in Appendix C.

issues of leadership are addressed in the next chapter. What the concept can realistically hope to achieve, however, is to inject a vital flow of fresh opinion and disciplined action into today's bureaucracies—in sum, to connect them with the forces of creative destruction in their environment.

CONTROL OF LIVING ORGANIZATIONS

Effective strategic management, then, cannot be simply sophisticated planning, bold leadership from brilliant CEOs, or enlightened people working in teams. These will only be useful if they are part of a dramatically different organic institution expressly designed to produce strategic change rapidly, effectively, and continuously. The head of the Xerox Palo Alto Research Center said, "The most important invention that will come out of the corporate research lab in the future will be the corporation itself."[23]

Constant Responses Everywhere to External Forces

I don't think we appreciate the full implications of what these organic systems would be like. Truly organic organizations will not be simply "flexible," "empowered," or otherwise "better." They will be as fully alive as a colony of bees, a tree, or a market. Only living systems operating on self-organizing principles will be able to sustain themselves through the whirlwind ahead.[24]

The most distinguishing, and perhaps the most troubling, feature is that they will have to operate beyond the control of management. One can control a machine and a hierarchical organization, but not a bee colony, a tree, or a market. Even if one could, it would defeat the organic system's purpose because its very nature is to adapt through a free flow of creative responsiveness. Think of the Internet; who could possibly control this vast ocean of communication? Kevin Kelley, editor of *Wired* magazine, described the outcome of today's race to information networks that will soon merge into a global web of commerce:

> As we unleash living forces into our machines, we lose control over them. . . . This is the dilemma. [Humans] can no longer be sovereign over their finest creations. . . . [Systems] will become autonomous, adaptable, and creative but, consequently, out of our control. I think that's a great bargain.[25]

Indeed, some of the corporations I've worked with did lose control of innovative practices. One firm showed a burst of vitality after moving to a market system that spawned numerous ventures, but poor control of the risks resulted in serious business failures. This problem might have been avoided with stronger leadership, but it illustrates both the challenge and the potential that are involved. Organizational freedom unleashes great reservoirs of creative energy, and this energy must be carefully channeled into constructive avenues.

When I claim that the New Management represents a source of greater power, I am not being rhetorical. The introduction of democracy and enterprise will charge today's organizations with new life, and managers will have to learn to guide this life more carefully. The task should be comparable to operating a nuclear reactor. Enormous power is available to serve useful purposes, but pull the rods out too far and the reaction will run out of control.

This does not mean that organic organizations will be out of control in the sense of behaving in wild, unpredictable ways. It means that the locus of control will move out of the hands of top executives so that it can be shared by operating managers, workers, clients, and others who are involved. An organic organization can be under far more *effective* control because decisions are made throughout the system by people close to the action.

The strength of an organic system is that it is more sensitive to the need for change because control is exercised constantly all about in response to the ebb and flow of environmental forces. People ordinarily resist change, not because they are obstinate, but because they are fearful when change is forced on them. If change originates *from* them, however, they can accept it because they are in control of their lives. Many thrive on self-created change because it gives them a sense of mastery over their future.

We like to think that leaders bring about change, especially in business, where dynamic executives are admired for their ability to take charge of corporations and turn them around. Managers certainly strive to formulate strategies by introducing new products and changing their organizations. But these are more like the random mutations that Darwinian evolution presents when searching for an adaptive fit between the organism and its environment. The fact is that managers face such uncertainty in trying to survive a turbulent world that their efforts often amount to an informed gamble, almost as though they were placing bets. Out of all the diverse strategies that various companies devise, the environment selects those that represent a functional advantage.

For instance, Paul Allaire is reviving Xerox only by accepting the fact that analog photocopiers have been made obsolete by the digitalization of data, and the company was then able to define a new product line based on digital documents. Think of other recent changes—the fall of Communism, the environmental crisis, the rise of a global economy. We can't possibly control these historic turning points, but we can use their power.

Facing Uncertainty

Here's what this chapter has concluded about the critical need for a more effective approach to strategic change:

1. Organizations are like other organisms in that they are dependent on their surroundings for all resources and information.

2. Most attempts to create strategic change fail because they use mechanistic elements of the Old Management that isolate organizations from environmental forces.

3. The New Management incorporates an organic approach to strategic change because internal markets, corporate community, and an intelligent infrastructure integrate the organization into the external forces that drive change.

4. Managers will have to learn to control these organic systems in subtle ways that influence and guide their self-organizing behavior.

Acknowledging that we are not in full control may provoke anxiety, but it will also make management a far more exciting, creative adventure. I know my experience managing aerospace projects, business start-ups, conferences, and even the publication of books has always been "organic." When contemplating a new venture, I may try to "plan" it in the sense of estimating its feasibility, the obstacles ahead, and other concerns. But once under way, every important project I have ever accomplished has taken on an unpredictable life of its own.

Managing a new venture is like giving birth to a child. One creates this living creature, and it then takes over to run its own life. I have the sense that I am not in charge of the venture, but the venture is in charge of me. I have unwittingly become its servant, holding on for dear life as it roars ahead. Yet somehow things usually work out just about as they should. If the venture is not a great success, I find there were good reasons that I can learn from. But most often I am amazed at the good fortune I receive. Despite my fears, the right people seem to appear at the right time, events unfold in ways I could not have imagined, and crises usually turn out to be blessings in disguise.

By learning to face the inevitable reality that management involves huge amounts of uncertainty, we may find the awareness needed to influence those wispy forces in the environment that shape events, and we would certainly be better prepared to react when they surprise us. All those external energies that now pose such threats to our sense of control could then possibly be used to move projects ahead. Just as the martial arts convert the strength of an aggressor to one's benefit, this ability to connect more solidly with that invisible, fleeting, often mysterious environment may allow managers to convert its external threats to their strategic advantage.

Notes

1. Although the United States spends more per capita than any nation, longevity, child mortality, and other health indices are only average. Forty million Americans with no insurance use expensive emergency clinics for their routine care, which we all pay for. Those who are covered have no incentive to reduce costs, and there is little comparative information available to guide choices anyway. These problems have increased health costs to 14 percent of GNP, and expenditures could reach 20 percent soon, as the population ages.
2. Eli Ginsberg, *Medical Gridlock and Health Reform* (Boulder, Colo.: Westview Press, 1994), C. Everett Koop, "The Health Care Mess," *Newsweek* (August 28, 1989).
3. See Michael Rothschild, "Why Health Reform Died," *Wall Street Journal* (September 22, 1994).
4. Kathryn Troy, *Change Management* (New York: The Conference Board, 1994). *Reinventing America,* a special issue of *BusinessWeek* (1992).
5. Peter Vaill, *Managing as a Performing Art* (San Francisco: Jossey-Bass, 1991).

6. William E. Halal, "Strategic Management: The State-of-the-Art & Beyond," *Technological Forecasting & Social Change* (May 1984).

7. Walter Kiechel, "Corporate Strategists Under Fire," *Fortune* (December 27, 1982).

8. See Daniel Gray, "Uses and Misuses of Strategic Planning," and Robert Hayes, "Why Strategic Planning Goes Awry," In Arthur A. Thompson, Jr., et al. (eds.), *Readings in Strategic Management* (Homewood, Ill.: Irwin, 1990). Also see Ian Wilson, "The State of Strategic Planning," *Technological Forecasting & Social Change* (1990), Vol. 37.

9. A good summary of the current state of the art is John Kotter's "Leading Change," *Harvard Business Review* (March-April 1995).

10. Noel M. Tichy, "Revolutionize Your Company," *Fortune* (December 13, 1994).

11. Frank Swoboda, "Up Against the Wall," *Washington Post* (February 27, 1994).

12. Dana Priest, "Where Health Care Reform Effort Failed," *Washington Post* (September 15, 1994). Brian O'Reilly, "Agee in Exile," *Fortune* (May 29, 1995).

13. Peter Senge, *The Fifth Discipline* (New York: Doubleday, 1990).

14. Gifford and Elizabeth Pinchot, *The End of Bureaucracy and the Rise of the Intelligent Organization* (San Francisco: Berrett-Koehler, 1994).

15. Brent Schendler, "What Bill Gates Really Wants," *Fortune* (January 16, 1995).

16. Andrew Grove, "From the Front," *Fortune* (September 18, 1995).

17. Michael Porter, "The State of Strategic Thinking," *The Economist* (May 23, 1987).

18. Ronald Henkoff, "How to Plan for 1995," *Fortune* (December 31, 1990).

19. William E. Halal, *Strategic Planning* (College Park: University of Maryland, 1991).

20. Amar Bhide, "How Entrepreneurs Craft Strategy," *Harvard Business Review* (March-April 1994).

21. Robert Howard, "The CEO as Organizational Architect: An Interview with Paul Allaire," *Harvard Business Review* (September-October 1992), pp. 107–121.

22. See John Bryson, *Strategic Planning for Public and Nonprofit Organizations* (San Francisco: Jossey-Bass, 1988).

23. John Seely Brown, "Research That Reinvents the Corporation," *Harvard Business Review* (January-February 1991).

24. Michael Rothschild, *Bionomics* (New York: Holt, 1990).

25. Kevin Kelley, *Out of Control* (Reading, Mass.: Addison-Wesley, 1994), p. 4.

9

Inner Leadership

How to Handle the Coming Power Shift

Reading the previous chapters, you've probably wondered how in the world managers like yourself are going to accomplish all these difficult innovations. The ideas may make sense, but how will you restructure today's bureaucracies into market systems? Unite diverse interest groups into a political coalition? Reorient sales to serving people? Organize work teams that manage themselves? Transform operations so that they are ecologically benign? And keep this entire system constantly adaptive to change?

You are not going to do it using authority, but by drawing out the talents of others. I was privileged to witness a vivid demonstration of this type of leadership when visiting a manufacturing company. In contrast to the antagonism between various groups that was once rife in industry, this organization had learned to work together by confronting its differences in a constructive spirit. Seated at a conference table were managers, labor leaders, suppliers, distributors, and even officials from the local government. Most striking was that the president of the company did not seem a particularly imposing person. He had no commanding presence, was not a genius, and showed little charisma. How, I wondered, did he manage to pull this diverse group of big egos together into a harmonious team?

As the meeting progressed, it became apparent that this was a different type of leader. He saw his role as encouraging the talents of the people in the organization, and so he rarely spoke himself but was more intent on asking others for their views. Remarkably, he really listened. Unlike almost all other leaders one usually meets, this man was genuinely humble in the sense that he focused on understanding the reality of the situation. It was like a breath of fresh air! A leader who cares what people really think? Who wants to hear the messy truth? Who does not impose his solutions? Surely this was either a ruse or it didn't work, I thought.

But it did work. It energized the meeting. People brought out their problems, their ideas, their doubts, their misunderstandings, and all the other hidden agendas we normally keep contained within us. The president simply asked an occasional question, made a few suggestions for the group to consider, and tried to clarify what they were doing. Otherwise, the group controlled the meeting. Most importantly, the meeting affirmed that this was their organization. They were responsible for its success or failure, so they did whatever was needed to make it work.

OK, this humble approach really works, but what about the leader, I worried? He was obviously not "in charge," and in fact he seemed a bit awkward and uncomfortable at times. Little wonder when people would say harsh things directly to him, such as complain about some aspect of the company and criticize his behavior occasionally. They even called him by his first name! How could he possibly maintain his dignity and self-respect, much less the power needed to be effective?

Beneath this appearance of casual disregard was a deep sense of respect and affection. Not because this leader held the power of the president, but precisely for the opposite reason. He had voluntarily yielded his authority. The heart of this relationship was that the president was genuinely concerned about the needs of the people in that organization, and he provided a subtle, supportive guidance that helped them find the way ahead. Ironically, by giving up his formal power, he was given far more real power. They would do things for this man that no ordinary boss could even ask for.

He was not simply another member of the team, however. At times he had to bear the responsibility for taking some difficult action on their behalf, such as asking for discipline or bringing up a serious issue. But because he was a true leader rather than a boss, he was able to do this with their willing support, rather like a "servant leader" or a "good father."

This is only one example, of course, of the many different ways that good leaders work. But I think it highlights a key principle of leadership today: *In a world of escalating complexity and empowered people, leaders must cultivate the art of helping others to share the responsibilities of management.* And the price of their support is to relinquish that comfortable old sense of control.

Genuine participation is an intense, creative act in which people step out of their comfortable roles to engage their differences. If this painful exploration can be sustained through its twists and turns, a new clarity of awareness, or a "vision," may be given us to guide the way ahead. Because this process involves nurturing an expanded sense of awareness, it can be said to be "spiritual." Participative leadership, then, is the fusion of human spirits that releases new energy and vision.

This chapter explores this inner dimension of management in which participative leadership occurs. We begin by clarifying the illusive nature of power to show that both leaders and followers mutually shape each others' awareness. Then we examine how a historic shift to a form of shared power is under way today that exposes all of us to stress and uncertainty. But if leaders can draw on their inner resources to keep the organization alert in the midst of problems and crises, creative solutions may emerge beyond the powers of either the leader or the followers.

THE CHANGING ILLUSION OF POWER

Whenever people discuss leadership, attention invariably gravitates to that illusive issue of power. The very essence of leadership is to get others to do something, so leaders must focus on the skillful use of power, influence, or whatever one chooses to call this force that propels action. Warren Bennis put it this way: "Leadership is the wise use of power."[1]

In this broader sense, everyone acts as a leader. Under some circumstances, we all try to influence our co-workers, bosses, spouses, children, and other relationships. Thus, power is an everpresent reality, since people always attempt to exert influence, and the result of all this mutual influence is what social scientists call "the social construction of reality." Power is not some fixed, official authority held by one person, but a changing, somewhat arbitrary way of organizing society—an illusion.

This fluid nature of power is seen in the wide variation it takes. In the example at the beginning of this chapter, for instance, the company president showed that power can easily be shared with followers if they feel committed to the leader or the organization. In fact, this benign type of power is usually far more influential because people feel united by a common sense of personal empowerment. Witness the mutual empowerment shared by great leaders and their followers: Gandhi and his Indian countrymen, Martin Luther King, Jr., and his black brothers and sisters, Pope John Paul II and the Catholic Church.

Such examples are fairly common because people want to feel a sense of their own power. Psychologists identify this as a healthy drive to be effectual, to have an impact on the world, and to see one's actions as meaningful. This need can be perverted into "dominance," of course, which is why an open, aggressive drive for power is often taboo in society. But we should acknowledge that all people have a healthy need to feel powerful and to influence others.

Power Is an Inner Experience

The widespread, changing pursuit of power is, however, often accompanied by conflict, confusion, and doubt, largely because it is so often a forbidden subject and is usually pursued alone and in silence.

A few years ago when I was a consultant to a major company, I experienced an exhilarating but painful lesson in the ways of power that helps clarify this problem. I had been asked to advise their managers about the New Management, and they were intrigued to see that a more effective type of corporation could be developed using these principles. I was then asked to help implement this concept in their operations.

Well, you can imagine that I was flying high at the prospect of seeing my ideas brought to life. It made me realize the attraction—no, the addiction, that grips those who taste great power. Using one's abilities to sway the opinion of others is a heady, delicious feeling. In contrast to the struggle of daily life, power conveys a sense of mastery over our environment. As the political TV talk show host John McLaughlin put it, "Power is an experience as intense as sex."

But the story gets better. The company asked me to conduct a project that required gaining the support of twenty-five other big corporations. When the project was completed, I organized a meeting of all the managers to discuss the results. At the meeting, I strode to the podium savoring the thrill of accomplishment, made some brief remarks, and noted that this project had succeeded because they had all worked together cooperatively.

Unfortunately, I made the mistake of taking my observations too far by saying that they should develop a similar cooperative spirit with their employees, customers, and other stakeholders. Suddenly, looking out at all those faces, I felt waves of resentment flowing toward me. They rightly felt that I was misusing my role to lecture them. When the full force of their anger hit, I was plunged into the nightmare that haunts speakers, a panic attack. In front of all those important people who I had wanted to impress, I just stood there, wordless, unable to find a way out of my terror. It was only a few seconds really, but it seemed like an endless ordeal.

I describe both the highs and the lows of this experience, even though they are both embarrassing in different ways, to illustrate how deeply we often experience the use of power. Think of a time when you handled a tough interpersonal situation well and felt a glowing sense of achievement or when you mishandled a situation and felt the power drain from you. Such deep feelings are common because jousting in the arena of power is a fact of life, and today the game is played at a psychic level as we test our beliefs, knowledge, and will against one another. It would be great if we could all work together cooperatively, but that does not happen very often.

Entire libraries have been written on leadership traits, styles, and skills to clarify these murky matters.[2] This "outer" view, focusing on the leader's *behavior*, is useful, but it misses the *inner reality* from which power emanates. In the experience described above, my outer behavior and that of my audience makes no sense without understanding the inner forces at work: my pushy need to change these managers, their sense of resentment, my fearful reaction in the panic attack, and so on. Here's how Robert Rabbin, head of a consulting firm that helps managers cultivate this type of inner understanding, describes it:

> Learning about awareness teaches us that life is actually an "inside job." Our experiences and abilities are an imprint of our awareness. . . . The quality of our awareness determines the quality of our life and actions.[3]

The Coming Shift in Power Structures

The inner domain of leadership is becoming especially important now because a historic shift in the use of power is disrupting the old relationship between leaders and followers.

Figure 9.1 illustrates the evolution of power over the long term, showing how the dominant form of leadership has changed in response to two central factors. As noted in Chapter 6, increasingly complex technologies create a fundamental advance in the economic foundation of work, which, in turn, drives the prevailing culture toward higher-order values. The result has been a slow but steady increase in freedom at each stage of development: from the absolute rule of feudal lords, to the authority of industrial bosses, to the human relations leaders of today's service economy, and soon, to self-managed teams of knowledge workers.[4] This is only a general tendency, of course, but a quick scan of history bears out this trend.

Agrarian societies are usually marked by autocratic leaders because these are primitive cultures in which people do simple work and live at a subsistence level. It is no coincidence that most undeveloped nations are still governed by kings and dictators.

Industrialization generally moves power up a notch to the use of formal authority for instructing profit maximizers—"economic men"—at routine jobs. Industrial bosses did not rule by sheer force, but developed a rational form of control to manage factories efficiently.

As automation replaced industrial jobs, a service society developed in the 1950s to focus on personal services. Because work was mainly concerned with managing social relationships among white-collar employees harmoniously, a "human relations" style of leadership emerged. The leader was still in charge but had to cultivate a warm emotional atmosphere among a unified corporate family. This model generally prevails in most organizations today.

Now, as robots and information systems automate factories and offices, teams of skilled professionals must manage complex business ventures, solve technical problems, and probe the boundaries of a knowledge economy. Not only are economies becoming unusually complex, a more educated, sophisticated breed of knowledge worker is appearing that is motivated by achievement, creativity, and, especially, control over their work.

FIGURE 9.1. THE EVOLUTION OF LEADERSHIP.

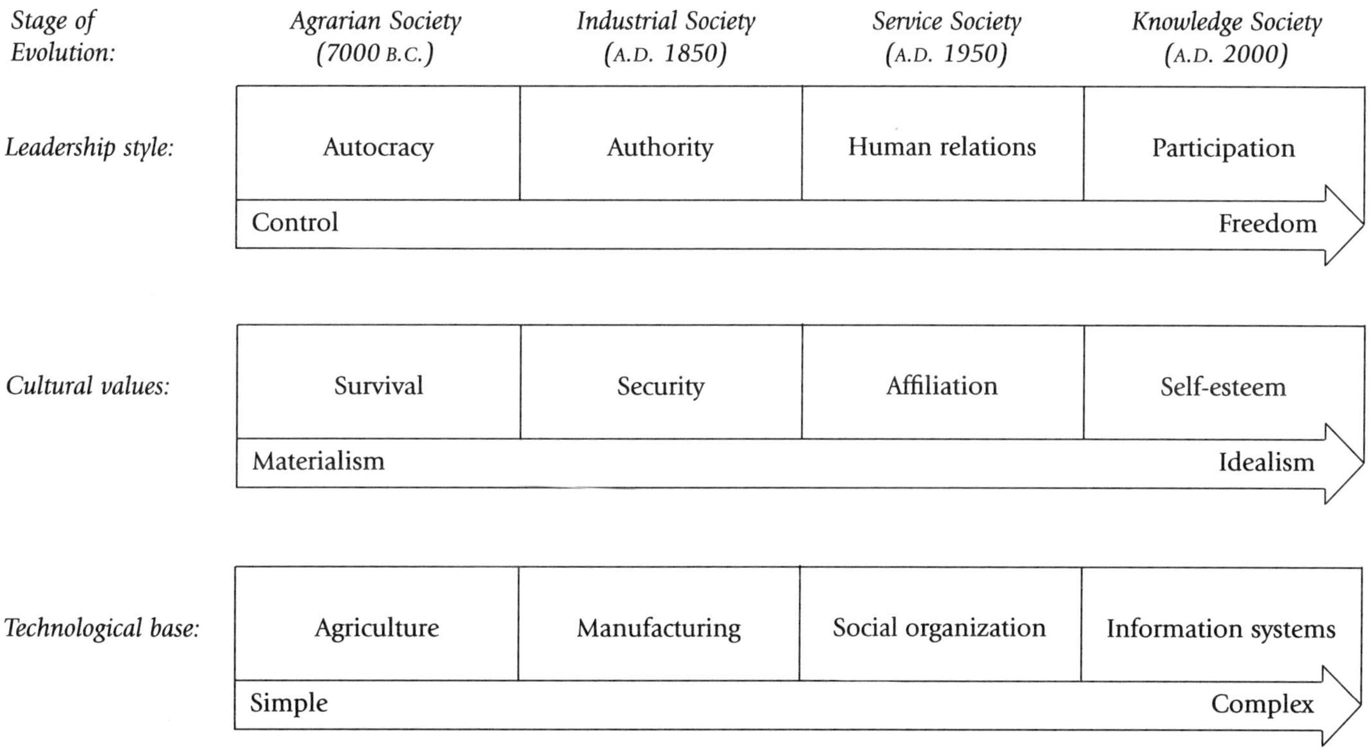

Stage of Evolution:	Agrarian Society (7000 B.C.)	Industrial Society (A.D. 1850)	Service Society (A.D. 1950)	Knowledge Society (A.D. 2000)
Leadership style:	Autocracy	Authority	Human relations	Participation
	Control →			→ Freedom
Cultural values:	Survival	Security	Affiliation	Self-esteem
	Materialism →			→ Idealism
Technological base:	Agriculture	Manufacturing	Social organization	Information systems
	Simple →			→ Complex

The result: a historic upheaval in power structures is under way. Jack Welch, CEO of GE, summed up the need: "In a [world] where we must have every good idea from every man and woman, we cannot afford management styles that suppress and intimidate." Frank Doyle, GE's vice president for human resources, added: "Power in the nineties will be people power. Power will go to employees with adaptable minds and flexible skills." Here's how Alvin Toffler described the coming power shift:

> The entire structure of power that held the world together is now disintegrating [due to] the rise of a radical new system for wealth creation in which information plays a dominant role. The essence of the new economy is innovation.[5]

This power shift amounts to a peaceful revolution that could prove as unsettling as the great revolutions that created modern democracy in the United States and Europe. Even now employees are gaining control over their time schedules, they often have access to the company's financial records, determine how to perform their jobs, choose co-workers and suppliers, challenge unjust firings, and even evaluate their superiors.[6] As power moves to workers, how will managers guide all this raw energy into useful directions?

Rise of the Informal Organization

These demands for sharing power are likely to prove emotionally volatile. The problem can be understood by comparing the "formal" and "informal" levels of organization to the "conscious" and "unconscious" levels of human thought. From a systems perspective, both organizations and individuals manifest outward behavior that seems rational. For most of us, the conscious level of thought seems fairly coherent, and most organizations appear to be managed in an orderly fashion. But beneath the surface of both systems lies a sea of turbulent energy.

The unconscious level of thought comprises that inner domain of fantasy and primal urges, which Sigmund Freud identified as lying deep within the human mind. Its counterpart in management is the informal organization that the Hawthorne studies discovered at roughly the same time Freud's work was gaining influence. It is the unofficial, hidden, and somewhat zany way organizations actually behave beneath the formal surface:

the bootlegged jobs and "skunk works," unofficial leaders, the grapevine, and all of the other natural, raw behavior that emerges spontaneously within any social system.[7]

A popular example of the informal organization is at the heart of the famous movie and TV series *M*A*S*H*. Two surgeons, Hawkeye and BJ, make bathtub gin to tolerate the horrors of war. The company clerk, Radar, actually runs the unit because the CO, Colonel Blake, is always busy fishing. And everyone accepts the fact that one of the medical corpsmen, Klinger, is a cross-dresser. Yet the bizarre behavior of this military unit somehow has a logic of its own that allows its members to work together effectively.

Although managers know that informal activity goes on underground, today's power shift is causing the informal level to surface. As authoritarian control yields to participation, the informal organization rises to challenge the formal system. Educated employees insist on controlling their work. Customers make greater demands for quality and service. Major investors replace CEOs.

The problem is especially visible on the communication networks that will soon dominate. In the Internet, great time and energy is devoted to "flaming" because the anonymity of networks brings out the hidden impulses in people. When personality clashes occur, people often unleash those impulses, spewing bile in cyberspace. The same happens in business. One CEO convened an "electronic meeting" to spur open discussion, only to see top management attacked so viciously that he had to pull the plug.[8]

The saving feature is that this rise of the informal organization also presents a vast new source of creative energy. In fact, this union of the formal and informal organizations is what makes the New Management "organic." Hal Hinson, a journalist, has claimed that "we are on the brink of a renaissance of spirit that will make the '60s look like a dress rehearsal. The signs of this cultural revolution are everywhere."[9] The signs can be seen in the "liberated" women who pursue careers; the "men's movement" that aims to nurture male sensibilities; and a wave of interest in spirituality. *Fortune* said of this perspective: "The new paradigm puts people at the center of the universe."[10]

Obviously, managers will have to be far more skillful to direct this raw energy into productive directions. They will have to shed their mask of authority to meet people directly, facing all the stinging criticism, outrageous demands, and other displays of human nature that have been suppressed by authoritarian controls. And employees will be equally unsettled at seeing that managers are not really demigods with all the answers but fallible humans like themselves; they will then have to assume the responsibilities that managers are being asked to relinquish. With managers and employees stripped of their old illusions, both parties may then be able to settle in for the hard but realistic task of making participation work.

PRINCIPLES OF INNER LEADERSHIP

As illustrated in this chapter's opening example, the participative leader plays a neutral role of facilitating a shared decision-making process: encouraging open discussion, clarifying issues and resolving conflicts, summarizing key themes, and drawing out a satisfactory conclusion. Table 9.1 shows that managers generally accept the need for participation now, and it is even being practiced in politics. Oregon's Governor Barbara Roberts organized a "Conversation with Oregon" program in 1992 using widespread opinion polls and electronic town meetings to engage citizens in a public debate over crucial state issues.[11]

TABLE 9.1. ADOPTION OF PARTICIPATION PRACTICES.
(SAMPLE = 426 CORPORATE MANAGERS.)

Practice	Not Practiced (0–3)	Partially Practiced (4–6)	Fully Practiced (7–10)	Mean (0–10)
The leadership style of management is participative in most respects.	13%	24%	63%	6.9
The corporate mission is well-defined and generally accepted.	8	20	72	7.5
Major decisions and disagreements are discussed openly among those concerned to reach consensus.	11	20	69	6.7
Means	11%	23%	66%	7.1

Source: William E. Halal, *Corporations in Transition* (an unpublished study in progress). Note that data in the first three columns ("Not Practiced," etc.) are aggregated by collapsing portions of the questionnaire scale as shown ("0–3," etc.). See the questionnaire in Appendix C.

While the concept is simple, its execution is surprisingly difficult because the outcome may be so trying that it tests the skill of the best leader. That's why managers continually agonize over the problem of getting employees to assume responsibility for their behavior. There is no really good solution, obviously, but the following sections describe the benefits of learning to live with problems, to listen for understanding, and to trust one's inner wisdom.

These approaches make even better sense when we see that they reflect the themes of democracy and enterprise running through the New Management. The purpose of participation is twofold. One goal is to engage knowledgeable parties in managing the organization more effectively; this "enterprise" dimension requires a sharp focus on problem solving and accountability for performance. The other purpose is to ensure that members of the corporate community are involved so that the outcome reflects their interests; this "democratic" dimension leads to the need for listening carefully to one another and to our inner wisdom as well.

Living with Problems and Crises

As the routine work of the Industrial Age yields to the complex demands of the Information Age, the very essence of work is increasingly concerned with problem solving on a regular, continuing basis. After all, the purpose of a knowledge economy is to gain better information and to use it in solving problems more effectively. Thus, managers today must accept the reality that the central task of their organization is to live with problems.

Now, this is tough because problems are usually defined in negative terms. They are seen as deviations from the normal order and satisfaction we want, bringing instead the stress and confusion we try to avoid. Managers who responded to the CIT survey described the typical situation this way: "Problems are not openly addressed, which causes much dissension," and "Disagreements frequently escalate and have to be taken behind closed doors."

However, problems are actually natural events in the process of change. A crisis in some institution, for instance, highlights the limits of the system so that all can see their dangerous significance in stark clarity, thereby mobilizing opinion to move the system to its next stage of development. The United States is a crisis-driven society because acting on crisis is practical. It would be nice if crises could be averted, but that requires unusual foresight and it would not trigger the attention needed to drive serious change.

Moreover, problems are prevalent because the world is passing through a period of upheaval, so it is only realistic to accept this turbulent state of affairs and learn to live with it gracefully. We might then find that living with problems has its benefits. One of the greatest testaments to the powers of the human spirit is the remarkable way people find the courage not only to endure but also to find meaning in poverty, failure, and even terminal illness.[12] We may never enjoy problems, but they help us shed our preconceptions about the world so that we may accept reality instead.

I was shocked at the election of Ronald Reagan in 1980 because it violated my liberal instincts. But after pondering the meaning of this crucial vote, I came to see the debilitating problem of big government and the fundamental importance of individual freedom. This crisis in my intellectual life has proven central to my present focus on synthesizing liberal and conservative philosophies. Indeed, this book would be far weaker if I had avoided facing the meaning of the "Reagan Revolution."

Thus, problems serve the essential purpose of demanding that we learn to cope with a complex world. They force us to grow in character and wisdom. Without problems, we would remain children, and our institutions would be primitive, boring places, rather than the exciting arenas of action they are today. The New Management challenges us to accept problems as an essential part of creative work. Rather than resist their demands, problems can be welcomed as an invigorating discipline from which we can draw strength.

One of the most effective lectures I've ever given was delivered during a personal crisis. My infant son was in intensive care, struggling to survive the threat of a grave disease. I have never been so terrified in my life, but I had a class to teach and thought it might help divert my mind from this ordeal. I felt numb going to the classroom, yet once there an extraordinary calmness carried me through the meeting. Because I had transcended my normal worries about doing a good job, the lecture went far better than I could have imagined. Without trying or thinking, point after point flowed between me and my students, back and forth in a gentle, accurate rhythm that left us all a little high.

My son survived and is fine now. I learned that there is a small center of peace within even the most devastating ordeal, a place where we must surrender our will to events beyond our control, hopefully to be cared for by some higher power. This must be the way John Kennedy felt during the Cuban missile crisis as he waited to see whether the Soviets would start World War III.

Creative managers go through a similar process. Springfield Manufacturing faced the loss of a contract that threatened to idle one-third of its labor force. As Box 9.1 shows, the CEO took the decision to his employees, and after a grueling year of all-out effort, they avoided layoffs and gained a sense of purpose. In Box 9.2, William Peace (I am not making this name up) finds that confronting sensitive problems produces surprising benefits, even though he is often embarrassed and pained by the experience.

Feeling vulnerable is increasingly common because nobody really knows how to handle the upheaval of the Knowledge Revolution. Yes, a few

---

BOX 9.1. SPRINGFIELD MANUFACTURING'S MOMENT OF TRUTH.

Springfield Manufacturing was thriving due to a large contract with General Motors. Suddenly, GM cancelled its plans to have 5,000 engines rebuilt, threatening to lay off one-third of Springfield's 500-person work force. After agonizing over the crisis, Jack Stack, Springfield's CEO, thought, "Why am I sitting here trying to make this decision for all these people? They should decide for themselves."

The Companywide Decision. The CEO called a companywide meeting at which he explained the situation as candidly as possible, pointing out the alternatives. If Springfield did not carry out layoffs and was unable to generate 50,000 hours of new work, the resulting loss of income would require laying off even more people. The unanimous decision was to "go for it."

The Struggle. The entire workforce struggled to bring in new work, venturing into products and markets unknown to them. People worked such long hours under stress that some broke down in tears. But the result was an increase in revenue over the previous year.

The Realization. The CEO realized that the company might have died if it had accepted the layoffs and that he was right to have taken the decision to the workers: "I couldn't make the decision myself. It was their future. Maybe that's why we're here. I'd felt for a long time this company ran on divine intervention, that there are higher laws in this world we don't understand."

Source: Jack Stack, "Crisis Management by Committee," *Inc.* (May 1988).

BOX 9.2. THE HARD WORK OF BEING A SOFT MANAGER.

William Peace calls his approach to leadership being a "soft manager": "I try my best to be tentative, and I cherish my own fair share of human frailty. Openness, candor, sensitivity, and a willingness to suffer painful consequences are productive management approaches. Being vulnerable to the give-and-take of emotional cross fire and intellectual disagreement makes us more human, more credible, and more open to change."

Facing People You Have to Lay Off. As a general manager of a Westinghouse division, Peace had to lay off fifteen people. Rather than have a staff member tell them, he told them himself. "It was without a doubt one of the most painful meetings I've ever attended. Yet, I felt a certain new closeness to those people." Later he noticed the remaining employees seemed determined and cheerful, and when he had an opportunity to rehire the fifteen fired workers, they all came back in good spirits. "I am more and more convinced that the 'success' of that meeting was due to the fact that it made me vulnerable to the criticism and anger of the people we laid off."

Confronting Union Opposition. On an occasion of union conflict, Peace held a meeting with the union membership to ask for support. The presentation was a nightmare. They heckled him mercilessly, they shouted abuse and threats. But later he was treated with respect. "They would listen to what I had to say—really listen." Because he opened himself to criticism, people were inclined to believe him.

Source: William Peace, "The Hard Work of Being a Soft Manager," *Harvard Business Review* (November-December 1991).

---

outstanding people are smarter and braver than most of us, but they also have the same unavoidable doubts. Good leaders will often admit that they really do not know what to do in difficult situations. Randy Berggren, manager of the Eugene Water & Electric Board in Oregon, was restructuring a large public utility to meet new competition when he found himself acknowledging that he needed help from his fellow workers: "I just came out and said, 'I'm confused and a little scared.' It isn't what people want to hear, but I'm not all-knowing. I help people to help me."[13]

As Box 9.3 shows, social scientists understand that people involved in creative problem solving almost always pass through this type of intense, painful process in order to gain a vision of some fresh innovation. Leading old institutions into a new era is one of the most creative tasks of our time, so managers will have to learn how to live in the midst of formidable problems and crises.

BOX 9.3. THE NATURE OF CREATIVE PROBLEM SOLVING.

The following comments from the study of creativity illustrate that struggling through a turbulent, painful problem-solving process is essential to produce creative solutions:

Ira Progoff: "There is no such thing as a creative act without anxiety, depression, or difficulty preceding it."

Ernest Becker: "The creative person becomes the mediator of natural terror and develops a new way to triumph over it."

Rollo May: "One needs courage to bring anything new into the world, to confront the "nothingness" of one's future . . . and give it meaning."

Sources: Ernest Becker, "The Denial of Death, *Co-Evolution Quarterly* (Fall 1977); Rollo May, *The Courage to Create* (New York: Norton, 1975).

Really Listening

The second requirement for participative problem solving is to really listen in order to fully understand the messy complexity of problems and the wildly different ideas others hold about them.

The art of listening is often discussed but seldom practiced because it is a demanding discipline. It is unfortunately true that most people feel chronically deprived of being heard in a deep way that fully appreciates their unique views and struggles. When some caring soul does come along to really listen, the average troubled individual will so eagerly unburden him- or herself that the listener may have a hard time disengaging. The beneficial effects are so great that an entire school of psychotherapy has thrived based on nothing more than listening.

It may be OK for a therapist to patiently wait for a client to probe the winding recesses of his psyche, but how do action-oriented, hard-driving managers handle aimless talk? I am struck with the evanescent quality of most discussions, the unpredictable way that a group's mood can form out of nothing, meander about, and move in improbable directions on what appears to be sheer whim. It is common to see a group reach consensus, when suddenly some small event will swing the mood dramatically to an opposite conclusion.

I vividly recall when Ronald Reagan was debating Walter Mondale during the 1984 presidential election campaign. Reagan had been showing signs of old age, and public opinion was poised to leap at any further hint of weakness as confirmation that he was now too old for office. When Mondale brought up the issue of age, Reagan summoned his masterful wit to announce that he was not going to take advantage of his rival's youthful lack of inexperience! The audience roared at this clever reversal, and even Mondale joined in the laughter, thereby burying the issue for good. Walter Mondale's campaign went steadily downhill after that turning point, leaving a distinct sense that the reelection of Ronald Reagan to his second term was decided by that trivial bit of humor.

How can managers cope with such flighty behavior? Some of it is pure froth, but I have found that there is usually a deep wisdom to group discussions that is not readily apparent. Groups may pursue circuitous logic, but if the leader gives up prior expectations and listens with a careful, receptive mind to capture subtle meanings, the most outlandish points can prove to be nuggets of good fortune dropped quietly into one's lap.

For instance, there is no better way to confirm an argument than to be challenged by an especially strong objection, and then to turn that objection into support. As a teacher, I have anguished over objections, and time and time again, I invariably find that they were opportunities to learn. If one can contain the fear of being proved wrong in order to listen carefully and ask probing, honest questions, a resolution usually appears.

The role of a wise leader is to nurture this greater truth and present it as a gift to his or her followers. The resulting sense of their gratitude and heightened trust can be palpable.

Finding That Inner Wisdom

Listening to others in order to understand them is essential, but participation is a two-way street, and the most profound source of understanding is likely to be found within oneself. The inner experience of leadership, then, ultimately takes us to the spiritual domain from which all power emanates.

Without approaching that controversial realm known as the "divine," we can adequately discuss the spiritual domain as consisting of the *human* spirit, that vast inner world of perception, knowledge, emotion, intuition, and other subtle sources of understanding that creates our unique sense of awareness. Managers are approaching spirituality today because it is becoming apparent that this is the source of all values, beliefs, and other transcendent qualities that govern the way we live. Listen to how Jerry Rosenbaum, president of an affiliate of Connecticut Mutual and a former Green Beret, described it: "I'm convinced that life is a manifestation of my subconscious thoughts. So I have to develop a belief system that will allow me to create [the type of life] I want."[14]

As Rosenbaum suggests, today's interest in spirituality is distinctive because it is often seen as a means to control one's life more effectively. That may explain why Americans—despite a long history of cynicism—are embracing spirituality in record numbers. It is estimated that almost half of Americans are actively involved in some way. This is not the "old-time religion" but a personal, practical variety learned through personal development, meditation, twelve-step programs, and other approaches.[15] A major reason society is awash in irresponsible behavior—crime, drug abuse, violence—is that we have ignored these realities, and so at least part of the solution lies in some form of spirituality. William Raspberry, a Pulitzer Prize–winning journalist, notes that only spiritual conversion seems to cure drug addicts.[16]

Speaking as one who has practiced this form of spirituality for two decades, I see a growing hunger for making peace with one's inner self and for finding meaning beyond material gratification. As we saw in Chapter 4, society is always evolving, and beyond the Information Age we are likely to discover an infinite world of the spirit.

As Box 9.4 shows, a number of leading-edge managers now use methods for shaping awareness with the same fervor they have previously embraced other management practices. Some of these methods may prove to be passing fads, but the domain of the spirit is so powerful that it seems likely to become a central part of management. Lotus, AT&T, Boeing, and other companies are forming various spirituality programs to examine their approach to management. A Boeing manager's first reaction was "What a waste of time." He later admitted it "helped us to think differently than we ever had before. We had to look inside of ourselves."[17]

If business more fully develops its use of vision, reflection, and other essentially spiritual disciplines, managers may come to resemble samurai warriors as they draw on these higher powers to transform a large company, introduce a global product, or take other heroic actions. Here's how a

BOX 9.4. MANAGEMENT PRACTICES FOR SHAPING AWARENESS.

While "spirituality" might seem different from other management techniques, it is remarkable how spiritual practices lend themselves to business use. The following examples can be thought of as "management tools for shaping awareness."

Strategic Vision. The idea of "vision" was once restricted to mystics. But now the concept is so ingrained in business that IBM's CEO, Louis Gerstner, created a scandal by announcing, "The last thing IBM needs is a vision."

Corporate Cultures. Some of the most successful corporations have corporate cultures infused with spiritual meaning. For instance, Mary Kay Cosmetics has grown from $198 million sales in 1963 to almost $1 billion in 1993 as a result of a spiritual philosophy and the CEO's charisma. "She is revered. . . . The giver and receiver of true love. Cynics do not remain cynics in her presence for long," said *Fortune*.

Process Facilitation. One of the main purposes of process facilitation is to clear up interpersonal tensions in order to create a more productive sense of awareness and to release constructive energy. Many practitioners of organizational learning and HRD make their spiritual agenda quite explicit.

Creativity Training. The onset of an economy driven by innovation has made creativity essential to success, so consultants have been conducting creativity training that employs various exercises to liberate the mind and otherwise induce a creative state of awareness.

Management Intuition. Studies show that intuition correlates strongly with management success. The field has spawned various approaches, books, and professional societies for training managers to use their intuition better.

Meditation. A growing number of managers are meditating because the practice relieves stress, clarifies thought, and encourages insight. The chairman of John Gibbs Associates says, "Through psychic attunement, we're in the right place at the right time. That's the big thing in business."

Prayer. Jerry Harvey reports that 90 percent of CEOs pray during difficult decisions, roughly the same proportion of Americans that pray. One manager claims prayer "does wonders for your colleagues, clients, and the company."

Quiet Reflection. Some organizations interrupt discussions for a few minutes of quiet reflection. One CEO described the need: "An enormous amount of facts have to pass through your mind to make a decision. That takes time and quiet."

Management Study. A new type of business book has been gaining attention during the 1990s focusing on human and spiritual values. Examples include Tom Chappell's, *The Soul of a Business* (New York: Bantam, 1993) and Carol Osborn's *Inner Excellence: Spiritual Principles of Business* (New World Library, 1993).

Sources: Alan Farnham, "Mary Kay's Lessons in Leadership," *Fortune* (September 20, 1993). Alan Farnham, "How to Nurture Creative Sparks," *Fortune* (January 10, 1994). Franz-Theo Gottwald, "Creating Synergy Through Meditation," *ICIS Forum* (Winter 1993). "God at the Workplace," *Newsweek* (March 10, 1986).

woman manager described the advantages of her spiritual practice in work: "I feel plugged into the fundamental power of the universe."[18]

Many will think this constitutes corporate brainwashing or religious indoctrination. There is a danger of conformity because spiritual life can be such a powerful experience that some people become zealots. But that is a small detour on the journey to enlightenment. In fact, the reverse of mind control is more usual. With increasing awareness, we are less likely to impose our morality on others and more likely to appreciate the diversity of life, to see the richness of this subtle inner world, and to accept its own sense of order. A consultant described the change in managers this way: "Once they become self-reflective, they realize they don't know all the answers."[19] Ed McCracken, CEO of Silicon Graphics, who has been meditating for a decade, sees it this way:

> We all have the fantasy that we control what happens to us. But in fact none of us has that kind of control. Meditation helps [by] giving me more confidence that I can let go of the feeling that I have to control everything and things will still turn out all right.[20]

Speaking from my own experience, I have come to realize that the very stuff of life is inherently mysterious. In spite of many years of study and reflection, every day is somewhat puzzling precisely because it all remains so open. As I grow older, life becomes a more thinly disguised apparition, a teeming blend of images, memories, and feelings, somewhat like a "cosmic soup" with such substance that I can savor its flavor and texture.

My main task increasingly seems to involve paying careful attention to this flood of experience in order to select what seems right at the time. And my best guide is an inner wisdom that I have come to respect. I do not know where it comes from or what it is, and I suppose we all do this without giving it much thought. But, still, I don't know how I would cope without it. Many managers, such as Willow Shire, a vice president at DEC, also rely on their inner voice: "When you need an answer, if you listen to yourself and just trust the process, the answer will come."[21]

As I have grown more familiar with this inner wisdom, I find that it is utterly dependable if I listen carefully and interpret it faithfully. That does not mean all will be smooth sailing, because it gets me into serious trouble now and again, as in the speech that bombed. Frankly, at times I wish it would leave me alone. But I call on it when I need guidance, such as right now as I write this book. I've learned that my inner voice can cut through the confusion about all the things that *could* be said in order to focus on the things that *should* be said.

MAKING PARTICIPATION WORK

Despite my espousal of living with problems through listening to others and to one's inner wisdom, I want to avoid imputing sacred meanings to this inner world of management, as if it were "altruistic" or "holy." It may be these things for many people, and at times it certainly is for me. But for our practical purposes here, it is primarily an ethereal domain of thought and action that has largely been ignored up to now. Today, the advance of a world based on knowledge offers an opportunity to come to grips with its special power. Progressive managers are cultivating this domain of the human spirit because it is the terrain on which they must lead competent employees, successful ventures, and strong organizations.

I do *not* think this means that "spiritual" leaders will be less powerful. Quite the contrary, inner leadership seems to offer leaders *more* power, even though it is usually benign. The difference is that power is not exerted through force or formal authority, but through the higher awareness and sheer will of the leader. And precisely because this type of power is hard to understand, there is always a serious risk that such leaders will go astray. Hitler was an unusually powerful charismatic leader.

To ensure that this power is not misused and to draw out the talent needed for a knowledge society, managers will have to reverse what was once considered admirable. Rather than acting with bold determination and extending a brilliant vision to guide others, today's leaders must direct attention *away* from themselves to focus on their followers. They should certainly offer their own ideas. But if they can unite their vision with the many other visions also waiting to be realized, the resulting synthesis of views is invariably far richer and more powerful.

So far we've focused on the advantages of this inner power; it also involves demands that are formidable. There is little tolerance for feel-good human relations or sham participation; people cannot be fooled, so leaders must be honest if they hope to maintain credibility. Respondents in the CIT survey often reported that empowerment was "just a lot of talk." An especially unpleasant task is holding people accountable for their performance. Here's how one manager put it: "One of the most painful things is to point out to someone that they are not coming up to expectations." It's also essential to avoid getting carried away with grandiose visions. Listen to how Gerald Langeler, president of Mentor Graphics, described the escalating rhetoric of their corporate vision: "As I sat in a meeting, it dawned on me that we were not converging on a product, we were circling endlessly around a dream. We no longer had a vision, the vision had us. We were no longer making [business], we were making poetry."[22]

Perhaps the most difficult challenge is to reconcile two opposing needs that seem inevitable. Managers increasingly know they must yield control, but this very process often releases such chaos and personal discomfort that they may have to reassert themselves to keep the organization from flying apart. This continual oscillation between freedom and control forms an uncertain dilemma because there is no good solution. The only feasible approach is to grant people room to grow, try to guide them skillfully, and trust that time and experience will lead them to increasingly responsible behavior. It should be obvious that this relationship closely parallels the ambiguity parents face in raising children. James Autry, a Fortune 500 executive, called the comparison "a touchy subject, but one that all managers come to understand at some point in their careers."[23]

The Need for Fresh Understanding

If we can hang in there long enough, we may be blessed with a gift of understanding that opens up new possibilities. This fresh sense of awareness, this vision that the world could operate in some different way, is the stuff that finally leads to all human advances. After fifty years of hostility between the United States and the former U.S.S.R., the onset of a unified world helped Mikhail Gorbachev envision the Soviet Union as an integral part of a global community, ending the cold war. It took two hundred years of civil rights conflict before Americans could understand that women, African-Americans, and other minority groups should be equal members of a diverse society. After fifty years of controversy over authoritarian institutions, now managers can see their way to shared governance.

We are still a long way from realizing this vision because an outmoded form of power continues to pose serious obstacles. I meet countless working people, and many of them are still suffocating under coercive bosses, complex bureaucracies, and meaningless jobs. It is estimated that one-fourth of employees are so abused by authority that they call in sick, limit productivity, and deliberately sabotage operations.[24]

The most discouraging thing about the misuse of power is that we usually do not face it openly. The obstacles seem so huge, so pervasive, so beyond the ability of mere individuals, that most people have given up hope that things will change. To maintain a semblance of sanity and peace, we have come to accept these assaults on our humanity as an inevitable part of organizational life. Management culture seems swathed in a sort of emotional fog where these abuses are concerned, a polite nonsense of human relations pumped out everywhere to blanket the harshness of authority, make life bearable, keep things working, and render us all powerless.

But as more managers, employees, customers, and others are thrown together by the historic shift in power that is gathering force, this interaction between diverse views should carry the collective spirit of modern institutions to new vistas. Even now people are voluntarily submitting to unprecedented open communications, such as "360-degree evaluations" from employees, peers, and bosses. We have long known that managers hold faulty perceptions of how others see them, and now those blind spots are being exposed to accurate feedback.[25]

Scholars and intellectuals likewise persist in holding on to their limited views of reality because they have invested a lifetime in developing some particular mode of understanding. I have numerous colleagues who insist that the solution to the world's ills lies in accepting *their* particular theory, and I suppose I do the same. Over my desk hangs a cartoon showing a psychotherapist telling his patient on the couch: "But you can't go through life explaining *everything* with Heisenberg's Uncertainty Principle."

Therein lies the greatest limitation the world is struggling with today: we are all creatures of belief, and we are usually trapped inside of our own heads by limited, outmoded beliefs. The first responsibility of a leader in the Knowledge Age is to understand that it is OK to admit we don't have all the answers. Leaders should make the search for understanding not only acceptable but also praiseworthy and show the way by modeling the ability to learn through honest interaction, thus helping others do the same.

When thinking about this, I realize how little we understand the wisdom of traditional sayings, such as the biblical prophecy "The meek shall inherit the Earth." The very thought seems ludicrous in today's high-stakes power games. But the real message is not that "weakness" will become widespread, but that a gentle, trusting humility is more realistic than self-pride in a world that is too mysterious to fully comprehend. Rather than a sign of weakness, humility is a virtue of strong people who do not need to prove their might, so they are open to new understanding.

Breaking Mental Barriers

The following conclusions focus on how an inner form of leadership can help managers in difficult situations:

1. The New Management creates a shift in power that is causing the informal organization to surface and challenge formal authority.

2. Effective managers lead in this situation by listening carefully to their followers and their own inner wisdom as they focus attention on solving difficult problems.

3. Participative leadership draws on the organization's full range of talent to release creative energy for improving performance and creating a stronger corporate community.

Participative leadership is nothing less that a means by which isolated souls can touch one another to set off sparks of insight and initiative. As we briefly noted in Chapter 4, this synthesis, which lies at the heart of the New Management, is a creative process for releasing social energy, and God knows we will need vast new amounts of social energy to cope with a far more demanding world.

Considering the enormous challenges posed by today's revolution in information technology, an emerging global order, a looming tenfold increase in environmental demands, and the social upheaval all this implies, more creative institutions are sorely needed. Only a new social order based on participation can provide the knowledge and will needed to solve this growing host of nagging problems. Patricia McLagan and Christo Nel call it the "Age of Participation."[26] Managers, then, are challenged to redirect the energy now wasted in crime, violence, drugs, and just ordinary social turmoil toward useful purposes.

For all its pain and peril, coming to grips with all these unpleasant realities, and with each other, is essential to create the needed break-throughs in awareness.

Notes

1. The central role of power is described by Fernando Bartolome and Andre Laurent in "The Manager: Master and Servant of Power," *Harvard Business Review* (November-December 1986).
2. For some of the better works, see Warren Bennis and Burt Nanus, *Leaders* (New York: Harper & Row, 1985); John Gardner, *On Leadership* (New York: Free Press, 1990); and John Renesch (ed.), *Leadership in a New Era* (San Francisco: New Leaders Press, 1994).
3. Brochure of the Hamsa Institute, Mill Valley, California.
4. For a fuller explanation of this model, see Halal, *The New Capitalism* (New York: Wiley, 1986), pp. 162–166.
5. Welch is quoted by Mark Potts in "A New Vision for Leadership," *Washington Post* (March 8, 1992). Alvin Toffler, *PowerShift* (New York: Bantam, 1990).
6. Sue Shellenbarger, "Companies Experiment with Flexible Schedules," *Wall Street Journal* (January 13, 1993); Timothy O'Brien, "Company Wins Loyalty by Opening Its Books," *Wall Street Journal* (December 20, 1993); Frank Swoboda, "Motorola Experiments with Letting Peers Weigh Their Pay," *Washington Post* (May 22, 1994).
7. This same dichotomy between the formal versus informal levels of organization is seen in entire economic systems. The Peruvian economist Hernando de Soto, for instance, has shown that the informal economy suppressed by government controls rivals the formal economy. See his book *The Other Path* (New York: Harper & Row, 1989).
8. See Amy E. Schwartz, "Learning Civility in Cyberspace," *Washington Post* (December 16, 1994), and Michael Schrage, "How to Take the Organizational Temperature," *Wall Street Journal* (November 7, 1994).
9. Hal Hinson, "And the Winner Is . . . Us," *Washington Post* (November 1, 1992).
10. A wonderful survey of the rise of human focus in academic disciplines is by James Ogilvy, "Future Studies and the Human Sciences," *Futures Research Quarterly* (Summer 1992). The *Fortune* quote is from Frank Rose, "A New Age for Business?" (October 8, 1990).
11. See Judy Rosener's article, "Ways Women Lead," *Harvard Business Review*

(November-December 1990), and her book *Styles of Leadership* (Washington, D.C.: National Foundation for Women Business Owners, 1994). See also Michael Abramowitz, "Oregon Governor Gets an Earful from the People," *Washington Post* (April 10, 1992).

12. For instance, see Jeanne Mandelker, "Shifting into High Gear," *Venture* (April 1986).

13. Thomas A. Stewart, "How to Lead a Revolution," *Fortune* (November 28, 1994).

14. Don Oldenburg, "Zen and the Art of Making Money," *Washington Post* (January 9, 1987).

15. For instance, a half million 12-step program meetings are held weekly in the United States to help 80 million Americans overcome addictions to drugs, alcohol, and food, and to solve other problems. Robert Wuthnow, director of the Center for American Religion at Princeton, says 40 percent of Americans now participate in various programs. "The Spirituality That Moves Us," *Washington Post* (August 27, 1994).

16. Conservatives have long claimed as much, and progressive liberals such as Hillary Rodham Clinton have recently called for a "politics of meaning— redefining who we are as human beings in this postmodern age." Martha Sherrill, "Hillary Clinton's Inner Politics," *Washington Post* (May 6, 1993). William Raspberry, "The Power of Spirituality," *Washington Post* (December 7, 1992).

17. "Companies Hit the Road Less Travelled," *BusinessWeek* (June 5, 1995).

18. "PR Exec Strives for 'Continual Consciousness,'" *New Leaders* (March-April 1995).

19. Stratford Sherman, "Leaders Learn to Heed the Voice Within," *Fortune* (August 22, 1994).

20. Sherman, "Leaders Learn . . ."

21. Sherman, "Leaders Learn . . ."

22. Gerald Langeler, "The Vision Trap," *Harvard Business Review* (March-April 1992).

23. James Autry, "Random Observations After Twenty-Eight Years of Managing," in John Renesch (ed.), *Leadership in a New Era* (San Francisco: New Leaders Press, 1994), p. 15.

24. "Good-Bye Mr. Dithers," *BusinessWeek* (September 21, 1992).

25. Brian O'Reilly, "360-Degree Feedback Can Change Your Life," *Fortune* (October 17, 1994).

26. Patricia McLagan and Christo Nel, *The Age of Participation* (San Francisco: Berrett-Koehler, 1995).

10

Managing a Unified World

Global Order out of Local Institutions

While previous chapters have focused on the United States, similar economic transitions are under way in other countries throughout the world. East Europe, Russia, and China are struggling to make market systems work, and the European Union is beginning to dismantle its welfare state. Even Japan, once thought to be invincible, is being forced to free its economy from overregulation and social conformity.

Just as the New Management uses a wholistic perspective to view organizations as complete socioeconomic systems, these global changes can be best understood by seeing the Earth as a whole system in its own right. Today, a fragmented world is coming together as the electrifying force of knowledge, technology, and capital flows instantaneously around the globe. Throughout history the idea of a unified world was unthinkable. But just within the past few years the Earth has been integrating before our eyes.[1]

In 1994, the Asia Pacific Economic Cooperation (APEC) forum, which includes the United States, Japan, China, and fifteen other nations, making up half the world's economy, agreed to eliminate all trade barriers over the next two decades. The European Union is planning to introduce a common

Note: Portions of this chapter are adapted from William E. Halal and Alexander Nikitin (of the Russian Academy of Science), "East Is East, and West Is West," *Business in the Contemporary World* (Autumn 1992), pp. 95–113.

currency by the year 2000 as it expands to include almost one billion people. And the leaders of thirty-three nations pledged to unify economically the American continent from Alaska to Argentina by the year 2005. In a decade or two, the same self-interested cooperation now driving the growth of these regional blocs should merge them together into a single global market. Akio Morita, former chairman of Sony, has called for the removal of all trade barriers between North America, Europe, and Asia.[2]

This chapter offers a global perspective to help managers guide their organizations through the complex world system that is now evolving.[3] We examine the revolutionary forces that are integrating the Earth into a global *order* and others that are creating global *dis*order: both the unification of markets and communications, as well as the disintegration of corporations and governments into a maze of global networks. The emerging global economy is becoming a churning ocean of small enterprise operating across diverse cultural regions, producing a tidal wave of creative destruction that could sweep away the comfortable communities of the past. An empirically grounded framework shows that this dilemma of capitalism versus community could be resolved as managers around the world create a human form of enterprise.

My guiding premise is based on the synthesis described in Chapter 4 but carried to a global level. *Today's upheaval is merely the onset of a profound transition to a new economic order governed by two central imperatives: markets, entrepreneurship, competition, and other principles of* enterprise *are essential to manage an explosion of complexity, while cooperation, human values, the public welfare, and other ideals of* democracy *are also being adopted because it is equally important to integrate enterprise into a productive, harmonious whole.*

Thus, the most distinguishing feature of the world system seems to be synthesis: the synthesis of economies into a unified global market, the synthesis of democracy and enterprise, and—in time—the synthesis of capitalism and socialism.

THE DILEMMA OF CAPITALISM VERSUS COMMUNITY

The fall of communism has made it clear that markets will dominate the new economic order, but the abandonment of central planning and welfare states is opening a Pandora's box. Without the support of big government, people are being left to struggle alone with unemployment, poverty, conflict, and other social disorders, causing mounting insecurity and political unrest. Thus, the same forces that are decentralizing corporations into internal markets are decentralizing governments as well, posing an urgent need for some way to create civil order. How will civilized communities be restored in a decentralized world governed by capitalism?

This dilemma is exacerbated by the collapse of faith in the familiar old ideologies that guided nations through the past epoch with good success. With the U.S.S.R. now defunct and the United States struggling through an identity crisis, the lack of superpower leadership has left a vacuum of power, ideas, and moral guides at the very time when the world is facing Herculean new challenges. To avoid chaos, a new paradigm of political economy must somehow be formed that allows us to make sense of today's radically different global realities. The CEO of Japan's NEC Corporation has said: "It won't be easy because nobody has really come to grips with the shift to an information economy."[4]

This critical need is not helped by the common belief that the collapse of communism proves that socialism is dead and capitalism reigns triumphant. Yes, the era of central planning is over, but markets are not the same thing as capitalism. The competitive strength of Japanese business flows from a collaborative type of corporation called a "Human Enterprise System," and other nations also have widely differing market economies.[5] The real question is what type of market would be best in post-Communist states—and even in Western nations like the United States itself?

Challenge to the East: Inventing Post-Communist Markets

A serious example of this dilemma can be seen in the former Communist bloc. There is little doubt among East Europeans and Russians that there is no going back to the old system of central planning and one-party politics—the "Old Socialism." However, these nations have communitarian cultures that encourage social welfare and economic security, and so the abrupt shift to a market system based on competition for personal gain has left people unable to cope with risk and inequality. Now that the euphoria of overthrowing communism has faded, these once functioning societies are suffering severe poverty, crime, and alienation as an overdose of raw capitalism threatens the body politic.

Even East Germans, who were expected to adapt immediately because of their ties to West Germany, now often long for their socialist roots. Polls show that only 30 percent of East Germans support the policies of their Western counterparts. Here's how many see the change: "The revolution benefited only 10 percent of us," and "I realize to my deep resentment that we have lost something of much more value." One person summed it up this way: "You may have freedom in the West, but we had security in the East, a feeling of being cared for. It is less cutthroat here."[6]

The tenacity of this "socialist ethic" is proving a major obstacle to economic reform, as seen in Box 10.1. On the supply side, a frenzy of new ventures has been unleashed by entrepreneurs and former Communist officials, but the privatization of state enterprises has faltered because of limited economic prospects, the lack of infrastructure, and poor business skills. Now great plants that were once productive backbones of the old Soviet economy are running at a fraction of their capacity, and workers sit idle.

On the demand side, the loss of productivity has plummeted living standards to half of the meagre lifestyles Communists once enjoyed. A middle class is emerging that is eager to buy cars, televisions, and the other goods of a consumer society, but those who can afford such luxuries amount to a mere 10 percent or so of the population while one-third or more are impoverished.[7] Understandably, resentment is mounting as people see the old Communist elites simply replaced by capitalist elites with still more wealth and privileges (see Box 10.1). Peter Reddaway, former director of the Kennan Institute for Soviet Studies, described the problem as follows:

> Why is shock therapy not working? Because Russia's deeply political culture is highly unsuited to free markets. Yeltsin now realizes he made a mistake in opting for a rapid transition to capitalism.[8]

Meanwhile, the Russian economy is being run by former Communist apparatchiks, Mafia bosses, and financiers seeking their own fortunes rather than creating jobs and goods, reminiscent of the "robber barons" of American capitalism. George Soros, the famous Hungarian-born American financier, called it "robber capitalism." It is ironic that seventy-five years of Soviet propaganda about the "evils of capitalism" were never really believed by the Russian people until they tried it themselves. Now the impoverished proletariat that Marx warned of is rising in his own homeland.[9]

Of course, the East Europeans are doing better generally. And some

BOX 10.1. THE POST-COMMUNIST CRISIS: OBSTACLES TO ADOPTING CAPITALISM.

The following passages summarize the obstacles that Russia and Eastern Europe are facing in the transition to capitalism:

Attitudes Against Capitalism Persist. Many Russians continue to dislike markets, and they reject the idea of profit making. A 1994 poll found that 30 percent think capitalism will improve their lives, 33 percent think it will make them worse, and 37 percent are unsure. Another study concluded: "There is little evidence that the Russian public is ready, willing, or able to adapt to a market economy."

Economic Progress Has Been Meager. Although 70 percent of state enterprises have been privatized, most are failing economically, yet they continue to be subsidized to avoid mass layoffs. The result is that economic production has fallen 10 to 20 percent per year since 1990, for a total decline of roughly 50 percent. Former East Germany, even with the support from West Germany, experienced a 50 percent drop in employment as its GNP declined 40 percent.

Standard of Living Has Fallen Drastically. Inflation has increased prices a hundredfold while wages only doubled, pricing most goods out of reach for average people. It is estimated that a third to half of the post-Communist bloc now lives in severe poverty. Here's how a Russian engineer described his plight: "This is how we live now. We think every day of how to sell ourselves." And a teacher said: "Now I am just a beggar. I cannot afford to buy anything to eat."

Resentment of the Rich Is Growing. The rise of capitalist millionaires flaunting flamboyant lifestyles is igniting keen resentment. A Pole objected, "The new system is turning out to be best for the rich and strong." And a Russian said, "We have some rich people, while the rest of us get poorer and poorer."

Needs for Capital Are Enormous. Former East Germany will require $1 trillion to turn its economy around. The sum needed to do the same for Russia, a nation roughly twenty times the size of East Germany, with less business experience and no comparable support, is inestimable.

Source: William E. Halal and Alexander Nikitin, "East Is East, and West Is West," *Business in the Contemporary World* (Autumn 1992).

Russians are optimistic because they think the worst is over, so these problems could be alleviated in time.[10] But many others think the nation is in serious trouble. The chief economist of the World Bank noted that "zealous reformers underestimated the task," and a Russian politician worried, "The situation is worsening. Some other way must be found." George Soros is even more dour: "I was hoping to see a market-oriented democratic system. That attempt has basically failed. [The present situation] is creating a tremendous sense of social injustice."[11]

By embracing the icon of capitalism held up by the West, communism has shed its old ideology only to submit to a new ideology. Many Russians bitterly condemn the blind faith in capitalism that now imprisons them as badly as communism used to. George Bernard Shaw put it best: "Revolutions have never lightened the burden of tyranny. They only shift it to another shoulder."

Challenge to the West: Inventing a Human Capitalism

While the virtues of capitalism were being promoted to cure the Russian malaise, the same system was suffering in the land of its chief proponent. America has entered a period of social decline because it seems *too* concerned with free markets, profit making, and other capitalist ideals being advocated for socialists.

No one denies that the American system has extraordinary virtues. U.S. citizens enjoy an exceptional degree of freedom, which has flowered into a vibrant, creative culture and one of highest living standards in the world. These strengths have long attracted a flood of eager immigrants to American shores, and they have inspired today's revolutions around the world.

But freedom entails a price, and the price Americans pay is the absence of that essential sense of community. The competitive stress, lack of social support, and sheer materialism of American life are major causes for the rampant crime, drug use, violence, and other social problems that are the highest in the world; that's why the "Land of the Free" has more of its people in jail than any other country. One study ranked the United States' overall quality of life at the bottom of a list of industrialized nations.[12]

Yes, productivity and corporate profits are doing well, but layoffs have demoralized employees, people are overstressed, loyalty is dead, wages are still falling, most wives must now work, and marginal workers struggle to survive. In the midst of all this loss, CEOs are awarding themselves lavish pay increases, as *BusinessWeek* announced record corporate earnings: "Hot Damn! Profits surged another 45 percent."[13] The resulting disparity of incomes between the top and bottom levels of American society exceeds that of all other industrialized nations, and it has returned to the levels reached prior to the Great Crash of 1929.[14]

Now, it is true that income differences are unavoidable, and profits are needed for capital investment. But without addressing such mounting concerns, today's upbeat faith in the Old Capitalism may prove a temporary lull in the long decline of America's economic dominance. During the past three decades, the share of worldwide sales by U.S. firms fell from 83 percent to 38 percent in autos, 71 percent to 11 percent in electrical goods, and 74 percent to 21 percent in steel. Even computer sales fell from 95 percent to 70 percent.[15] Since 1985, the American dollar has declined 70 percent against the Japanese yen and 60 percent against the German mark.[16] Can this system thrive in a Knowledge Age that demands the support of educated, motivated people?

The same loss of social support is occurring in government as the Republican Revolution rolls back the federal programs that have been relied upon since the New Deal. Of course, this is an indispensable part of the historic move to decentralize all institutions for a new era. But decentralization cannot simply abandon people to fend for themselves. Some form of local control must be devised to take up the slack left by eliminating federal regulations, social assistance, and other forms of support. Pious claims that this will be done by "the market," the "states," and "voluntary institutions" are little more than wishful thinking.

As shown in Box 10.2, the resulting loss of confidence over government, corporations, and other institutions has caused the American system of political economy to be widely questioned as well.

The Democratic Party does not show much talent for exploring new directions, and the Republican Revolution seems destined to roll on because it has history behind it. Thus, a serious question is being raised: How will Americans avoid the trauma that seems likely as a harsh economy and the dismantling of federal programs leave the nation bereft of social support?

A similar conflict is seen in other Western nations that also practice a more pure form of capitalism. The Thatcher Revolution may have halted the growth of the welfare state in the United Kingdom, but polls show the British people are concerned that crime, greed, and poverty have replaced the qualities that made England a great civilization, and the economy remains weak.[17]

BOX 10.2. THE AMERICAN CRISIS: LOST CONFIDENCE AND SIGNS OF CHANGE.

The following passages indicate that the United States has entered an identity crisis that could produce significant change:

Americans Think the Nation Is Heading in the Wrong Direction. The number of people who think "the country is heading in the wrong direction" rose from 40 percent during the 1980s to 80 percent in 1995.

Employee Confidence in Corporate Management Has Fallen. Surveys show that employees are angry over the incompetence and excessive pay of corporate executives at a time when they are forced to make great sacrifices. Robert Swain, CEO of a New York consulting firm, says, "Everybody is exhausted and nobody thinks it will get better. They're hanging on by their fingernails." *Fortune* reported that "confidence in top management is collapsing."

American Quality of Life Ranks Below Advanced Nations. Studies place the United States' quality of life below that of Canada, West Europe, Scandinavia, and Japan. Although their material standard of living is highest in the world, Americans are the only people in an advanced nation who do not have universal health care or protection against worker firing; they have the highest rates of infant morality, illiteracy, crime, drug use, homelessness, and out-of-wedlock births. The United States has the lowest rates for saving, voting, and recycling; the greatest gap between rich and poor; and the poorest public education and transportation systems.

A Populist Revolt Is Under Way. Kevin Phillips, the Republican political analyst who forecast the Reagan Revolution, counsels that a "political counterreaction" is under way, "a resurgence of economic populism based on resentment of the rich combined with a concern over the decline of the U.S. economy."

A New Paradigm Seems to Be Coming. There is growing acceptance of the idea that the United States must adopt a new economic–political paradigm. *Time* magazine noted: "The 1990s have become a transforming boundary between one age and another, between a scheme of things that has disintegrated and another taking shape."

Sources: Richard Morin and Paul Taylor, "Polls Show Plunge in Public Confidence," *Washington Post* (October 16, 1990); Anne Fisher, "Morale Crisis," *Fortune* (November 18, 1991); Alan Farnham, "The Trust Gap," *Fortune* (December 4, 1989); Joani Nelson-Horchler, "The Pay Revolt Brews," *Industry Week* (June 18, 1990); Spencer Rich, "U.S. Ranks Sixth in Quality of Life," *Washington Post* (May 18, 1993); Michael Wolf, *Can America Make It in the Global Race for Wealth, Health, and Happiness?* (New York: Bantam, 1992); Kevin Phillips, *The Politics of the Rich and Poor* (New York: Random House, 1990); Lance Morrow, "Old Paradigm, New Paradigm," *Time* (January 14, 1991).

These problems are not as dramatic as the collapse of communism, but they are also serious and they stem from the same cause—outmoded economic beliefs. The ideological flaw in capitalism is the wishful fantasy that rugged individualism in a struggle for profit will somehow be sublimated into healthy progress by the magic of an invisible hand. This may have worked in an industrial past, but it ignores that vast realm of human and social realities that now drives a knowledge-based economy.[18]

The Ideological Crisis of Our Time

These problems are formidable because they emanate from a profound ideological crisis facing the entire globe that is most clearly seen in Russia and the United States. Historian Charles Maier finds that both the collapse of Soviet Communism and the decline of American capitalism are a result of the same historic transition to a new era that is rendering all past ideologies obsolete.[19]

There is an intriguing symmetry to these dilemmas of East and West that is seldom understood. Both socialism and capitalism produce serious distortions, but in opposite directions. Generally speaking, socialism is in crisis because it bought secure but meager lives at the expense of freedom; but capitalism is in crisis because it has bought a prosperous freedom for some at the expense of security and community for all. Socialism suffers from scarcity, while capitalism suffers from overconsumption. Socialism produces angry dissidents, capitalism produces crime and lost souls.[20]

Even moderate nations are struggling with this dilemma. Almost all European governments are under extreme economic pressure to dismantle their welfare states and to rejuvenate enterprise. For instance, Italy, Spain, and France are running massive annual government deficits. Germany has inflated wages to almost twice the levels of the United States and Japan, so capital investment produces less than half of normal returns. The CEO of a German company said: "We cannot go on supporting high wages and benefits. Either we change fast, or we do not survive."[21] In Japan, the collapse of the "bubble economy" is forcing a move to accept foreign competition, reduce regulation, and create more dynamic companies.[22]

The conflict between capitalism and community is not so easily resolved, however, because these nations are also under enormous political pressure to continue supporting their citizens. In France, 54 percent of the

TABLE 10.1. MANAGERS' ATTITUDES TOWARD THE NEW MANAGEMENT (TNM).
(SAMPLE = 426 CORPORATE MANAGERS.)

Question	U.S.A.	Europe	Japan	Mean
Do you think these practices making up The New Management (TNM) are needed?				
No	5%	2%	0%	4%
Yes	77	93	83	82
Unsure	18	5	17	14
Why are some firms not using TNM?				
Resistance to change	54	70	68	61
Short-term focus	20	18	17	19
Ideas are unacceptable	8	2	4	6
Unsure	18	10	11	14
What will happen to firms that do not adopt TNM?				
They will survive	20	3	2	12
Marginal existence	38	65	27	45
Likely to fail	14	20	54	33
Unsure	28	12	17	10
When is TNM likely to enter the mainstream of business?				
1995	9	12	5	11
2000	38	40	45	41
2005	17	29	20	22
Later	6	14	13	9
Unsure	30	5	17	17

Source: William E. Halal, *Corporations in Transition* (an unpublished study in progress). See the questionnaire in Appendix C.

public wants *more* state control of the economy and only 11 percent wants less. A German businessman said: "We understand that poverty and other social ills are morally unacceptable and economically harmful." The Japanese share a similar view: "We simply cannot fire people," said Norio Ohga, CEO of Sony. "It would only contribute to the worsening of the economy, and we really can't afford that."[23]

The same confusing dilemma persists in other regions. Latin America suffers from chronic political unrest because wealth is so concentrated that a form of monopoly capitalism often exploits an impoverished working class. Development in the Middle East has stalled because free markets conflict with Islamic principles that require serving the community.

ECONOMIC IMPERATIVES OF THE INFORMATION AGE

It is easy to be pessimistic over the enormity of this challenge, but the imperatives of the Information Revolution seem to be driving nations toward a new global order based on enterprise and democracy that may resolve the conflict between capitalism and community. Here's how Lech Walesa explained the way this revolution occurred in Poland: "How did all these reforms appear? The result of computers, communication satellites, television."[24]

A Global Network of Local Enterprise and Community

Chapter 3 showed that these same forces of democracy and enterprise are also transforming organizations. This is happening not only in the United States but also throughout the globe. European companies, such as ABB and Siemens, are being restructured to spur entrepreneurship, while the virtues of corporate community were showcased as Japanese firms captured foreign markets by cultivating harmonious working relations. Table 10.1 shows that American, European, and Japanese managers tend to agree that this trend toward a New Management is likely to enter the economic mainstream between 2000 and 2005.

As a result, corporations are becoming global entrepreneurial networks organized into pockets of local community. They now operate hundreds of internal enterprises internationally (such as ABB's 5,000 profit centers), each forming collaborative alliances with foreign suppliers, distributors, and other business partners to raise capital, launch new ventures, acquire technology, and gain access to local markets. These complex operations are managed by an international class of professionals drawn from all over the world who can adapt to a diverse tapestry of politics and cultures by working effectively with local employees, unions, and governments. Thus, a seamless web of entrepreneurial community is increasingly joining and rejoining over a worldwide information grid to tame a complex, changing global society, as shown in Box 10.3.[25]

BOX 10.3. THE KNOWLEDGE-BASED GLOBAL ECONOMY.

The following examples illustrate trends that are defining the central features of a knowledge-based global economy.

Rise of a Global Middle Class. Middle classes with discretionary buying power are forming huge new consumer markets in China, India, Russia, and other once-slumbering giants that are ten times the size of American markets. *Fortune* magazine noted "From Singapore to Santiago, customer wants and needs are converging."

Worldwide Retail Chains. McDonald's is extending its network from 15,000 to 42,000 restaurants serving local tastes around the world. Toys "R" Us is growing internationally at a 35-percent annual rate. Wal-Mart is now the world's biggest retailer, operating sixty-seven discount stores in Mexico alone. Italy's Benetton operates in 120 countries. The Chinese company, Yaohan, is expanding to 1,000 stores; one will handle a million shoppers each weekend.

A Global Information Revolution. Businesses in less-developed regions are buying computers, cellular phones, fax machines, and other information systems faster than developed regions because they are unhindered by investments in old systems. For instance, Chile has only three PCs per hundred people, compared with thirty PCs in the United States.

The Truly Global Corporation. Ford's chairman (Scottish) and CEO (Lebanese) manage the company from a jet aircraft equipped with video conferencing systems connecting them to thirty manufacturing plants spanning the globe, which use standard automotive subsystems (frames, engines, and so forth) to produce custom cars for markets in 230 countries. GE is focusing its strategy on joint ventures in China, India, South America, and other emerging markets.

Teleshopping Around the World. Long-distance shopping using such services as CompuServe and telephone networks is attracting buyers from around the globe. L. L. Bean now has 200 foreign language operators taking orders, boosting global sales from $25 million in 1990 to $130 million in 1994. Microsoft obtains more than half of its revenue from international sales. Retailers say they are merely nibbling at the edges of an enormous market.

The Global Travel and Tourism Industry. Tourism is now the largest industry in the world and growing rapidly. Airlines are deregulating and forming alliances to provide far more convenient, inexpensive, and safe transportation to anywhere.

Sources: Rahul Jacob, "Middle Classes Explode Around the Globe," *Fortune* (May 30, 1994); Carla Rapoport, "Retailers Go Global," *Fortune* (February 20, 1995); "GE Sees the Future," *BusinessWeek* (November 8, 1993); Warren Brown and Frank Swoboda, "Ford's Brave New World," (August 12, 1994); *World Investment Report* (U.N. Conference on Trade and Development, 1994); Sharon Waxman, "Global Shopping Booms," *Washington Post* (June 21, 1994).

Governments are also moving in this same direction. In 1994, voters in Italy, France, Sweden, Japan, Canada, and the United States revolted against political systems that ruled the cold war era with cumbersome regulations, poor services, high taxes, and corruption. U.S. Congressman Robert Andrews acknowledged, "We are in the midst of a middle-class political revolution. The public is absolutely right. Government is out of control."[26]

Caught between political opposition to raising taxes and cutting services, growing deficits are now forcing the restructuring of government throughout the world in roughly the same way that business has been doing: by privatizing operations, introducing competition to improve services, and collaborating with public stakeholders.[27] These forces are also disaggregating nations into smaller communities. The number of independent states has doubled in the past few decades, and some claim the world will hold a thousand nations soon, each with numerous independent regions and cities. Henry Cisneros, U.S. secretary of housing and urban development, says the need is to "decentralize with a vengeance."[28]

The emerging role for government is to provide a cooperative economic infrastructure that supports sound economic growth. As a global economy enables firms to locate anywhere, governments are under increasing pressure to attract responsible business formation by providing low taxes, information superhighways, minimal regulations, access to advanced technology, educated workers, product markets, and social amenities.[29] Cultivating this new role made Singapore one of the most prosperous regions of the world. With no natural resources and a small population, the city has attracted three thousand corporations by creating the most advanced public IT system and economic infrastructure anywhere.

Further, the need for both enterprise *and* social support is encouraging a symbiotic relationship between these two pivotal institutions, which can be seen in the wave of business-government partnerships. Governments are eager to help business rejuvenate their economies, and business can only thrive in healthy societies. "The government can't do it by itself," said Governor George Voinovich of Ohio. "The private sector has to get involved."[30]

Remember that this emerging form of economic cooperation is not altruism but mutual self-interest that benefits all parties. Ray Norda, former CEO of Novell, called it "coopetition—cooperating, often with one's rivals, out of enlightened self-interest." In fact, it is precisely the height-ened level of competition that drives a corporate community together. The battle for economic survival is no longer waged between single firms, but takes the form of competition between these "clusters of entrepreneurial community."

It's obvious that only a leading edge of progressive managers are adopting these innovations, especially the idea of corporate community. And there will always be a crucial role for the United Nations and other international institutions. But *the most likely scenario for maintaining social order in a complex, changing, decentralized global economy is through cultivating community among local institutions.*

The revolutionary forces described in this chapter and the many examples cited in this book highlight the power of today's technological earthquake that is causing a global upheaval. Information technology exerts a force as revolutionary as that of industrial technology two hundred years ago. The Information Revolution requires free enterprise to manage a rising tide of complexity, while economic cooperation is also necessary to unite this complexity into productive communities. Driven by these twin demands, managers around the globe are transforming corporations and governments into the same form of entrepreneurial, collaborative institu-tions needed to maintain a civilized although turbulent world.

The Tendency Toward Divergence and Convergence

I do not claim that this new economic system will become universal. Figure 10.1 depicts how the relationship between enterprise and democracy forms complex, changing patterns in response to two opposing trends: a tendency toward *divergence* caused by differences in cultural values, and a tendency toward *convergence* caused by the common imperatives of information technology.[31]

Studies indicate that nations develop diverse economic systems that are compatible with their cultures. Figure 10.1 shows how countries like the United States, the United Kingdom, Canada, Taiwan, South Korea, and the South American states favor entrepreneurial freedom and other economic values, which characterize the lower-right end of the political spectrum. At the upper-left end of the spectrum, China, Russia, East Europe, Sweden, India, Africa, and the Middle East lean toward social values like security and public welfare. It is hard to categorize nations neatly, and all this is changing, of course. But culture, one of the most powerful forces in the world, seems to produce these broad, general patterns.[32]

While wide variations will remain, over the long term the imperatives of information should continue to urge most nations toward a roughly similar combination of democracy and enterprise that integrates social and economic values. The attraction toward this center position is illustrated by the fact that the most productive economies tend to favor a combination of enterprise and collaboration; Switzerland, Germany, France, Italy, Scandinavia, and Japan have created the highest overall quality of life in the world during the past few decades, although they too are now facing new adjustments. A European manager explained:

> The competitive battle senior managers face is a struggle among [market] systems, each with its distinctive set of values. I believe our European system of alliances among workers, suppliers, distributors, and government is better suited to meet the economic and social challenges ahead.[33]

Although differences will flourish to suit cultural tastes, this diversity is likely to evolve into variations on the same organizing principles because all nations are pressured by common economic realities of the Information Age. The instantaneous flow of electronic capital around the globe is now forcing interest rates and wages to converge and governments to adopt similar economic policies. In 1995, for instance, the Mexican peso fell precipitously because of a large trade deficit, while the Japanese yen climbed due to a trade surplus.[34] This convergence may be most pronounced in the developing countries that are searching for a middle way. Mujmul Saqib Khan, a Pakistani ambassador, claims that "leaders of developing countries will blend capitalist and socialist models."[35]

This perspective on the emerging global economy, then, offers managers some insights into the complex problems they must solve around the world. Not only must they learn how to operate across wildly different economies, laws, currencies, and cultures, they must also adapt to a wide variety of deeply rooted political ideologies, which should increasingly combine various blends of enterprise and community. While this global order is sure to grow even more intricate, it should help to keep in mind that this

FIGURE 10.1. THE EVOLUTION OF POLITICAL ECONOMY.

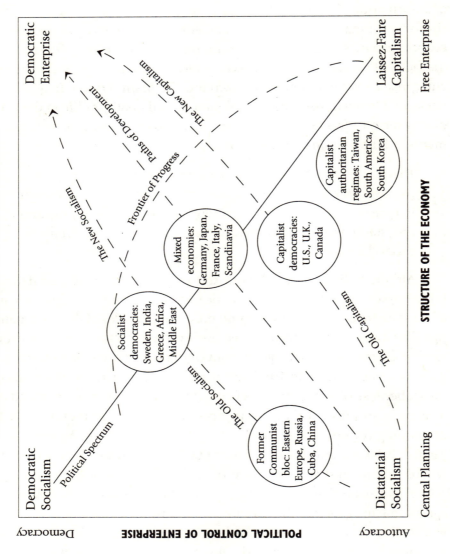

confusion can be sorted out by using New Management concepts. I hope this chapter shows that the same forces are at work in a global context.

These trends are as yet limited to an avant garde, of course, but their implications are profound. As shown in Figure 10.1, the concept of Democratic Enterprise may eventually integrate socialism and capitalism into compatible but somewhat different versions of this same overarching global paradigm. We could then witness a breakthrough in political economy that fosters the formation of robust local community while simultaneously creating a more productive type of enterprise. A new economic epoch is at hand in which enterprise and human values are *efficient*, so such a system may become commonplace, making it possible for managers to operate more easily throughout a truly unified global economy.

I realize that there is much cynicism over such prospects, but consider the changes the Industrial Revolution brought to the average agrarian peasant, who suffered a short, grueling life of labor in the fields under servitude to a dictatorial monarch. Average people living in developed nations today certainly bear hardships, but they are white-collar workers enjoying the freedom of market economies and democratic government. Why should the Knowledge Revolution be less dramatic?

THE EMERGING SHAPE OF THE NEW ECONOMIC ORDER

Projections of these trends provide some intriguing forecasts that defy conventional wisdom.

Democratic Enterprise in the East: A New Socialism?

The main obstacle facing the former Soviet bloc is today's antisocialist fervor, which blinds us to the more subtle truth. As we have shown, most people in socialist cultures, and even many Americans, dislike the harshness of capitalism and prefer the human values that have inspired socially oriented economies now thriving in Western Europe, Japan, and other leading economic areas. That's why half the world moved to socialism in the first place.

The key to resolving the crisis gripping Russia and Eastern Europe, then, is to recognize that socialism was not an aberration but an important advance. In the heat of today's reforms, it is easy to forget that socialist philosophy was once praised as a constructive response to the exploitation of labor, monopoly control of markets, and other injustices of early capitalism. Communism was a harsh system, certainly, but the capitalism of the robber barons was equally harsh, and even the capitalism of today can be harsh. What morality tolerates a system that rewards people like Michael Milkin with more than $500 million per year while a quarter of its infants live in poverty? The present love affair with capitalism is likely to run its course in a few years as excesses mount, taking the political cycle back toward social policies.

Rather than expect socialists to abandon their heritage, therefore, it is more useful to view the Russian dilemma as roughly comparable to the transition Americans experienced during the Great Depression of the 1930s, which threw the viability of capitalism into question. The Depression resulted from a severe failure in the market system, but it was corrected with insured savings, unemployment benefits, and other *social welfare* programs that stabilized the American economy.

Economic progress in Russia lags behind that of the United States by about fifty years, so the nation is making a similar transition at roughly the same point in its development. Just as Americans did not abandon capitalism during the Great Depression but corrected its flaws by adopting some elements of socialism, Russians may in time develop an advanced form of socialism incorporating markets and democratic enterprise—it could be thought of as a "New Socialism."

Many economists dispute the concept of a "Third Way," yet some trends are moving in this direction. Polls show that most Russians and other post-Communist people favor a democratic, market socialism. A Czech politician said: "We do not talk about 'social markets' to avoid headlines, but the condition for our success is to keep public support." In Poland, the Democratic Left Alliance that won the 1993 elections based its success on combining the best features of socialism and capitalism: "The big mistake that Solidarity made was to throw out everything from the past," said the party chairman. And a Chinese official said, "Capitalism doesn't have a patent right over markets. We're trying to establish a socially oriented market economy."[36]

Just as markets are not necessarily capitalism, then, socialism is not necessarily government planning. The concept of Democratic Enterprise offers a logical solution to the current Russian crisis because it could provide the advantages of free markets while retaining some sense of harmonious social control. In terms of traditional socialist thought, this type of socially guided market economy would serve the public welfare through *decentralized* planning, conducted at the level of the individual enterprise rather than the state, and managed *democratically* by stakeholders.[37] The main obstacle to revitalizing the post-Communist bloc is building viable institutions, and this approach could draw on their communitarian culture to form productive business corporations and other social institutions.

Let's sketch out what this system might look like. The private sector in Russia should continue to be managed with free markets, but this is basically a socialist society, so government could assist with employment, medical care, housing, and pensions to buffer its citizens from the vicissitudes of markets. It might also be best to maintain strategic control over banking, utilities, transportation, and other quasi-public industries, either through regulation or state ownership. A 1995 poll of 4,000 Russians found that 66 percent want more state control of the economy.[38]

The most crucial strategy would be to help Russian managers develop a form of democratic governance in which workers, business partners, government, and customers share control of organizations. This crucial step would allow a fresh application of socialist values to form an acceptable type of communitarian enterprise able to thrive in a vibrant market economy. Box 10.4 shows typical practices.

The path these nations follow is certain to be messy, and today's raw capitalism will likely continue until the public demands reforms, following the American experience. However, opinion polls show the following probabilities for three alternative scenarios: Russians believe there is a 22 percent chance that the nation will develop an American type of capitalism; a 15 percent chance that it will revert back to central controls; and a 63 percent chance it will follow the middle path of Democratic Enterprise. Other studies show similar results for China.[39]

Democratic Enterprise in the West: A New Capitalism?

An interesting feature of this thesis is that the capitalist world may move toward a roughly similar system, although it would be viewed in terms of Western values and it would be approached from the opposite direction, as shown in Figure 10.1.

BOX 10.4. DEMOCRATIC ENTERPRISE IN THE EAST.

The following examples illustrate new practices in Russia and Eastern Europe in which "democratic" enterprises operate in a free market system.

Democratic Centralism. To meet their two cultural needs for democratic policy making and centralized control, Russian managers periodically engage their subordinates in a free debate to produce a consensus on policies, after which the decision is implemented in an authoritarian manner. Thus, leadership alternately moves from democracy to dictatorship, in keeping with different needs at different times.

Worker Councils. Worker councils have been formed in large enterprises to participate in the selection of managers and in policy formation, roughly similar to the German and Japanese approaches, which are famous for creating productive organizations.

Diverse Approaches to Corporate Control. Poland, the Czech Republic, and Russia have adopted privatization plans that offer different types of economic control: selling companies to private investors, cross-ownership among suppliers and distributors, giving stock to employee-owners, and distributing vouchers that allow citizens to buy shares of different businesses.

Employee Stock Ownership Plans. ESOPs are gaining popularity. One of Russia's largest lumber mills, the Ust Llimsk Wood Industrial Complex, recently sold shares to its 12,000 workers, who now boast of being the mill's owners. At the Konveyer plant, a similar system has been running smoothly for years, and employees received a 20 percent dividend recently.

Joint-Stock Companies. Joint-stock companies offer a democratic form of governance in which all stakeholders share in ownership and control of the enterprise. A good illustration is the famous GUM Department Store on Red Square, which has been converted into a "joint-stock society" whose shares are held by employees, financial backers, suppliers, and the Moscow City Council.

Self-Managed Teams. Russians have organized self-managed teams that share responsibility and financial rewards. At a famous hospital, for instance, surgical teams are jointly managed by doctors, nurses, and technicians, and receive incentive pay that differs by no more than a factor of three among team members.

Sources: William E. Halal and Alexander Nikitin, "East Is East, and West Is West," *Business in the Contemporary World* (Autumn 1992); Paul Lawrence and Charalambos Vlachoutsicos, *Behind the Walls: Decision-Making in Soviet and U.S. Enterprise* (Cambridge, Mass.: Harvard Business School, 1990).

America is a crisis-driven society, so the driving force for such a difficult change seems likely to be the identity crisis that grips the United States. But the American potential for meeting new challenges is enormous. After Pearl Harbor forced America into World War II, the United States emerged as the most powerful nation in the world. When *Sputnik* launched the space race, America soon landed the first man on the moon. And the Arab oil embargo produced such a burst of energy conservation that the United States became glutted with cheap oil. The demand for change during the 1992 and 1994 elections suggests that a similar surge of reform could emerge over such ideas as "Human Capitalism" or a "New Capitalism."

Americans are practical people, and a continuation of today's social decline may convince them that the nation's obsession with profit, capital investment, taxes, and other economic policies misses the real issue. The great need facing the United States is to make a subtle but crucial shift from a *capital*-centered system to a *human*-centered system that would create a sense of common purpose to unify its institutions and the nation. Herbert Stein, former chairman of the Council of Economic Advisers, says America needs to establish a new goal of "improving the quality of life."[40]

Some movement has been building in this direction for years. As summarized in Box 10.5, the trends reported in this book show that many American managers realize that a collaborative form of business is needed because economic success hinges on gaining the support of their various stakeholders. Why should tough-minded executives want to do this? Because it is more productive.

Moreover, business is the leading institution that sets the tone for society today, so its example could encourage government, education, and our other social institutions to do the same. The crisis in American education, for instance, could be resolved as public schools move further along the path toward internal markets and corporate community being blazed by innovative corporations. A dozen or so states allow parents to choose schools; roughly twenty states now permit teachers to form charter schools, and many offer merit pay. Likewise, participative governance is being adopted to manage schools by bringing administrators, teachers, and parents into policy making. In short, the principles of the New Management are at work revitalizing education.

BOX 10.5. DEMOCRATIC ENTERPRISE IN THE WEST.

The following trends summarize concepts presented throughout this book to show that Western economies are combining democratic cooperation with creative enterprise.

Participative Employee Relations. Various types of employee participation are under way at roughly half of American companies. Also, about 15,000 firms have employee ownership plans covering 20 million workers because they improve productivity and provide a defense against hostile takeovers. As a result, no-nonsense executives who abhor any whiff of idealism are moving toward the democratization of the workplace.

Client-Driven Marketing. As foreign competition has entered American markets, almost all American firms have begun shifting attention from selling goods to serving genuine customer needs; they emphasize quality and customer satisfaction, and bring clients into the policy-making process. *BusinessWeek* magazine summed up this move to client-centered marketing: "Entire companies are being reorganized around giving customers what they want."

Strategic Alliances. Almost all corporations are being connected by strategic alliances, even with their competitors. About 250 research consortia of competing companies and 1,600 business-government research agreements have been formed recently in the United States. The auto industry alone has twelve consortia in which all three major carmakers work together, often with government support, on developing everything from new fuels to electric cars.

Government-Business Partnerships. American cities like Baltimore, San Antonio, and Indianapolis, and states like Michigan and Pennsylvania, are forming working partnerships among local corporations, universities, labor unions, and civic groups. Roughly forty states are developing collaborative government roles that facilitate the successful operation of free markets.

Democratic Model of the Firm. The trends noted here are creating corporate communities that unify workers, clients, associated firms, governments, and investors, as illustrated by GM-Saturn, the Body Shop, and other progressive firms. More than 80 percent of managers in the CIT study say their companies cooperate with these stakeholders (see Table 3.3). William Andres, CEO of Dayton-Hudson, put it best: "We find no conflict in serving all our constituents because their interests are mutually intertwined. Profit is our reward for serving society."

A powerful new form of government is also needed that assists the responsible operation of a fast-moving, high-tech society. Creative politicians today could be more effective by helping corporations, schools, and other institutions develop a human form of enterprise that draws on America's democratic heritage. One striking possibility is to form a *Democratic* "Contract with America." Where the Republicans gained power by seizing the iron need to decentralize, the Democrats could gain power by ensuring the iron need for responsible local governance. Governments could offer corporations and other institutions freedom from regulations and taxes—if they adopt democratic governance systems that assume responsibility for their social impacts.[41]

If a decentralized society is to work, this type of sound local governance will be needed to create self-regulating, vibrant communities that replace federal controls and welfare programs.

A Global Race to Invent the Economy of the Future

This chapter has defined the following major dilemma and how managers can best operate in the new global order:

1. Although the world is moving toward unification, the emerging global economy is increasingly characterized by widespread disintegration of corporations and governments.

2. This decentralization is causing a serious dilemma between capitalism and community, although each nation may experience it differently.

3. Managers have an opportunity to create a new form of political economy that draws its strength from creating pockets of entrepreneurial community at the grassroots level.

Events will not evolve this neatly, since a race is under way to discover the secrets of success for a new economic era that nobody really understands. It almost seems as though the globe has become a great laboratory in which competing nations and corporations must work feverishly to invent new economic prototypes for the future before disaster strikes.

If Russians and Americans are unable to meet this challenge, Germany, Japan, and China seem most likely to emerge as the dominant global powers. Germany is poised to become the gateway between East and West. Japan is forming alliances throughout Asia and the rest of the world. And China's great size almost ensures it a central role in the world economy. Without major changes, the United States may become a marginal global actor that celebrates innovative freedom and extravagance, albeit accompanied by increasing poverty, crime, and other social problems. Russia would probably sink further into its present quagmire of outlaw capitalism, unworkable bureaucracy, and poor living standards, punctuated by periodic social revolts that are brutally suppressed.

But I am more impressed by the imperatives of information technology which are now forming a new global order. Something similar to Democratic Enterprise seems inevitable for the same reason today's economy replaced the feudal system two hundred years ago: not because of good intentions, altruism, or even sound planning, but because a more productive blend of markets and democracy is now essential to meet the demands of an Information Age. The inexorable logic of this historic development is likely to prevail over the next ten to twenty years, and the big question is who will provide the leadership for moving in this direction?

Capitalism and socialism suffer severe disadvantages because of structural limits in both systems: economic freedom is productive but socially disruptive, while government controls are orderly but economically stifling. It seems to me that the next great step in human progress is the transformation of these two fading ideologies into modern equivalents that can integrate social and economic values. And a seminal new idea is emerging that may finally resolve this nagging old dilemma. Managers around the globe are redefining the very nature of enterprise to incorporate social values democratically at the grassroots level.

Notes

1. See the special issue of *Futures, The Global Economy,* edited by William E. Halal (December 1989).
2. C. Fred Bergsten, "Clinton Makes the Pacific Connection," *Washington Post* (November 13, 1994). John Goshko and Peter Behr, "Leaders of Western Hemisphere Agree to Form Free Trade Zone," *Washington Post* (December 11, 1994). Akio Morita, "Toward a New World Economic Order," *Atlantic Monthly* (June 1993).

3. See Heidi Vernon-Wortzel and Lawrence Wortzel, *Global Strategic Management* (New York: Wiley, 1992), and the special issue on global strategy published by *Strategic Management* (Summer 1991).

4. Emily Thornton, "Japan's Struggle to Restructure," *Fortune* (June 28, 1993).

5. Robert Ozaki, *Human Capitalism: The Japanese System as a World Model* (Tokyo: Kodansha International, 1991). For a good analysis of differences in market systems, see "The Many Faces of Free Enterprise," *BusinessWeek* (January 24, 1994).

6. Peter Gumbel, "East Germans Can't Shed Communism," *Wall Street Journal* (September 29, 1994). Jane Mayer, "Many East Germans Find There Is No Place Like Home," *Wall Street Journal* (December 8, 1989).

7. Steve Liesman, "More Russians Enter Middle Class," *Wall Street Journal* (June 7, 1995).

8. Peter Reddaway, "Next From Russia: Shock Therapy Collapse," *Washington Post* (July 12, 1992).

9. Fred Hiatt, "Historic Chance to Aid Russia Said to Be Slipping Away," *Washington Post* (March 1, 1993).

10. The president of ABB Russia said: "In another five years young Russians will have the same work habits as the West," and the Russian government claims that real incomes rose 11 percent in 1994. But there are doubts about the validity of these statistics. See "In Poland, Reform Brings Painful Progress," *Washington Post* (September 6, 1993), and "Russia's Strivers," *BusinessWeek* (1994, special issue).

11. Hobart Rowen, "Soviet Iceberg," *Washington Post* (May 21, 1992). Soros is quoted in *BusinessWeek* (October 3, 1994), p. 105.

12. Guy Gugliotta, "Index of Social Health," *Washington Post* (October 25, 1994).

13. The headline is from *BusinessWeek* (November 14, 1994), p. 108. For an analysis of this conflict between business and society, see "We're No. 1, And It Hurts," *Time* (October 24, 1994). The editorial page of *BusinessWeek* (April 26, 1993) notes that average CEO pay rose 56 percent from the previous year to $3.8 million; the editorial concluded: "CEO pay continues to climb to ridiculous heights. . . . The disparity tears at the social fabric."

14. An authoritative analysis is provided by Gary Burtless and Timothy Smeeding, "America's Tide: Lifting the Yachts, Swamping the Rowboats," *Washington Post* (June 25, 1995).

15. Lawrence Franko, "Global Corporate Competition," *Business Horizons* (November-December 1991).

16. Michael Dobbs, "Who Won the War?" *Washington Post* (May 7, 1995); Judy Shelton, "A Flat Tax for a Strong Dollar," *Washington Post* (September 6, 1995).

17. Based on a Gallup Poll conducted for *The Daily Telegraph* (April 1989).

18. See Amitai Etzioni, *The Moral Dimension: Toward a New Economics* (New York: Free Press, 1988).

19. Charles Maier, "The Collapse of Communism" (Working paper, Center for European Studies, Harvard University, 1994).

20. See Clark Kerr, *The Future of Industrial Societies* (Cambridge, Mass.: Harvard University Press, 1983).

21. "Europe Faces Pressure to Cut Social Spending," *Wall Street Journal* (May 8, 1995). Rick Atkinson, "German Workers Getting Stiff Shot of Reality," *Washington Post* (February 22, 1994).

22. Ichiro Ozawa, *Blueprint for a New Japan* (Tokyo: Kodansha International, 1994).

23. Herbert Henzler, "The New Era of Eurocapitalism," *Harvard Business Review* (July-August 1992). Brenyon Schlender, "Japan: Is It Changing for Good?" *Fortune* (June 13, 1994).

24. Walesa's statement is from *Newsweek* (November 27, 1989), p. 35. A good account of the role of television in bringing about the fall of the East German Communist government is provided by Tara Sonenshine, "The Revolution Has Been Televised," *Washington Post* (October 2, 1990). Alexander King and Bertrand Schneider, *The First Global Revolution* (New York: Pantheon, 1991).

25. As noted by John Naisbitt, *Global Paradox* (New York: Morrow, 1994), p. 14.

26. Robert Andrews, "Democrats: Change or Die," *Washington Post* (November 10, 1994). Also see John Fund, "The Revolution of 1994," *Washington Post* (October 19, 1994).

27. "America's Heartland: The Midwest's New Role in the Global Economy," *BusinessWeek* (July 11, 1994).

28. David Broader, "The Power of Our Discontent," *Washington Post* (September 6, 1995).

29. Michael Porter, *The Competitive Advantage of Nations* (New York: Free Press, 1990).

30. David Vise, "Comeback on Lake Erie," *Washington Post* (November 11, 1994).

31. See William E. Halal, "Political Economy in an Information Age," in Lee Preston (ed.), *Research in Corporate Social Policy and Performance* (Greenwich, Conn.: JAI Press, 1988).

32. Samuel Huntington, "The Clash of Civilizations," *Foreign Affairs* (Summer 1993).

33. Herbert Henzler, "New Era of Eurocapitalism."

34. See the special issue of *BusinessWeek*, *21st Century Capitalism* (1994), and Joel Kurtzman, *The Death of Money* (New York: Simon & Schuster, 1993), which describe the effects of today's $200 trillion volume of annual trade in global finance markets, which is roughly ten times the entire output of the world's economies.

35. "Japanese Fusion," in the special 1994 issue of *BusinessWeek*, *21st Century Capitalism*.

36. "Soviets Reject U.S. Style Capitalism," *Washington Post* (July 26, 1991). "Prague's Progress" *Wall Street Journal* (July 6, 1994). "Poles Split in Vote for Parliament," *Washington Post* (October 28, 1991). Lena Sun, "China's Party Sees Threat from the West," *Washington Post* (November 12, 1991).

37. The rationale for a socially oriented form of market economy was first described by Oskar Lange in *On the Economic Theory of Socialism* (New York: McGraw-Hill, 1964), pp. 57–143, and Pat Devine in *Democracy and Economic Planning* (Boulder, Colo.: Westview Press, 1988).

38. Reported in *Washington Post* (November 12, 1995).

39. John Bradford, "The Prospects for Change in the Soviet Economy" (Unpublished research report, George Washington University, 1990). Zhihua Chen, "The New China: Capitalism or Market Socialism?" (Unpublished research report, George Washington University, 1991).

40. Herbert Stein, "The Show Is Over," *Wall Street Journal* (October 25, 1994)

41. Robert Kuttner, "Good Corporate Citizens," *Washington Post* (August 23, 1995).

CONCLUSION

Drawing on the Power of Heritage

Although my goal in this book has been to define a comprehensive approach to transforming institutions, I expect that readers will see their goal differently. You have your own unique problems, your own ideas about what is needed, and your own set of principles. I also realize that you are flooded with lots of advice that differs enormously, so why should my concepts be special?

MAKING SENSE OF MANAGEMENT TODAY

I hope you have found it useful to see that a New Management is emerging and that its underlying concepts of internal markets and corporate community offer unusual insights. *What sets this book apart, however, is that it focuses very sharply on what really counts. Management could be far more effective if we drew on the power of our American heritage: democracy and enterprise.*

It seems to me that we have become trapped in a great irony. At the very time when American ideals are creating revolutions around the world, our own institutions are still suffering from authoritarian control. The unpleasant truth is that we have relegated our principles to lofty occasions, such as presidential elections, while ignoring their relevance to our workplaces, schools, hospitals, churches, and other ordinary aspects of daily life. This problem is compounded by today's jumble of incompatible frameworks that scatter attention in many other directions: Peters and

Waterman's "Eight Attributes of Excellence," "Deming's Fourteen Steps to TQM," "The Eight Principles for Reengineering," "Five Disciplines of Organizational Learning," on and on in an endless stream of mind-numbing lists.

I wonder if we realize how confusing the practice of management has become today? As one who instructs in this field, I often feel embarrassed that it lacks a solid body of knowledge and accepted principles. Yes, I know that's because management is more art than science, and some confusion is unavoidable because management will continue to change.

But the concept of hierarchy effectively organized management through throughout the Industrial Era, so why can't we define a conceptual foundation for the Knowledge Era? Rather than struggling to sort out the useful ideas from today's maze of management fads, almost everything we need can be found in the two great principles of democracy and enterprise America has given the West:

- Is your corporation under pressure to improve quality? Restructure into small internal enterprises that are held accountable for serving their clients.

- How are you going to empower employees while maintaining a sense of control? By helping them organize into self-supporting teams that are managed democratically.

- Are alliances and networking making hash of your organization chart? Set up a common economic infrastructure, and let internal markets do the rest.

- You say the demands of different constituencies are pulling you apart? Bring them together to create a democratic system of governance that sorts out all their rights and responsibilities.

- Your competition is relentless? A dynamic market system of small internal enterprises guided by skilled stakeholders would be a powerful competitive advantage.

I realize that not all problems would fit into this framework, lots of situations will always require firm control, and freedom is a messy, difficult thing to manage. But the evidence summarized in this book shows that democracy and enterprise offer a universal, enduring, readily understood foundation that integrates today's bewildering blur of management innovations into a coherent whole.

MANAGING THE DAILY NEED FOR COMMUNITY AND FREEDOM

If this heritage is so great, then why do we have such a hard time accepting such a basic idea? I am not entirely sure, but I do know that people feel ambivalent about community and freedom.

I experienced a personal example of this problem recently. My extended family has held a one-week reunion for many years, which my brothers and their families attend faithfully. Not one of us, even the teenagers who are so eager to dissociate from their parents, would think of missing this annual feast of community. It is a veritable orgy of reminiscing, telling stories, hugging and kissing, working on family problems, exchanging photos, admiring each other's kids, swapping advice, and making future plans.

Yet there is always a subtle but solid resistance to integrating our lives beyond a certain point. Who wants to take the responsibility for organizing next year's reunion when they are struggling to keep their own lives under control? I would love to help my brother's son with his college studies, but I'm worried about my own kids. And does anybody really want to go through all the arguments that are part of a closer relationship?

A family is not a large organization, but I think the same two opposing forces are at work in all social systems. Most of us want to be a close part of a group, but we also insist on retaining our individual freedoms. For instance, employees should be part of the corporate team—but they may not agree with each other. Citizens want strong government support—but they also want to avoid rules and taxes. The basic problem is that we rarely acknowledge these conflicting needs for community and freedom, so they are not addressed very well, leaving everyone confused and irritated. I know our family reunions go far better if we make explicit plans for common gatherings and block out time for individual activities.

These two basic needs are strong and growing stronger, and the only real solution is to plan how to serve them better. Bringing democracy and enterprise inside organizations will not magically dissolve the fears, doubts, and other complex issues we experience over this dilemma. But I do think the New Management will provide a framework for dealing with these matters more effectively.

THE UNIVERSAL POWER OF THE NEW MANAGEMENT

I would like to conclude this book with a personal experience that helped me appreciate the essential nature of the New Management more fully. It's easy to discuss what we should do in the abstract, but somehow things always look differently when put into practice—"management from the inside out." That's what happened when I helped make a major change to my neighborhood.

I live in a lovely old community of English Tudor townhouses. It is conveniently located in Georgetown, close to downtown Washington, D.C., yet it retains the spacious feel of a suburb. One of the great legacies left by the builders is three parklike "circles" that dot the community. The one in front of my home is a 150-foot circle surrounded by other homes, creating a large, gracious open space that resembles a public square.

Although living in such magnificent space is rare in any city, this circle had grown into a useless lot over the years. Large bushes and trees were planted in the center, which became overgrown and choked with weeds, making the entire circle an impenetrable jungle. The only purpose this prized piece of real estate served was as a convenient place for people to walk their dogs—it had become a latrine. The problem persisted because, like most communities, mine consists of a wide variety of people with strong beliefs, and the difficulty of achieving consensus had left the neighborhood immobilized into inaction. The sad state of the circles was merely a symptom of this political paralysis.

Becoming desperate over this growing jungle, two neighbors and I took the lead in relandscaping it, which led to a great adventure in community building. After much discussion, there seemed to be agreement that the circle should be changed. But who was going to do all the hard work? Where would the money come from? How would we ever agree on a new design that all could live with? In short, we faced the typical obstacles that paralyze most organizations.

It occurred to me that we could ignite some energy by organizing a small group of neighborhood men to begin by moving the trees and bushes in the circle. The idea was appealing because there is a symbolic power in "gathering the neighborhood men to work on their common land." This was a huge, difficult task, but it was also a very visible goal that, if completed, would make an equally huge impact on the way neighbors viewed their community.

Sure enough, it worked. About ten men showed up the first Saturday; they made a large dent in the job and had a great time together. Once everyone saw what could be done, the rest was fairly easy. I organized a half dozen such work teams, which transformed the circle into an open, useful space. As the neighbors watched this progress and came out to discuss it, they became convinced we were serious and began donating money to support the work. And, although we haggled over details, these conflicts were resolved along the way as we allowed the project to evolve of its own accord.

This former eyesore is now carefully laid out with paths leading to shaded spaces for sitting and playing, all enhanced by appropriate landscaping. The effect has been to inject a vital new spirit into the community. People now interact in ways they rarely did before, especially because this gorgeous new public space invites them to be together. The greatest achievement, however, is that an empowering example has been set. Neighbors now think, "If we can do this, why can't we _____?"

This task was not as challenging as many business projects, but it nicely illustrates the basic elements needed to create organizational success today. The first thing to notice is that this project was not initiated by formal authorities, but sprang up from the grass roots. I cannot imagine how it could have moved successfully through the complex steps our small community association requires for formal action. Even more bizarre is the thought that it could ever be done by—God forbid—the D.C. or federal governments. No, it was accomplished by the voluntary efforts of a small team that had a better idea. I like to think that this highlights my skills as an entrepreneur, although my wife calls me "a madman" for taking on such challenges. But madmen are exactly the stuff that all good entrepreneurs are made of, and the greatest task facing managers across the globe today is to unleash the entrepreneurial powers of ordinary people.

The other major point to observe is that the entrepreneur cannot accomplish the task alone but is utterly reliant on others. Our efforts would have failed without the willing efforts of many men who volunteered to do the hard work, without the financial backing of my neighbors, and without the collaborative sense of community that allowed us to reach tough decisions amicably. Despite all the attention showered on heroic CEOs, the reality is that managers and organizations can do very little by themselves; local pockets of collaborative community are needed to provide the energy, support, and vision that drive all human efforts.

We could show how this simple example illustrates the other concepts of the New Management, but I think the point is clear. Managers around the world are struggling mightily to discover new principles to cope with a changed world, yet the key ideas that are needed lie waiting in our common heritage we take for granted.

Society is adrift in various crises today because business, government, education, medicine, and all other institutions lack a way of dealing effectively with a technological and economic revolution, that is creating a decentralized global order, of 10 billion industrialized people, who all share a fragile Earth. I suggest that the common model needed to manage this huge, far-flung, enormously complex global system is the humble blend of local democracy and enterprise at work in communities like mine around the world. No, it will not solve all the world's problems by a long shot. It would, however, establish a solid foundation of two well-established, easily grasped principles that offer enormous new prospects because they can harness the power of ordinary people spontaneously from the bottom up.

IT ALL BEGINS WITH YOU

In view of the struggle that goes on within most of us over such issues and the massive momentum of the status quo, I must admit that prospects for creating a New Management do not appear overwhelming. It may be that there is limited potential for this type of management. Nobody really knows.

But the genius of markets and democracy is that it is not necessary for anyone to really "know" how to manage this system. The system manages itself by drawing out the talents and energies of ordinary people. It is open ended, rich in unlimited possibilities. Leaders only have to create such a system and then allow people to do what they can with it. That basic freedom is responsible for the remarkable achievements America has realized during its short 200-year experiment in self-governance. If this principle can be extended into institutions, we may be even more surprised by the creative talent that is unleashed as these ideals penetrate down to the nitty gritty of daily life.

There are many formidable obstacles, of course, but the path to a New Management starts with managers like yourself who are willing to reconsider their basic ideas about the way organizations work. Business leaders in particular have a great opportunity to show the way by developing the New Management for all to see. It is said that John Adams told Thomas Jefferson what he thought was the pivotal factor in the success of the American Revolution: "The Revolution originated in the minds of the people."

Consider the exciting possibility that we could actually manage our institutions in a manner that is consonant with our most cherished ideals—the belief that members of all organizations should have the freedom to start and manage their own internal enterprises and to control their corporate communities democratically. If we could simply acknowledge that these ideals are as appropriate within organizations as is society at large, the world could take a great step forward.

So managers are the people to take on this challenge, and American managers should lead the way because of our special heritage. After all, even Russia and other post-Communist countries are beginning to embrace democracy and free enterprise now. Can we do anything less than live up to our own ideals?

Appendix A

The Organization Exercise

This exercise is designed to allow participants to experience the effects of different tasks on organization structure.

METHOD

The instructor should assign participants to groups of 3 to 7 people and have each group select a leader. The leaders are then asked to have their groups perform two different tasks, and the results are posted on a chalkboard or flipchart.

The first task is to add up a page full of random numbers and produce a total. (See Exhibit 1. The correct answer is 161,280.) The instructor should make it clear that group leaders are free to go about this assignment any way they choose and that they are competing against the other groups to obtain a reasonably close answer in the shortest time possible. After starting, the instructor notes the elapsed time as each group produces a good answer, and posts the time. Groups are then asked to describe how they organized themselves on a scale of 0 (mechanistic) to 10 (organic). These results are posted under the heading "Organization Structure."

Groups are then instructed to complete the second task, which involves a more complex assignment of assembling a puzzle, such as the cutout shown in Exhibit 2. The instructor again notes completion times and obtains descriptions of group organization ranging from 0 to 10, and posts these results, as before.

RESULTS

With these data posted, the instructor then moves to the analysis phase of the exercise.

The data for "organization structure" are averaged for each task, and groups are asked to describe how they experienced the two tasks, focusing on the type of organization structures they created. Based on the assumption that the two tasks present challenges of differing complexity, these data usually show that the more complex task (the puzzle) encourages more organic structures.

The instructor can also demonstrate more sophisticated results by plotting "organization structure" versus "performance time" and other relationships. Many different and instructive scatterplots of this type can be used, especially if additional data are obtained from groups, such as "satisfaction" measures. It is also useful to encourage groups to discuss and compare their experiences.

CONCLUSION

This exercise tends to consistently demonstrate a few central conclusions. First, more complex tasks tend to require more organic structures. Second, people tend to prefer working in organic structures. Finally, organic structures, such as networking and internal markets, should be more effective for organizations generally because of the complexity of most task environments and because of personal preferences of most workers.

EXHIBIT I. A SIMPLE TASK: ADDING NUMBERS.

2856	2658	5639
9487	4979	4769
3756	3759	5638
7658	4579	3479
3467	4738	5048
4529	3602	4930
2389	4869	2958
4760	3960	4768
3406	4869	2385
5689	2649	4769
4579	9586	4768
2306	4869	2130

EXHIBIT 2. A COMPLEX TASK: COMPLETING A PUZZLE.

A puzzle as shown below can be made very easily by simply cutting sheets from a magazine roughly as shown. Pages with photos and advertisements are especially useful.

Appendix B

The Stakeholder Meeting

*A Role-Play Simulation of the Organization
as a Socioeconomic System*

This exercise is designed to simulate a stakeholder meeting that approximates the reality of organizational life as an extended socioeconomic system consisting of various "subsystems," "constituencies," or "stakeholders," as described below. The managers of this organization should open the meeting, define the agenda, conduct the proceedings, and close the meeting. Although managers should behave as they see fit, the simulation is most valuable if they allow each group to be heard, address the issues raised, and generally encourage a lot of interaction. Total time for the exercise should be limited to about thirty minutes.

The objective is to engage in a fresh learning experience that simply allows us to explore how such a system would work, its strengths and weaknesses, points of conflict and agreement, and how the system could be managed more effectively. Simply do what seems reasonable from the perspective of the role you are playing.

SOME ISSUES TO CONSIDER

Management

This would be the CEO, president, or general manager of a corporation; the secretary or director of a public agency, and so forth. Managers have the central role in a stakeholder meeting because they serve as the hub of this extended system, so ideally, their job is to reconcile all stakeholder interests and draw these groups into a unified, productive coalition. To do this, it is useful if they can present a coherent, stimulating vision of the organization that will inspire people to work together, and then to help iron out differences: the need for capital from investors, productivity and service of employees, needs of clients, assistance from associated organizations, regulatory relief and support from government, and so on.

Investors

Officers from a financial institution may represent stockholders of a corporation; congressional representatives would stand up for taxpayers in the case of a government agency. Investors typically think they "own" the organization, so they tend to impose their concerns about poor performance, focusing on profit in the case of business and taxes in the case of government. Management's challenge is to help investors to acknowledge that other groups have equally legitimate claims on the organization's performance and that these interests do not necessarily conflict with making money.

Employees

Employees are usually represented by labor leaders and/or ordinary workers in stakeholder meetings. This group typically feels abused by management's authority and concerned about low wages, dull jobs, layoffs, and lack of dignity, so they usually make unreasonable demands and oppose management proposals. Their main issue is to find a way to be involved as constructive partners in raising productivity, quality, and the like, in return for higher pay and other benefits.

Clients

This group might be represented by average clients or possibly a consumer advocate. Clients are usually critical and hard to please, often threatening to take their business elsewhere if they can. Yet they can be a source of creative ideas since they usually know their needs best, even if they have difficulty articulating them, and their faithful patronage is essential, obviously.

Associated Organizations

In business, associated organizations are suppliers, distributors, partners, and the like, while in government they are private contractors and other agencies. These groups tend to feel defensive because they are dependent upon the larger host organization for their survival, whereas the reverse is also true.

The Public

Politicians usually represent the public at local, state, and federal governments. They provide the infrastructure but also control organizations through regulations and taxes, so a constructive relationship is needed that enhances the benefits for the various levels of government and the organization.

SOME QUESTIONS TO CONSIDER FOLLOWING THE EXERCISE

Was this simulation realistic?

What is common to all these relationships?

Is the investor's relationship unique?

To what extent are all these interests compatible?

How could their interests be better served?

What should be the goal of the organization?

What information, type of governance, etc., is needed to manage this system better?

How do you personally feel about this system?

What do you think will happen over the long term?

What are the implications of this type of organizational governance for national economies? Would it still be capitalism? Free enterprise? Socialism? A worker's democracy? A consumer cooperative? Are other terms more meaningful?

Appendix C

Corporations in Transition Study

The questionnaire in this appendix was used to survey 426 managers from the United States, Europe, and Japan. Results are referred to throughout this book.

The questionnaire is reproduced here to allow you to see how the study was conducted and to invite you to extend the study to your organization. So please feel free to copy the next few pages in order to have the questionnaire completed by you and your colleagues. You can then compare your results with those of the entire sample in this book, use the data to analyze your management approach and that of your organization, and consider what changes you would like to make. I would be extremely pleased if you could send me copies of your responses to add to my growing data base, along with any suggestions, criticism, new questions, or any other feedback you care to offer. A larger, more up-to-date collection of data would greatly help in understanding how the New Management is evolving. I can be reached at the following address:

Professor William E. Halal
Department of Management Science, Monroe Hall
George Washington University
Washington, D.C. 20052
PHONE: 202-994-5975
FAX: 202-994-4930
E-MAIL: Halal@gwis2.circ.gwu.edu

CORPORATIONS IN TRANSITION STUDY

This survey is intended to assess the transition from the "Old Management" to the "New Management." The Old Management is defined as the hierarchical, authoritarian form of business that worked well in the Industrial Age, while the New Management is defined as the entrepreneurial, collaborative form of business now emerging for an Information Age. The results are to be used for university research, which may then be published in business journals. Naturally, your responses will be treated with strict confidence and only aggregated data will be used.

Instructions: Each question below describes a "New Management practice" as clearly as possible and asks you to indicate how your company is now managed. Circle one number along the scale for 0 to 10 that best describes the extent to which this type of management is "Not Practiced at All" versus "Practiced Completely." Please try your best to make an accurate estimate, but leave the question blank if you really do not know or if this does not apply to your company for some reason. We would also appreciate any comments you can offer to explain your answer, to describe a new management practice that does not fit our categories, offer suggestions for improving the study, or anything else. If you need more space, use the back of this form.

My graduate students and I thank you sincerely for your help. In return, we will be happy to share the results with you.

PROFESSOR WILLIAM HALAL

Background Data

Name of your organization:

Number of employees:

Annual revenue:

Type of industry:

Your position:

Country in which the operations you are describing are located:

ORGANIZATIONAL STRUCTURE

1. Operating units are treated as semiautonomous enterprises that have control of their own operations and keep most of their revenue.

NOT PRACTICED AT ALL   0   1   2   3   4   5   6   7   8   9   10   PRACTICED COMPLETELY
COMMENTS:

2. Staff and support units (HRD, Legal, IS, etc.) are treated as profit centers that obtain revenue by selling their services to other units.

NOT PRACTICED AT ALL   0   1   2   3   4   5   6   7   8   9   10   PRACTICED COMPLETELY
COMMENTS:

3. Operating units are generally allowed to buy products and services from any organization, inside or outside of the company.

NOT PRACTICED AT ALL   0   1   2   3   4   5   6   7   8   9   10   PRACTICED COMPLETELY
COMMENTS:

4. Staff and support units are generally allowed to sell their services to any organization, inside or outside of the company.

NOT PRACTICED AT ALL   0   1   2   3   4   5   6   7   8   9   10   PRACTICED COMPLETELY
COMMENTS:

5. Apart from proprietary secrets, employees have access to central information systems that contain all available company information.

NOT PRACTICED AT ALL   0   1   2   3   4   5   6   7   8   9   10   PRACTICED COMPLETELY
COMMENTS:

GOALS AND GOVERNANCE

I. The company strives to maintain cooperative working relationships with important stakeholders. (For instance, investors, employees, customers, suppliers, distributors, the local community, and possibly other groups.)

NOT PRACTICED AT ALL   0   I   2   3   4   5   6   7   8   9   10   PRACTICED COMPLETELY

COMMENTS:

2. The company's primary goal is to serve the interests of important stakeholders, including making money for investors.

NOT PRACTICED AT ALL   0   I   2   3   4   5   6   7   8   9   10   PRACTICED COMPLETELY

COMMENTS:

3. In addition to profitability, corporate performance is evaluated by a formal system that assesses how well important stakeholders are served.

NOT PRACTICED AT ALL   0   I   2   3   4   5   6   7   8   9   10   PRACTICED COMPLETELY

COMMENTS:

4. The board of directors includes employees and other important stakeholders.

NOT PRACTICED AT ALL   0   I   2   3   4   5   6   7   8   9   10   PRACTICED COMPLETELY

COMMENTS:

5. Apart from proprietary secrets, employees have access to central information systems that contain all available company information.

NOT PRACTICED AT ALL   0   I   2   3   4   5   6   7   8   9   10   PRACTICED COMPLETELY

COMMENTS:

MARKETING AND SALES

I. In addition to sales levels, customer satisfaction is evaluated by customer surveys and interviews, monitoring complaints, and other formal systems.

NOT PRACTICED AT ALL   0   I   2   3   4   5   6   7   8   9   10   PRACTICED COMPLETELY

COMMENTS:

2. The views of customers are solicited by product designers, managers, or other personnel when making decisions about products and services.
NOT PRACTICED AT ALL   0   1   2   3   4   5   6   7   8   9   10   PRACTICED COMPLETELY
COMMENTS:

3. Customers can use a toll-free line for information and to have problems corrected.
NOT PRACTICED AT ALL   0   1   2   3   4   5   6   7   8   9   10   PRACTICED COMPLETELY
COMMENTS:

4. Advertising is designed to provide useful information rather than inflated claims.
NOT PRACTICED AT ALL   0   1   2   3   4   5   6   7   8   9   10   PRACTICED COMPLETELY
COMMENTS:

5. A significant portion of operating managers' pay is based on customer satisfaction.
NOT PRACTICED AT ALL   0   1   2   3   4   5   6   7   8   9   10   PRACTICED COMPLETELY
COMMENTS:

EMPLOYEE RELATIONS

1. A significant portion of employee pay is based on performance incentive systems.
NOT PRACTICED AT ALL   0   1   2   3   4   5   6   7   8   9   10   PRACTICED COMPLETELY
COMMENTS:

2. Employee attitude surveys are conducted periodically.
NOT PRACTICED AT ALL   0   1   2   3   4   5   6   7   8   9   10   PRACTICED COMPLETELY
COMMENTS:

3. Employees are encouraged to develop their creative ideas into new ventures.
NOT PRACTICED AT ALL   0   1   2   3   4   5   6   7   8   9   10   PRACTICED COMPLETELY
COMMENTS:

4. Employees are organized into self-managed teams that choose their leaders, work methods, equipment, hours, co-workers, and most other aspects of their work.

NOT PRACTICED AT ALL   0   1   2   3   4   5   6   7   8   9   10   PRACTICED COMPLETELY
COMMENTS:

5. Employees can use information systems to "telework" from home, in the field, and other locations.

NOT PRACTICED AT ALL   0   1   2   3   4   5   6   7   8   9   10   PRACTICED COMPLETELY
COMMENTS:

ENVIRONMENTAL MANAGEMENT

1. Environmental impacts are studied as they affect product design, manufacturing processes, packaging, waste treatment, recycling, and other aspects of operations.

NOT PRACTICED AT ALL   0   1   2   3   4   5   6   7   8   9   10   PRACTICED COMPLETELY
COMMENTS:

2. Environmental costs and benefits are incorporated in management decisions.

NOT PRACTICED AT ALL   0   1   2   3   4   5   6   7   8   9   10   PRACTICED COMPLETELY
COMMENTS:

3. The company solicits advice from an environmental advisory committee and/or various environmental groups.

NOT PRACTICED AT ALL   0   1   2   3   4   5   6   7   8   9   10   PRACTICED COMPLETELY
COMMENTS:

STRATEGIC CHANGE

1. A formal strategic planning process is conducted periodically to determine how corporate strategy should respond to technological advances, economic conditions, social attitudes, and other critical issues.

NOT PRACTICED AT ALL   0   1   2   3   4   5   6   7   8   9   10   PRACTICED COMPLETELY
COMMENTS:

2. Unit managers are free to pursue their own strategies for their units.

NOT PRACTICED AT ALL   0   1   2   3   4   5   6   7   8   9   10   PRACTICED COMPLETELY

COMMENTS:

3. Top management encourages major structural changes when they are needed.

NOT PRACTICED AT ALL   0   1   2   3   4   5   6   7   8   9   10   PRACTICED COMPLETELY

COMMENTS:

LEADERSHIP

1. The leadership style of management is participative in most respects.

NOT PRACTICED AT ALL   0   1   2   3   4   5   6   7   8   9   10   PRACTICED COMPLETELY

COMMENTS:

2. The corporate mission is well defined and generally accepted.

NOT PRACTICED AT ALL   0   1   2   3   4   5   6   7   8   9   10   PRACTICED COMPLETELY

COMMENTS:

3. Major decisions and disagreements are discussed openly to reach consensus among those concerned.

NOT PRACTICED AT ALL   0   1   2   3   4   5   6   7   8   9   10   PRACTICED COMPLETELY

COMMENTS:

GENERAL

1. Generally speaking, do you think these practices making up The New Management (TNM) are needed?

NO   YES   UNSURE

COMMENTS:

2. Why are some companies not using TNM?

RESISTANCE TO CHANGE   SHORT-TERM FOCUS   IDEAS ARE UNACCEPTABLE   UNSURE

COMMENTS:

3. What will happen to firms that do not adopt TNM?

THEY WILL SURVIVE   MARGINAL EXISTENCE   LIKELY TO FAIL   UNSURE

COMMENTS:

4. When is TNM likely to enter the mainstream of business?

1996   2000   2005   LATER   UNSURE

COMMENTS:

Thanks very much for your time and thoughtful responses.

INDEX

for organizational learning, 188, 190

Inner leadership. *See under* Leadership

Institutions: authoritarian control in, 255; confidence in, 2; failure of, 1–2; shareholder, 62

Interdependence, 96, 157–158, 172

Interest rates, convergence in, 241

Internal market: adoption of practices, 19, 34, 43, 49; advantages of, 49–50; in business schools, 27–28; compared to free enterprise, 8–9; corporate community and, 14, 84–90; defined, 9; employment contracts and, 140; entrepreneurial energy in, 33–34; examples of, 31, 35, 37, 39; guides to reorganizing into, 48; inappropriate situations for, 45; leadership of, 41–42; mechanisms vs. economy, 49; political views of, 83–84; principles of, 33, 36–42; skepticism about, 33; strengths and weaknesses of, 36, 43–45. *See also* Enterprise

Internet, 30, 85, 209

Intraprises, 36–37

Intuition, spirituality in, 218

Italy, economy in, 235

Japan: collaboration in, 229; corporate community in, 65; downsizing in, 29; economic dilemma in, 235, 236; New Management challenges in, 94; role in global economy, 249–250

Jobs, loss in, 29, 85

Johnson & Johnson, 35, 41–42, 65, 69

Juran, J.M., 6

Kennedy, Allen, 5, 6

King, Martin Luther, Jr., 204

Kmart, 111

Knowledge economy: development of, 134–136; leadership in, 206, 207, 208; management's role in, 1, 41–42, 47, 67, 90; need for cooperation in, 86–90. *See also* Information Age

Knowledge work: adoption of entrepreneurial practices, 11, 15, 19, 151; employment contracts for, 139–143, 147, 151, 152–153; exemplars of, 138; jobs, 45–46, 143–148; new demands of,

148–153; self-management in, 137, 139, 141, 143

Koch Industries, 35

Kodak, 74–75

Kondratieff cycle, 133

Labor-management conflict, 132–134

Latin America, economic dilemma in, 236–237

Lawrence, Paul, 4, 5

Leadership: evolution of, 11, 206–208; inner domain of, 16, 17, 19, 203–205, 216–220; of internal markets, 41–42; need for global, 229; participative, 17, 201–203, 206–210, 223–224; principles of, 203; in serving organizations, 121–122; stewardship and, 75–76; strategic change and, 184–185; synergy from, 42; as wise use of power, 203. *See also* Authority; Power

Learning organization, 111

LeFauve, Richard, 12

Legal issues, in corporate governance, 62–63

Levi-Strauss, 69

Liberal and conservative synthesis, 83–84, 89, 212

Lifestyles, ecological health and, 171–173

Listening, problem solving and, 215–216

L. L. Bean, 121, 122–123

Lockheed, 138

Lorsch, Jay, 4, 5

Malone, Thomas, 44

Management: compared to science, 21; conflict with labor, 132–134; confusion over paradigms, 6–8, 18–19, 23n.11, 255–257; employee confidence in, 234; evolution of, 2, 4–6, 11; leadership and, 41–42, 201–224; mechanistic view of, 2; organic views of, 6, 196–198; rise in, 1, 22n.2; role in knowledge economy, 1, 41–42, 47, 67, 90; spiritual approach to, 217–219; stewardship and, 74–76; strategic, 182–185; use of democracy and enterprise in, 8–11, 255–257, 260–261. *See also* New Management

Marketing: centripetal vs. centrifugal, 111; client-driven, 116–119, 248; as enterprise unit, 38; focus

on selling in, 107–109; high-technology, 112–114; niche, 112; truthful, 114–116

Market organizations, 28–35, 46–47

Markets: compared to capitalism, 228; entrepreneurial energy in, 33–34; social values and, 167; sustainability and, 169–170; vs. central planning, 34, 49. *See also* Internal market

Marriott, 121

Marshall Industries, 142

M•A•S•H, 209

Maslow, Abraham, 4, 5

Matrix organizations, 31, 32

Matsushita, 35

Mayo, Elton, 4, 5

McDonald's, 121, 155–156

McGraw-Hill, 190

McGregor, Douglas, 4, 5

MCI, 12, 13, 35, 40, 41

Media, 59–60, 107–108, 114

Meditation, 218

Men's movement, 209

Mentor Graphics, 221

Merck Corporation, 35, 65

Middle East, economic dilemma in, 237

Miles, Ray, xi–xiii, 5, 6

Minnesota Mining and Manufacturing Company (3M), 164

Mintzberg, Henry, 4, 5

Motivation: organizational structure and, 44; for work, 140–141, 154n.12

Motorola: internal markets in, 35; knowledge work in, 138; organizational balance in, 92–93

Munger, Tolles & Olsen, 142

Murray, Charles, 149–150

MusicWriter, 113

National Bicycle Company, 138

Nations, disaggregation of, 239

NCR Corporation, 65

Networks: global, 47; information, 63, 190, 196; managed by markets, 46–47; as successor to hierarchies, 30, 52n.8

New Capitalism, 18, 245, 247–249. *See also* Democratic enterprise

The New Capitalism (Halal), xvii–xviii, 6

New Management: CIT study questionnaire on, 269–276; compared to old management, 6–8, 10–12, 78–79, 89, 270; confusion over,

THE AUTHOR

Bill Halal discovered the interest that led to this book while working as an aerospace engineer on the *Apollo* program. He had obtained a B.S. in aerospace engineering from Purdue, served in Europe for three exciting years as an Air Force officer, and then joined Grumman when the company was awarded the NASA contract to build the Lunar Module. It was the thrill of a lifetime to see that first "spaceship" land on the Moon. But he felt a keen need to become engaged in something that concerned people and society, some as yet undefined interest closer to the heart of life.

When the Free Speech Movement erupted at U.C. Berkeley, Bill was captured by the fresh, intellectually provocative spirit of the times. College students just had not acted this way previously. Drawn to this source of change, he attended Berkeley for six years, obtaining M.B.A. and Ph.D. degrees, and a wide range of experience in various organizations. His most significant gain, however, was a lasting fascination with today's transition to a knowledge-based society that started during those hectic years, swung abruptly to the right during the Reagan administration, and continues to seek out its resolution in a new social order.

Halal is now professor of management at George Washington University in Washington, D.C., and an authority on emerging technologies, strategic management, and institutional change. He has consulted for General Motors, AT&T, International Data Corporation, Japanese firms, the U.S. government, and many other organizations. His work has appeared in a variety of publications, including *The New York Times*, *The Christian Science Monitor*, *The Academy of Management Executive*, *The California Management Review*, *The Futurist*, *The New Portable MBA*, and several books, including The New Capitalism. One of his papers, "Beyond the Profit Motive," won the 1977 Mitchell Prize of $10,000.

Bill is not quite sure what this odyssey really means or where it will end. One thing that does stand out is the almost unpredictable nature of life. The human soul is so infinitely complex that it is almost impossible to fathom its destiny, especially when we get caught up in historic events. There is a grand sweep to the unfolding of the future today that seems determined to carry us beyond our present limits, regardless of all our confusion, doubts, and obstinence. In Halal's view, the prospect that the world may soon be organized to foster the advance of knowledge is truly a modern miracle.

Halal's abiding interest in the transition to a new epoch has also led him to work in other areas. He has formed a project within the World Future Society called WORLD 2000, which helps people around the world work together in shaping the new global system now emerging—"strategic planning for the planet." He is also producing a CD-ROM on "Knowledge Companies" and a book about the impact of the Information Revolution.

Bill lives in Washington, D.C., with his wife, Carol Lynn, and their two children. Finding his way through those tumultuous early years seems rather mild now when compared to the challenge of guiding a rebellious son toward college and ensuring that his lovely daughter makes the passage to womanhood safely. In Halal's view, these are all different faces of the same evolutionary flow of life, the same relentless search for meaning, the same energizing spirit that animates everything. It is at once both humbling and elevating to be part of this great drama.